WILLIAM O'BRIEN
AND THE COURSE OF
IRISH POLITICS
1881–1918

Photo, J. Russell & Sons.

William O'Brien

William O'Brien

AND THE COURSE OF

Irish Politics

1881–1918

by
JOSEPH V. O'BRIEN

UNIVERSITY OF CALIFORNIA PRESS
BERKELEY   LOS ANGELES   LONDON

ף٦
University of California Press
Berkeley and Los Angeles, California
University of California Press, Ltd.
London, England
Copyright ©1976, by
The Regents of the University of California
ISBN 0-520-02886-4
Library of Congress Catalog Card Number: 74-22970
Printed in the United States of America

... the task of William O'Brien's generation was well and bravely done. Had it not been so the work men are carrying out in this generation would have been impossible.

ARTHUR GRIFFITH,

Young Ireland, June 1920

To Gretta, Paul, and John

Contents

Illustrations

Preface

William O'Brien's career as an Irish Home Rule politician spanned the years 1881 to 1918. He was one of that small group whose long careers were set in motion by their association with the great Parnell. Moreover, he was a member of the smaller inner circle of policymakers who guided the destiny of the Irish Parliamentary party after Parnell's death in 1891. In fact, it was O'Brien who, almost single-handedly, saved the party from a lingering death in the general apathy and disgust that followed the recriminations and abuse of the 1890s between Parnellite and anti-Parnellite factions. Yet, despite his long and eventful career, O'Brien's fellow countrymen of today would scarcely know O'Brien's place in Irish history, much less be able to recount the details of those stormy episodes of his one-man war against the Irish administration during the 1880s which made him the darling of Irish peasants and the bane of successive Irish Chief Secretaries.

The reason for this neglect is easy to discern. O'Brien's generation was committed to the peaceful solution of the thorny Irish question. The essence of Home Rule politics was constitutional rectitude. Neither O'Brien nor any other major figure in the Irish party, before or after Parnell's death, disavowed the British connection or looked to an Irish Parliament's having other than a subordinate status within the Empire. This was the issue which was to test the credibility of the Irish Parliamentary party as the standard-bearer of Irish Nationalism in the opening decades of the twentieth century. The stillborn achievement of Home Rule in 1914 sealed the party's fate. Material success in domestic legislation—land reform, social reform, the achievement of local government—failed to avert the widespread contempt and indignation which greeted the party's palpable lack of success in the higher reaches of political endeavor. Thus, O'Brien, like his fellow Home Rulers and like Daniel O'Connell before him, forfeited the accolades of revolutionary and postrevolutionary generations by a principled commitment to constitutional agitation, which was doomed to be ineffective.

O'Brien's active career falls into three well-defined phases: agitation (1881–1889); organization (1898–1902); and conciliation (1903–1918). The first gained him notoriety, the second earned him the respect and gratitude of feuding Nationalists, while the last phase brought the progressive decline of his political hold on the Irish masses. In those latter years he believed that the policy of conciliating the Irish Unionists was the sole prerequisite to a workable independence for Ireland, shared by Protestants and Catholics alike. In theory it seemed a reasonable solution, but, alas, both the men and the times were unreasonable. For if politics be the art of the possible, then O'Brien during those years was certainly no politician as he pursued the chimerical aim of conciliating Protestant countrymen who turned a deaf ear to his entreaties. Yet, his fame will not rest on his failure but on the part he played in the Land War of the 1880s and in its solution twenty years later. That alone has earned for him a permanent niche in Irish history.

The basic sources for the study of William O'Brien's role in Irish affairs are the O'Brien Papers in the National Library of Ireland and in University College, Cork; his several volumes of memoirs; and the newspapers he owned or edited, particularly *United Ireland*. The correspondence, largely letters to and from the major figures in the Irish Parliamentary party, becomes interesting only from 1889 onward, mainly because his myriad public activities throughout the 1880s—his incessant speechmaking, his dodging of the police, his frequent jail terms, all coupled with his duties as editor and member of Parliament—were not conducive to regulated living and record-keeping. Not until his marriage in 1890 did O'Brien cease to be a man of "no fixed abode." From that period onward most of his illegible scrawls were copied faithfully by his wife, Sophie; our debt to her patient labors becomes apparent when we realize that no other source exists for O'Brien's correspondence with his Nationalist colleague Tim Healy or with his Southern Unionist collaborator Lord Dunraven, both of whose papers have apparently ceased to exist. Likewise, until the correspondence of John Dillon and Michael Davitt, now in private hands, becomes freely available to scholars, researchers can only resort to this transcribed material.

O'Brien, because of his importance in the Nationalist movement, looms large in any study of the Home Rule era. However, there has been no full-scale political biography of this highly individualistic man, in many ways one of the most interesting politicians of his day. True, his journalist friend Michael Macdonagh published an official life in 1928, shortly after O'Brien's death; but though he had access to all the private papers, he made little or no use of them, and what emerged was a piece of popular biography which left huge gaps and provided no critical assessment of O'Brien's activities and policies during the thirty-odd years in which he was a central figure in Irish politics. Scholars, therefore, have had to rely for their research on works in which O'Brien is not the central figure—in particular, on Professor F. S. L. Lyons's *The Irish Parliamentary Party, 1890–1910* (1951) and *John Dillon: A Biography* (1968); and on Dr. C. C. O'Brien's *Parnell and His Party, 1880–1890* (1957). O'Brien's own memoirs, comprising four volumes, betray the usual drawbacks of self-exculpatory reflection, especially the controversial later works, *An Olive Branch in Ireland* (1910) and *The Irish Revolution* (1923), whose sole purpose would appear to be to discredit his former colleagues in the Irish party.

The purpose of this study is to describe and evaluate O'Brien's career in Irish politics over a period when Nationalist Ireland developed its first serious challenge to British rule. Since O'Brien was in the thick of this contest, his story is interesting not only for its own sake but also for the light it throws on British policy toward her unruly sister island. Furthermore, his story is in part the story of the Irish Parliamentary party in those crucial years when it had to face two fateful issues—the unbending resolve of English politicians to deny Ireland full legislative freedom and the awakening distrust of Nationalistic Irishmen for any solution that accepted less.

I wish to express my thanks to Professor Herman Ausubel of Columbia University, who gave me the idea for this book and who provided much help and encouragement along the way. Professor Chilton Williamson of Columbia saved me from many errors and also made valuable suggestions, for which I am most grateful.

I also want to thank the keepers and assistant keepers of manuscripts who gave me permission to use the documents in their possession or care. Most of the research for this book was done in the National Library of Ireland, and it is a pleasure to express my particular thanks to its staff, perhaps the most cheerful and helpful group of librarians that any researcher could wish to meet. A generous grant from the Woodrow Wilson National Fellowship Foundation made possible my research expeditions to Dublin and London.

Finally, special thanks to my wife, who endured the grinding work of endless typing, editing, and proofreading.

Abbreviations

AOH Ancient Order of Hibernians
BM Add. MS. British Museum, Additional Manuscript
CDB Congested Districts Board
DM Divisional Magistrate
DMP Dublin Metropolitan Police
GAA Gaelic Athletic Association
IRB Irish Republican Brotherhood
LC Library of Congress
NLI National Library of Ireland, Dublin
NYPL New York Public Library
PML Pierpont Morgan Library, New York
PRO Public Record Office, London
RIC Royal Irish Constabulary
RM Resident Magistrate
SPO State Paper Office, Dublin
SPO, CBS Crimes Branch Special
SPO, CSO Chief Secretary's Office
SPO, DICS District Inspector Crimes Special
SPO, IG Inspector General
UCC University College, Cork
UIL United Irish League

Introduction

William O'Brien was born in the small town of Mallow, County Cork, on October 2, 1852. As the birthplace of Thomas Davis, the poet of Young Ireland, Mallow claimed its own special prominence in the annals of the Nationalist movement. Daniel O'Connell issued his famous defiance to Sir Robert Peel, the British Prime Minister, from Mallow in 1843, and William O'Brien's mother, daughter of a local shopkeeper, had helped to decorate the banquet room on that occasion. In later years, she was wont to regale her children with stirring tales of the Nationalist heroes of the 1840s. In his memoirs O'Brien relates that family gossip had it that the Nagle clan to which the mother belonged had once included Nano Nagle, founder of the Irish Ursulines, and also the great Edmund Burke, himself. There were more verifiable connections on his mother's side with the famous Nationalist Archbishop of Cashel Thomas Croke, a curate in Mallow when William was a boy. O'Brien's father, though a Nationalist sympathizer in his youth, became disillusioned by the failure of the 1848 uprising and the horror of the famine and appears to have had no part in encouraging a Nationalist outlook in his children. At any rate, the example the son chose to follow was that of his oldest brother, James, who had been "out" with the Fenians in 1867.

Until William was fifteen, the family's middle-class fortunes were secure enough to give him the type of education then denied to most Catholics—a good grounding in the classics and the liberating experience of attendance at the Cloyne Diocesan School, the Protestant high school for the district. Perhaps it was in this climate that he imbibed the spirit of religious toleration that eventually enabled him to marry a French woman of Jewish background and advance a broad conciliatory policy toward the Protestant minority in Ireland.

Bad luck beset the family from 1867 onward. The father lost his job

1

as a managing clerk in an attorney's office and died shortly thereafter. The oldest son, James, found it difficult to hold a job because of his association with the underground movement (he was part of the gunrunning operation which resulted in the long imprisonment of Michael Davitt, founder of the Land League). Thus, by the time he had turned sixteen, William had to take on his own shoulders the sole support of his widowed mother, his sister, and two brothers, a responsibility which put an end to a promising school career. His choice of work was fortuitous. A born journalist, he became a reporter on the Cork *Daily Herald,* winning that position by the power of his graphic description in reporting the trial of a Fenian for an obscure periodical. As a working journalist in Cork from 1868 to 1876, he experienced at first hand the rough justice of local magistrates, the autocratic disdain of ex officio Poor Law Guardians, and the nascent cry of the impoverished Irish farmer for "the three Fs" (the fair rent, fixity of tenure, and right of free sale ceded by the Land Act of 1881). He was to put the experience to powerful use in the next decade.

The years O'Brien spent in Cork coincided with the decline of the Fenian movement in Ireland. During that time he dabbled in the activities of that spent organization and even rose to the position of secretary for the southern counties.[1] According to the evidence he gave before the Parnell Commission in 1890, he never was a Fenian in the sense of having taken the oath and he claimed to have ceased contact with the movement around 1870. But it appears that he continued his clandestine associations for several more years, judging by a letter written to John Devoy, head of the Irish-American organization in New York, by one of O'Brien's fellow "conspirators": "William O'Brien used to be one of our gang. He left the I.R.B. about 6 years ago . . . He ought to be with us."[2] It seems that O'Brien, however, had already developed a capacity for erratic political behavior for, while on the one hand he had ostensibly committed himself to Fenian revolutionary ideals, he was at the same time manifesting a political outlook of a decidedly compromising tendency. In his memoirs he takes special pride in a letter he managed to get published in the London *Daily News* January 2, 1870, calling for "a conference of a few of the leading men of both nations to effect a compromise solution on the national question."

[1] W. O'Brien, *Recollections* (New York, 1905), 116.

[2] T. H. Ronayne to John Devoy, September 24, 1881, quoted in *Devoy's Post Bag, 1871–1928* (Dublin, 1953), W. O'Brien and D. Ryan (eds.), 2:101–102.

This approach was to be the leitmotiv of his political activity forty years later.

O'Brien's intellectual prowess and capacity for hard work was demonstrated when he matriculated for entrance to Queen's College, Cork, in 1871. The strictures of the Irish hierarchy against attendance at the "godless" colleges founded in Ireland by Sir Robert Peel apparently mattered as little to the adult O'Brien as had the fact that the Cloyne Diocesan School contained over 50 percent Protestant boys did to his father. But religious association has never been a consideration in the establishment of Nationalist credentials in Ireland, and these experiences, though unusual for a Catholic Nationalist, should not be construed as any evidence of O'Brien's antipathy either to the Catholic religion or to the strong clerical influence in Irish life. He was throughout his life a devout Catholic and even made his wife's conversion from Judaism a condition of their marriage. At any rate, he walked off with the Queen's College law scholarship despite stiff competition and his own abbreviated schooling and might have become a lawyer had not a serious attack of smallpox destroyed his chance of winning the scholarship, whose financial support he needed, for the second year.

His career finally began to take shape in 1876, when he accepted an invitation to join the Dublin *Freeman's Journal*. The respectable *Freeman* was then the only daily newspaper in Ireland espousing anything like an Irish Nationalist viewpoint. More and more this type of outlook was acquiring significance because of startling changes that were taking place in the political arena. True, the Home Rule movement founded in 1870 by the Protestant barrister Isaac Butt had hardly ruffled the surface of English politics. But from 1876 onward, the rise of Charles Stewart Parnell, yet another Protestant recruit to the movement for establishing an Irish Parliament, was opening a new and challenging chapter in Anglo-Irish relations. Not all the drama was being played out in the rarefied atmosphere of the House of Commons, however. There were ominous signs of impending disaster for Irish tenants in the mounting agricultural depression of the late 1870s. This trend was aggravated by the socially regressive imbalance in the relations between landlord and tenant. One of O'Brien's notable journalistic feats was to record at first hand the sufferings of more than two hundred rack-rented families on an estate near the Galtee Mountains in the South of Ireland. It was the experience of this venture during the winter of 1877/78 which afforded him, in his own words, "the first intimate and never-to-be-forgotten insight into the horrible realities of the Irish Land Question."[3] In order to appreciate the fanatical dedication with which William O'Brien championed the claims of the peasantry for the next twenty-five years, it is necessary to trace briefly the history of land tenure in Ireland.

The Land Question

The land problem in Ireland was the malignant legacy of the English conquest and plantations of the sixteenth and seventeenth centuries. Within a few generations the old Celtic aristocracy had been dispossessed and replaced by English and Scottish proprietors. By 1778 perhaps 5 percent of Irish land was in the hands of Catholic owners. The peasantry, previously tenants on an ancient type of communal landholding, were forced to adapt to English laws of private property, which absolved owners from any specific obligations to their unprotected tenants. A century of punitive laws against Catholics—exclusion from Parliament, from holding government office, from entering the legal profession, and from holding commissions in the army or navy—had already done much to widen the gulf between the two peoples: the one conquering, free, and Protestant; the other poor, servile, and Catholic. The lowest point in the deteriorating legal position of the tenant was reached in 1860 with the passage of the Landlord and Tenant Act (Deasy's Act) of that year. That act stipulated that landlord-tenant relations were to be fixed by contract and not based upon tenure or service. This extension of the free trade principle to the land question ensured a heavily-weighted bargaining power in favor of the landlord. Moreover, the landlord was empowered to evict tenants after arrears of rent amounted to one year and, in addition, seize crops and confiscate improvements without compensation to the tenant.

Contemporary writers and recent Irish historians have painted a dismal picture of the agrarian poverty and stagnation of the eighteenth century, generally attributed to the pressures of increasing population and the absence of a market economy.[4] Bad harvests were every bit as alarming as in the following century. In 1741 a vast famine killed an es-

[3]W. O'Brien, *Recollections*, 188.

[4]For a sharp criticism of the traditional gloomy picture of Irish economic history, see L. M. Cullen, "Problems in the Interpretation and Revision of Eighteenth-Century Irish Economic History" in *Transactions of the Royal Historical Society*, (January, 1967) 7:1–22. However, because of the paucity of research in this aspect of Irish history, it seems probable that the dismal account will die hard.

timated 400,000 people, or one in six of the population. The sharpest
peasant outcry was rebellion, modeled on the great Whiteboy disturbances in Munster in the 1760s. Most outbreaks were directed against
specific agrarian grievances—enclosure, tithe exactions of the Protestant clergy, rack-rents, evictions, forced labor, and unemployment. The
response of the English government was coercion, the name given in
popular parlance to any measure which increased the severity of the
criminal law in Ireland alone. The first such act was passed in 1765.
The canker of social distress and peasant retribution is well attested by
the survival of coercive legislation. Eighty-six coercion acts (fifty-eight of
them in the nineteenth century alone) preceded the much-hated Crimes
Act of 1887 directed against the agrarian agitation of William O'Brien
and the more daring of his colleagues in the Irish Parliamentary party.

Contemporaries, from Swift to Drummond, hardly erred in singling
out the Irish landlords as the *fons et origo* of Irish social evils. So little had
the landlords learned the dictum "property has its duties as well as its
rights," that many of their critics must have shared the view of Michael
Davitt that all landlords were morally entitled to in return for the use of
their land was "a single ticket, third-class, to Holyhead." The Irish
landlord is perhaps more maligned than any other miscreant in Anglo-
Irish history, excluding Cromwell. Among the more notorious
specimens was the Earl of Leitrim, whose coffin was almost dragged
from its hearse by a howling mob after his murder in 1878. Another was
the infamous Lord Clanricarde, who fought and goaded tenants,
Nationalists, and English cabinet ministers until he was compulsorily
dispossessed by the Congested Districts Board in 1914. *The* (London)
Times in 1852 damned them all as "a class which for selfishness and
cruelty has no parallel, and never had a parallel in the civilized world."
Parnell, himself a landlord, was more charitable: "The only good things
the Irish landlords have to show for themselves are their hounds and,
perhaps, in the Roscommon country, their horses."[5]

Of course, by Davitt's time not all landlords were absentee English
owners, for great changes had occurred in the ownership of land during
the nineteenth century. In 1801 the Act of Union abolishing the Irish
Parliament and placing control of the country directly under the Parliament at Westminster was passed. This ensured that the future
economic problems of the country would be viewed in the light of

[5]W. O'Brien, *Recollections*, 202; N. D. Palmer, *The Irish Land League Crisis* (New Haven,
Conn., 1940), 211.

prevailing English political philosophy and would not receive the special treatment they needed.[6] Next, a collapse in corn prices after the Napoleonic wars, coupled with the refusal of landlords to reduce rents, pauperized many well-to-do farmers and hurt the landlords themselves through diminished rents.[7] There was no attempt to encourage a capitalist agriculture, and even if there had been, tenants were too poor and holdings too small to expect English farming methods to prosper of their own accord. Land was consequently reconverted to pasture, which meant less was available to the tenants, a condition which could only be "solved" by subdivision or emigration. But the latter could never be a solution, given the remarkable growth in population in Ireland from 1780 onward. Naturally, subdivision and rack-renting reinforced the general deterioration of the situation of landlord and tenant alike.

In the wake of the Great Famine of the late 1840s, Westminster formally recognized that Irish landlordism needed an infusion of new blood and capital. The Encumbered Estates Act of 1849 allowed impecunious Irish landlords to break the English law of primogeniture and "make land in Ireland a marketable commodity." The aims of this act were not realized, however. Would-be English purchasers were discouraged by the diminished rent rolls resulting from the great clearances caused by death and emigration. Therefore, the purchasers were mostly Irish (over 90 percent of 7,500 purchasers), and the capital was speculative, not improving (practically all of the sales went to creditors).[8] Thus, land fell into the control of "gombeen men"—petty shopkeepers, who in spite of the Famine had managed to scrape some capital together by lending money. These purchasers were given full legal rights to determine tenancies and rents, with the result that more evictions took place in the six years from 1849 to 1854 than in the rest of the century. By the 1870s about 750 of the 20,000 existing landlords owned half the land of Ireland.[9] As a class, they had resisted all attempts to ameliorate the condition of their tenants. And their dominant position was hardly disturbed by the government's effort in 1870 to acknowledge the claim of the tenant to an interest in his holding. Nevertheless, their fate was sealed within a few short years when they refused to ally themselves under Isaac Butt's Home Rule banner.

[6]R. D. Collison Black, *Economic Thought and the Irish Question, 1817–80* (Cambridge, 1960), 246.
[7]J. E. Pomfret, *The Struggle for Land in Ireland, 1800–1923* (Princeton, 1930), 12.
[8]*Ibid.*, 44.
[9]Appendix B; Palmer, *The Irish Land League,* 9.

Instead of becoming the leaders of the people, the landlords remained a target of hate. It is only fair to note at this point that recent scholarship has gone some way to providing a more balanced perspective on the Irish land question and the landlord's place in it. It has demonstrated, for example, that rents in Ireland rose very slowly from the low levels that had been set in hard times by the valuation of Sir Richard Griffith, embodied in the Act of 1852; that rack-rents were rare and evictions small; and that landlords were at all times prevented either by tenure customs or by the threat of violence from executing the arrangements (consolidation of farms, for instance) necessary to merit capital investment to improve the land.[10] Nevertheless, landlords, good and bad, were to play the role of scapegoat for Irish nationalist agitation. By their refusal after 1870 to aid in the work of unraveling the legislative bonds that made their country (though perhaps few thought of Ireland as *their* country) a poor, despised appendage of the British lion, these landlords fully deserved the epithets hurled at them by Michael Davitt and by his successor, William O'Brien.

At the other end of the scale from the landlords was the peasantry. Their ability to survive on scraps of land "where a central European goat would die of hunger" amazed continental observers throughout the eighteenth and nineteenth centuries. A distinction must be made between the northern small farmer (usually a Protestant) and the Catholic tenants in the South. The former, in addition to being exempted from the harsh provisions of the anti-Catholic penal code during the eighteenth century, also enjoyed the benefits of the tacitly recognized Ulster custom, which secured to the holder an interest in the tenancy of his holding. In this way tenants who occupied such holdings became virtual owners of their farms and would not be evicted without proper compensation, such as by purchase of the "tenant right." For this reason the Protestant North was relatively free from the agrarian crime that left a trail of murder, assault, robbery, destruction of property, and intimidation in the rest of Ireland.

Completely opposite conditions prevailed for the Catholic peasantry. Throughout the eighteenth century those native Irish peasants were subjected to the brutality of the penal code, which, in addition to ensuring their social and political inferiority, also forbade them from buy-

---

[10]B. L. Solow, *The Land Question and the Irish Economy, 1870–1903* (Cambridge, Mass., 1971) 57, 83, *et passim*.

ing land or taking leases for longer than thirty-one years. Even after
these laws had been abolished or had fallen into desuetude, the
economic status of the Catholic farmer continued to be precarious. The
law supported the landlord's claim that he alone was the owner of the
land, including any improvements made by the labor or capital of the
tenant. The story of evictions highlights his plight. From 1816 onward,
the process of eviction was speeded up by legislation: evictions could
thereafter be effected at about one-tenth the cost and six times as fast as
a similar process in England.[11] The Industrial Revolution, at its height
in the 1820s in terms of new capital investment, touched Ireland only
indirectly through the siphoning-off of tens of thousands of the population, who fled their stagnating economy. Those who remained and who
later escaped death in the Famine filled the 500,000 mud cabins recorded in the census of 1871. The lowly cottiers were the worst off of all.
They were the laborers who grubbed a bare existence on tiny plots of
land, who paid their rent in labor and who saved themselves from annihilation by taking seasonal work (spalpeening) in England.

As a result of the changes brought about by the Famine, the total
number of holdings decreased from 827,000 in 1841 to 608,000 in
1851.[12] Twenty years later the census recorded a total of approximately
592,000 holdings. About 50 percent of those holdings were considered
uneconomic, being less than fifteen acres, while 80 percent of the occupiers were tenants-at-will, and the remainder held leases. Herein lay
the tenant insecurity that always kept agrarian agitation just below the
surface even in good farming years. Even the most moderate demands
for redress of the lopsided landlord-tenant relations were ignored by a
Parliament dominated by landlord interest, the *coup de grace* being
delivered by Lord Palmerston's comic rebuff, "tenant right is landlord's
wrong." Not until 1870 was the Ulster custom of tenant right extended
to the entire island. However, the Land Act of that year enveloped the
concession in legal bonds that rendered the measure worthless as far as
the tenants were concerned. Moreover, the justice dispensed by the
courts was class justice in favor of the landlords, so rack-rents and insecurity continued as before.

Before the decade of the seventies had run its course, however, the
land question took on an immediacy dictated by acute economic distress. The agricultural depression in England was disastrous when
translated to Ireland, where the virtual absence of industry decreed an

[11]Pomfret, *The Struggle*, 14.
[12]*Ibid.*, 42.

economic reliance on agricultural produce every bit as vulnerable as the agricultural reliance on the potato had been before the Great Famine. It only required bad harvests in 1877, 1878, and 1879 to bring matters to a head. The social distress and dislocation can be inferred from the bare statistics shown below:

Year	Families Evicted	Agrarian Outrages
1876	553	212
1877	463	236
1878	980	301
1879	1,238	863
1880	2,110	2,585
1881	3,415	4,439
1882	5,201	3,433

Such were the circumstances in which the land question entered its final phase.

The Home Ruler

While Parnell was consolidating his power within the Home Rule League, William O'Brien, through his work as a journalist, was establishing himself as the confidant of leading Nationalist spokesmen. He became intimately acquainted with Parnell toward the end of 1878. His diary records how profoundly that event affected him: "[Parnell] has captured me, heart and soul, and is bound to go on capturing."[13] Within a year, Parnell, aided by the newly-founded Land League of the ex-Fenian Michael Davitt, was also to captivate the peasant masses and emerge as the leader of an aggressive, minority wing of Irish M.P.'s. From that point onward, the contending forces of Irish discontent coalesced into one great movement on behalf of the tenants. This conjunction was manifested by the so-called New Departure of 1879, in which Irish-American dollars, Parnell's political acumen, and the grassroots Land League joined forces to make the solution of the land question the paramount issue in Anglo-Irish politics for the next quarter-century.[14]

[13]W. O'Brien, Recollections, 198.

[14]For an account of the controversial alliance between the American Fenian elements and Parnell, see T. W. Moody, "The New Departure in Irish Politics, 1878-79" in Essays in British and Irish History in Honour of James Eadie Todd, edited by H. A. Cronne, T. W. Moody, and D. B. Quinn (London, 1949), 303-333.

O'Brien played no part in the momentous resurgence of organized resistance to landlordism in those opening months of 1879. Indeed, a deep personal tragedy almost completely broke his own frail health at that juncture. Within a few hours of each other in December 1878, both his brothers succumbed to tuberculosis. A bare three weeks later, he had to witness the further horror of the death of his only sister, again due to the same "Irish" disease. It required a sojourn in Egypt to improve his own frail health and restore him to any sort of activity. But those sad events were not without effect in heightening O'Brien's importance to the Nationalist movement. For, as he later recalled, "this tragic episode coloured my whole life and character, and explains the recklessness (for it was not calm courage) with which I was afterwards accustomed to encounter personal danger, and which perhaps, alone made me in any degree a formidable element in a semi-revolutionary movement."[15]

O'Brien's formal adhesion to the semirevolutionary, or Home Rule, movement did not occur until 1881, but already he was marked for prominence in the developing organization. Never before had the political future seemed so bright for activist Irishmen restless under alien rule. In the preceding decade Irish Nationalist representation in Parliament had been recruited from those landlord, commercial, and professional elements whose principal qualification was their ability to pay election expenses. They were greeted across the Irish Sea as the harmless gentlemen from Ireland.[16] American dollars in the hands of Parnell changed this forever. The general election of 1880, though it returned but twenty-four Parnellites out of a total non-Ulster representation of seventy-four members, foreshadowed the complete turnover in that body six years later when "the eighty-six of '86" took their seats at Westminster under Parnell's leadership.

[15] W. O'Brien, *Recollections*, 208.

[16] The Nationalists of the 1880s, whose job it was to revolutionize the Irish representation, found the record of the more egregious type of Irish member grist to their mill. Charles Lever's popular broadside surely hit home in the unhumorous conditions of Land League days:

> To drink a toast
> A proctor roast
>   Or bailiff as the case is,
> To kiss your wife
> Or take a life
>   At ten or fifteen paces;
> To keep game-cocks, or hunt the fox,
>   To drink in punch the Solvay,
> With debts galore, but fun far more
>   Oh! that's the man for Galway.

A notable victory of the Land League agitation was Gladstone's Land Act of 1881, conceding the famous three Fs—fair rent, fixity of tenure, freedom of sale. This was the first great blow struck at the cherished sanctity of private property rights as it established the doctrine of dual ownership (i.e. copartnership of landlord and tenant) in the land. Soon, the names of the constitutional standard-bearers of Irish Nationalism became everyday words in farmhouse and mud cabin. Men like John Dillon, the Redmond brothers, T. P. O'Connor, Thomas Sexton, Tim Healy, and O'Brien, himself, first acquired the popular touch in the reflected glory of the charismatic Parnell. All of them were conditioned in their outlook by traditions maintained during the previous century—the revolutionary ideals of Wolfe Tone and the Fenians, the moderate Nationalism of O'Connell and George Gavan Duffy, and the agrarian yearnings of the peasant, expressed in social unrest.

William O'Brien's romantic nature (he proposed marriage to an actress in a traveling company at age sixteen) coupled with his Nationalist background rendered him particularly susceptible to the appeal of tradition. In a typical rhetorical outburst, he contended that "the driving force and vital breath of all our struggles, the consecration which lifts us above the paltry contentions of the hour, and makes even suffering and failure sweet—has its origin deep in the recesses of the past."[17] Like many of his colleagues, O'Brien was growing to manhood in the late sixties and could hardly avoid being touched by Fenianism. Young Ireland, the hope of his parents, was recent history, while the rebellion of 1798 was still revered as the apotheosis of national resistance to British rule.

Yet, the response of the Home Ruler to his past was the measure of his future political outlook. Justin McCarthy, the doyen of Parnell's party, judged the 1848 experience in much the same way as his younger political associates judged 1867:

From that time forth I became more and more convinced that the task of righting Ireland's wrongs was to be accomplished by earnest and incessant appeal to the conscience, the reason, and the manly feeling of England's best citizens.[18]

Fenian activity had the same salutary effect on O'Brien that the '48 call to arms had had on Justin McCarthy. O'Brien's writings afford

[17]W. O'Brien, *Irish Ideas* (London, 1893), 48.
[18]J. McCarthy, *An Irishman's Story* (London, 1904), 82.

several examples of his antipathy to violent solutions. In his memoirs he attributed his joining the constitutional movement to "the gloom of inevitable failure and horrible punishment inseparable from any attempt at separation by force of arms." Nor was this theme neglected in his novel, *When We Were Boys,* where comfort is taken that "Irishmen have discovered a saner resource than the wild weapons of boyish insurrection." And as late as 1917, a time when the doctrine of physical force had just been put to the test once more, he rejected it in a letter to the aged Frederic Harrison, stating, "it is not and can never be" a remedy.[19]

The political common denominator of the Home Rulers was that they were constitutionalist to a man. The recoil from the physical force used by the Fenians was complete and abrupt. It was as if a shudder of fear had swept through an entire generation. Such revulsion was sustained by the grisly, exemplary execution of three Fenians at Manchester in 1867 (the last English public hanging) and the numerous civilian casualties in the Fenian-inspired attempted jailbreak in London's Clerkenwell prison in that same year. Though Home Rule orators might romance their audiences with thrilling evocations of Meagher of the Sword, their own prototype was surely O'Connell of the Lichfield Compact. When agrarian agitation was at its height during the 1880s, the parliamentary leaders' condemnation of crime, violence, and secret societies was an echo of the Liberator's own attacks on the illegal associations thrown up by the social injustices of his era.

The Home Rule leadership was overwhelmingly middle-class, in fact or in pretension, at a time when that class formed a minuscule part of the population. Justin McCarthy refuted English accusations that Parnell's "lieutenants" comprised a "ragged regiment" by pointing out that they were all either journalists, like O'Brien, or well-to-do, like Dillon. Nor did this change with the infusion of new blood. The turnover was in the rank and file, not in the leadership. This probably accounts for the remarkable fact that, despite the close affinities of the movement with the discontented masses in Ireland, the leaders totally ignored the exploitation of Irish immigrants in England and Scotland. Similarly, the Home Rulers showed little but indifference to the cause of labor in Ireland, even though British trade unions had begun to organize Irish workers, an Irish Trades Union Congress was founded in 1894, and Dublin contained some of the worst slums in Europe.

[19] *Evening Memories* (Dublin, 1920) 443; *When We Were Boys* (London, 1890), 550; O'Brien to Frederic Harrison, July 17, 1917, NLI William O'Brien Papers, NLI MS. 8557/6.

It is important to grasp the fact that the Home Ruler was essentially a moderate, content to accept as gifts legislative concessions that were his by right, in the hope that Ireland could settle down in peace and prosperity under the mantle of the British Empire. This may not seem evident if one misreads the story of the fierce agitation of the 1880s, the Plan of Campaign years, when William O'Brien and John Dillon seemed the archetypes of socialistic and separatist intriguers to a Conservative Prime Minister and his Chief Secretary for Ireland. As events will show, the Home Rulers endured coercion, arrogance, and betrayal from English politicians without once deviating from the constitutional path. Their respect for parliamentary methods and the implicit acceptance of the hegemony of the Imperial Parliament reflected the bewilderment, anger, and distrust with which they viewed the separatist Nationalism of the early twentieth century.

The direction of their politics was prompted by two laudable, though narrow, goals—the emancipation of the peasant and a measure of legislative independence for Ireland, however emasculated. But, by the 1890s this conception of Irish Nationalism was being challenged by others whose vision transcended mere politics and who viewed the struggle against England as the much more vital one of Gaelic *versus* English culture. The political corollary of such aspirations was complete separation from England. Home Rule looked backwards to the bourgeois element in Young Ireland, leavened by peasant proprietary, not forward to the Socialist Republicanism of Pearse and Connolly. Indeed, the idea of an Irish republic would have seemed as absurd to William O'Brien as it would have to Parnell or any of his other followers. O'Brien, in a speech delivered in 1893, spoke for his own generation when he chided those who sought to erect such hopes:

There are men who would have us depreciate, ignore, and even reject all these priceless advantages for our country; who would throw up allies, Parliamentary weapons, and progress transcending our wildest hopes, and reduce the young men of Ireland once more to the bleak alternative of dreaming of an insurrection which could never come off . . .[20]

Yet, the younger generation was being lost even then, for in that same year the Gaelic League, that nursery of twentieth-century Irish Republicanism, was born.

---

[20]Address to Cork National Society, September 26, 1893, quoted in W. O'Brien, *Irish Ideas*, 162.

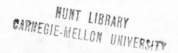

ONE

In the Public Eye

WILLIAM O'BRIEN was twenty-eight years old in 1881, when he was lured from the *Freeman's Journal* by Parnell in order to conduct the Nationalist organization's first adventure in journalism. O'Brien had been a special correspondent for the *Freeman* since 1876, but over the years he had become increasingly uncomfortable about the paper's timid Nationalist viewpoint: "[The editor] pressed me hard to become a regular leader-writer for the paper; but, apart from the drawbacks of incessant illness, the views of the *Freeman* were sometimes . . . of too indecisive a hue in National crises to make it possible for me to undertake any personal responsibility for them."[1]

True, the *Nation* and the *Freeman's Journal* were Nationalist newspapers, but their support of Parnell's advanced party was inconsistent, if not actually hostile. The *Freeman* had opposed Parnell's nominees during the 1880 election, and its owner, Sir John Gray, M.P., had voted for the moderate William Shaw against Parnell in the contest for the chairmanship of the Parliamentary party after the election. And when Parnell ordered his followers to abstain from voting on Gladstone's Land Bill in the summer of 1881, both the *Nation* and the *Freeman's Journal* attacked him for want of gratitude to the Liberal party. It was clear that Parnell could not depend for support on journals not under his own control,[2] and when the opportunity came that summer

[1]W. O'Brien, *Recollections* (New York, 1905), 185.

[2]May's British and Irish *Press Guide* for 1883 shows how weak the Nationalist press in Ireland was at this time.

Affiliation	Dailies	Other
Conservative	7	33
Liberal/Conservative	2	11
Liberal	6	32
Independent	1	34
Nationalist	—	16

The *Press Guide* classified the papers of the Freeman's Journal Co. as Liberal, thus leaving no avowedly Nationalist daily paper, since both *United Ireland* and the *Nation* were weeklies.

14

to buy Richard Pigott's publishing establishment, the *Flag of Ireland* was converted to *United Ireland,* with William O'Brien as editor and general manager at £400 per annum. The latter had refused £600 a year to remain with the *Freeman,* preferring instead a commission as another one of Parnell's lieutenants.[3]

O'Brien's selection as propaganda chief for the party machine was a foregone conclusion. An experienced and well-known journalist, an ardent Nationalist, a proven friend of the Irish tenants, and a devoted admirer of Parnell—these were qualifications that few could fill in 1881. But the idea of publishing a Parnellite newspaper did not receive unanimous support within the party. Dillon, Parnell's most extreme lieutenant and the son of the John Blake Dillon of '48, wrote to O'Brien on July 12 intimating his hostility to the venture, perhaps fearing the influence a newspaper could wield in propagating moderate courses of action.[4] He need not have worried. O'Brien, having apparently brought Dillon's objections to Parnell's notice, received the following reply from the chief:

I think the feeling you allude to would not be a persistent one, if the newspaper were managed on straightforward and advanced lines . . . it will, of course, always be my duty to conciliate all sections of opinion comprised in the movement—and to see that everything connected with it is conducted in such a way as to leave no room for complaint of backwardness by anyone.[5]

Parnell probably little realized how straightforward and advanced the paper would be in O'Brien's hands. The first weekly number of *United Ireland* appeared on August 13, 1881, and the first few issues certainly merit O'Brien's own description of it as "an insurrection in print." Rumor had it that W. E. Forster, the Chief Secretary for Ireland, on reading the first number, exclaimed, "Who on earth is this new madman?" The paper was an immediate success. It radiated from Dublin to virtually every town and hamlet and within weeks achieved a steady circulation of between 70,000 and 100,000 and a readership of probably half a million, evidence enough of how well the paper met a popular need.

The first number predictably invoked every militant spirit in Irish history, from the United Irishmen to the Fenians, and it, more daringly, also recalled the "true lesson" of the French Revolution for the cause of peasant proprietary. The heady prose and wild invective of the leaders

[3]O'Brien to M. Macdonagh, April 20, 1927, Macdonagh Papers, NLI MS. 11442.
[4]W. O'Brien, *Recollections,* 304.
[5]Parnell to O'Brien, July 15, 1881, Gill Papers, NLI MSS. 13478–526 (Box 1871–92).

THE PIG THAT WON'T "PAY THE RINT!"

The Arms Act of 1881 was directed against the agrarian crime associated with the Land League agitation.

and articles bear the unmistakable mark of O'Brien's volatile pen. According to himself, practically every number of the paper in the first two months of its existence was written entirely by him.[6] All in all, it was eight pages of unrelieved news and comment on the land problem and the activities of the branches of the Land League. It was a stark contrast to the cosmopolitan and inoffensive *Freeman's Journal*. Nothing quite like it had ever before been offered for the delectation of the village sages.

The next issue hailed the Greek war of independence for its example in encouraging "many another suffering nationality to similar efforts." The September 10 issue taught a new Irish Alphabet—an unrestrained tirade against the iniquity of the Irish Administration, with pride of place reserved for the Viceroy, Lord Spencer, and his Chief Secretary, W. E. Forster: "A is an Ass on the Viceregal throne/B is old Buckshot—boys! give him a groan . . . " Everyone was fair game for the paper's barbs, whether a visiting member of the royal family, "His Serene Humbug the . . . Duckling of Teck," or the Prime Minister himself—"a snivelling hypocrite." Nor was the Catholic church spared, as Archbishop McCabe of Dublin and sixteen bishops were denounced for their political pastoral against the Land League.[7] A cartoon, at the expense of Gladstone or one of his ministers, became a regular feature of the paper. Quite obviously, onerous tasks were in store for the recording clerks of the Crimes Branch in Dublin Castle, the citadel of British rule in Ireland.

The tone of the paper was vituperative and not a little tiresome, neglecting all news not directly connected with the Nationalist movement. Its more extreme exhortations were no doubt not meant to be taken seriously, but its pages were both an arsenal against the Dublin Castle regime as well as the exemplar of a revived Nationalist spirit of defiance. Perhaps unnoticed at the time was one item of amusing incongruity in an otherwise unrelievedly serious newspaper—advertisements offering cheap emigration and assisted passage to Australia, the United States, or Canada. This at a time when Nationalist M.P.'s were decrying the robbery of Ireland's manhood. A glaring example of the contradiction was the leader of August 18, 1883, condemning Trevelyan's proposal to grant £100,000 for purposes of emigration while the back pages carried several notices of assisted passage to the United States and Canada. In that year alone, close to 109,000 persons departed for America.

[6]W. O'Brien, *The Parnell of Real Life* (London, 1926), 32.
[7]*United Ireland*, October 8, 1881.

There was no shortage of axes for the paper to grind in the early years of the Parnellite movement. Government and people would need to be reminded of the social distress which had given rise to the Land League and was still rife in Mayo and the western parts of the country. The Administration would have to be damned for policies which added two new milestones to the long line of regressive legislation for Ireland—the Coercion Act of 1881 and the Crimes Act of 1882. The tenants would require guidance as a new land act sought to wean them from their traditional hatred of the landlords. And, of course, no excuse whatsoever would be needed to assail the enemies of the Nationalist movement.

The No-rent Manifesto

The Land Act which passed into law on August 22, 1881, presented O'Brien with his first real challenge as editor of *United Ireland*. This great measure provided for the establishment of "fair" rents, to be reduced periodically thereafter, and it secured to the tenant undisturbed occupation of his holding as long as those rents were paid.[8] Moreover, the landlord could no longer raise the rent, and an evicted tenant could sell his interest and claim compensation for his improvements. Its crucial faults were that the definition of a fair rent was left to the discretion of the Land Court judges, the question of arrears was not settled, and more than 100,000 leaseholders were denied recourse to the fair-rent clauses. However, the act posed a definite threat to Parnell's control of the Nationalist movement. On the one hand, to men like Dillon and Davitt the only fair rent was no rent, while moderates within the party, such as Justin McCarthy, T. D. Sullivan of the *Nation,* and John O'Connor Power, had earlier defied Parnell's advice to abstain by voting in favor of the bill. In the long run, Parnell succeeded in pleasing none of them by his neutral stance. Worse still, after the bill became law, the tenants, urged on by the clergy, flocked to the courts to have their rents fixed, ignoring Parnell's advice to await the Land League's submission of selected cases to the land courts in order to test the

---

[8]For an analysis of the Land Act, see J. E. Pomfret, *The Struggle for Land in Ireland, 1800–1923* (Princeton, 1930), 196–204. The contemporary Nationalist criticism is typified by M. Davitt, *The Fall of Feudalism in Ireland* (New York, 1904), 321–329. For treatment of the opposing pressures on Parnell, from the left and moderate wings of the party, see C. C. O'Brien, *Parnell and His Party, 1880–90* (Oxford, 1957), 65–9; F. S. L. Lyons, *John Dillon* (London, 1968), 49–51. Note also a recent revisionist treatment of Gladstone's measure, concerning its regressive effect on Irish economic advance in B. L. Solow, *The Land Question and the Irish Economy, 1870–1903* (Cambridge, Mass., 1971), 157–161.

fairness of the rent-fixing provisions of the act.[9] It was indeed too much to expect that sorely-pressed tenants would turn their backs on legislation which went a long way toward conceding the basic demands of the League. Nevertheless, Parnell now sought aid from O'Brien's *United Ireland* to stem the tide of defections.

Of all the prominent men around Parnell, O'Brien was closest to agreeing with the leader's estimate of the situation arising from the act. Like Parnell, O'Brien put his reliance on the tenants, firmly convinced that the act would leave most of their rents unchanged and would thereby disgust the farmers.[10] Throughout the summer, *United Ireland* denounced the Land Courts and publicized the handful of estates in the West, where arrears-ridden tenants, worked up by the more aggressive members of the Land League, were refusing to pay rents. Both men miscalculated. Within two months of the passage of the act, over 11,000 tenant applications for reviews of rents had been received at the Land Commission and the numbers continued to mount steadily. Even the government was surprised at the response.[11]

Unfortunately, the only allies who rallied to Parnell's speeches and O'Brien's exhortations were those who countenanced or promoted the growing violence attending demonstrations against evictions and land-grabbing. Forster's Coercion Act, passed in the previous February in response to a threefold increase in outrages, had failed to eradicate agrarian crime. Now, with crime still increasing,[12] the effect of the agitation could only be to persuade the government to regard Parnell and his associates as accomplices of criminal elements in the countryside. It was not unexpected, therefore, when on October 12, 1881, the British Cabinet fell in line with Parnell's strategy of inducing the government "to transmute him, by imprisonment, into a symbol of the Irish nation."[13] Several other members of the party joined their leader in Kilmainham jail. O'Brien could hardly escape the net, for the entire responsibility for *United Ireland* had been his ever since Parnell and his colleagues Joseph Biggar and Patrick Egan had withdrawn from their nominal directorships to sidestep the mounting libel suits against the

[9]Parnell could not even rely on his professed supporters. A. J. Kettle, M.P. advocate of a no-rent campaign, was one of the first to apply to the new Land Court for the fixing of a fair rent on his 150-acre home in County Dublin, see A. J. Kettle edited by A. J. Kettle, (Dublin, 1958), *Material for Victory*, xi.

[10]Parnell to Croke, July 22, 1881; O'Brien to Croke, August 11, 1881, Croke Papers, NLI microfilm, p. 6011.

[11]G. Shaw-Lefevre, *Gladstone and Ireland* (London, 1912), 162.

[12]In 1881, alone, the alarming total of twenty-two agrarian murders were recorded.

[13]C. C. O'Brien, *Parnell and His Party*, 72.

paper.[14] Within three days, therefore, O'Brien, too, was lodged in Kilmainham as "reasonably suspected of having since the 30th day of September, 1880 been guilty as principal of treasonable practices"—one more instance of the unerring facility of British governments, of whatever hue, for yielding martyrs and heroes to the Nationalist cause.

O'Brien's arrival at Kilmainham coincided with Parnell's decision to launch a "no-rent" campaign in Ireland. The time had arrived for another dose of Parnell's strategy. He had little to lose now that the testing of the act had failed. Besides, he even stood to gain in American circles. There, under the direction of Patrick Ford's *Irish World*, New York's literary vehicle for the fiercest sort of anti-English sentiment, many New Departure elements had become disillusioned by the failure of the movement in Ireland to organize a determined campaign. For drafting such a plan, Parnell selected the new arrival: "'O'Brien, of all the men in the world, you are the man we wanted' . . . and he [Parnell] begged of me during the dinner-hour to draft a No-Rent Manifesto."[15] O'Brien was eager to perform the task, believing that inaction could only result in the extinction of the Land League.

The manifesto appeared on the front page of *United Ireland* October 22 and called for the withholding of rents until Parnell and his fellow prisoners were released. It was not a repudiation of rent per se. It urged passive resistance by the entire population, asked the tenants to choose between "all-powerful unity and impotent disorganization," and assured them that "millions" of American dollars would be thrown into the fray. The document bore the signatures of the League executive board: Parnell, Davitt, Dillon, Thomas Sexton, Patrick Egan, A. J. Kettle, and Thomas Brennan. Apparently, it had not been easy to reach agreement on issuing so provocative a declaration. Kettle recalled that it took O'Brien all he knew to induce Dillon to sign.[16] Davitt, whose name was added by Brennan because he was then in an English jail as a result of his Land League activities, later expressed strong disapproval, complaining that the tough policy had come eight months too late and would prove ineffective.[17] The fears of clerical repudiation, which O'Brien rejected, were soon realized, however.

[14]W. O'Brien, *Recollections*, 308n.
[15]*Ibid.*, 362.
[16]A. J. Kettle, *Material*, 56.
[17]Davitt, *The Fall*, 309.

Archbishop McCabe of Dublin publicly blasted the document as "an indignity to the moral sense of our own people . . . [which] struck at the foundation on which society rests—the rights of property." Archbishop Croke of Cashel, who had read the manifesto "with the utmost pain" felt it would lead to nothing but disintegration and defeat.[18] The *Freeman's Journal* and the *Nation,* for the second time during 1881, echoed outspoken opposition to Parnell's tactics.

In the face of such an outcry, *United Ireland* had no hope of arousing the tenants to withhold rents. As long as their bishops blasted the party's advice as being akin to communism, the incarceration of Parnell and his colleagues seemed less horrendous to the tenants than the harm to their souls if they followed the manifesto's advice. It speaks more for O'Brien's courage than his political sagacity that he persisted. Possibly his courage was nurtured by a mild anticlericalism, which manifested itself some years later in the unfavorable portrait of Father McGrudder, a timeserving cleric in O'Brien's novel *When We Were Boys.*

The no-rent campaign proved, indeed, to be a complete failure. Its most serious annoyance to the landlords may well have been the decision of the Galway Blazers to skip the fox-hunting season because of the opposition of local tenants! In a comment some months later, Parnell put the best face on the episode when he explained:

I am not one of those who ever believed that the tenants of Ireland would refuse to pay rent at the outset. I never supposed that the policy of "no rent" would do more than effect good indirectly in enabling tenants to obtain large abatements and in this sense it worked.[19]

Defeat on particular issues, however, could not materially weaken the Nationalist cause as long as the real enemies—landlordism and Dublin Castle—remained. These O'Brien held up to constant abuse in *United Ireland.* Nor did the manifesto diminish the popularity of the paper or its editor. *United Ireland* throughout played an important role as the upholder of Parnell's political views, as a virulent critic of coercion, and, above all, as the standard-bearer of what then stood for Irish Nationalism.[20] Week after week, its pages kept the names of imprisoned

[18]*Freeman's Journal,* October 20 and November 4, 1881.

[19]*United Ireland,* December 23, 1882.

[20]This latter point becomes evident when set against the *cri de coeur* of the *Freeman's Journal* of January 14, 1882: "We are no advocate of extreme or visionary doctrines in connection with the distribution of land or of anything else. We are opposed to all violence and all illegality. We have never encouraged those who dream of a separation of Ireland from

M.P.'s and hundreds of other victims of coercion before the public, and it never missed the opportunity to praise rent-striking tenants (real or supposed) or to curse the "nominal" Home Rulers who voted with the government. O'Brien gained a notoriety all his own by successfully defying the authorities by having his "suppressed" newspaper published from London, Paris, Liverpool, and elsewhere until censorship was removed—all the time editing the paper from his cell in Kilmainham.

"United Ireland"

William O'Brien had served six months of his imprisonment under the Coercion Act when his release was ordered on compassionate grounds in April 1882. Tragedy again struck the family. His mother, another victim of tuberculosis, died soon after he reached her side: the last link with the past had been severed. A few weeks later a great tragedy also befell the Parliamentary cause. On that day, Lord Frederick Cavendish, the newly-appointed successor to W. E. Forster, and his Undersecretary, Thomas Burke, were brutally murdered while walking in Dublin's Phoenix Park. On the face of it, this attack by secret-society assassins blighted the hopes for the conciliation agreement worked out behind the scenes between Gladstone and Parnell which had secured the latter's release four days earlier.[21]

United Ireland on May 13 abandoned its weekly cartoon and used that space, bordered in black, to express its revulsion "for the stain cast upon the character of our Nation for manliness and hospitality." In the same issue, Parnell dubbed the murders "one of the most atrocious and unprovoked crimes ever committed," and Davitt called them "one of the most disastrous blows which has been sustained during the last century by the National cause in Ireland." Dillon echoed those sentiments, while Sexton even went so far as to attempt to counter popular feeling against Burke, one of the most hated men in Ireland.

The murders in Phoenix Park were the culmination of almost three years of agrarian violence of an intensity unusual even for Ireland. Such violence had posed a dilemma for the Nationalist leaders all along, com-

---

England . . . We did not identify ourselves with all the proceedings of the Land League nor have we approved of the No Rent manifesto."

   [21]For the background and analysis of this agreement, the so-called Kilmainham treaty, see C. C. O'Brien, *Parnell and His Party*, 76–78, 82.

mitted as those leaders were to using parliamentary methods for the solution of Ireland's problems. If, as most of them believed, the pressure exerted in Parliament should be supported by external pressure from the tenants, then that support would have to be of a kind sanctioned by morality. The disaffected tenants might be forgiven for thinking otherwise, considering the fiery language of O'Brien and the wilder utterances of John Dillon.

After May 1882, however, the situation changed radically. The Crimes Bill, introduced in the House of Commons on the evening of Lord Frederick Cavendish's funeral, became law during the summer and was harsh enough to keep Ireland under the firm control of Earl Spencer, the Lord Lieutenant, for the next three years. Under its terms the Lord Lieutenant could prohibit meetings and suppress newspapers; magistrates on summary jurisdiction were allowed to impose sentences of six months with hard labor; trial by jury could be abolished in serious cases; and power was given to the police to enter houses under warrant to search for the "secret apparatus of murder, for the dagger, for the documents, for the threatening letters, for the cape masks." A special provision—the power of removing foreigners—was directed at the American "emissaries of O'Donovan Rossa," the exiled Fenian. The trying of cases without juries never needed to be put in force, however, for a special clause enabled the government to frame amenable jury panels. This jury-packing device earned the special abuse of William O'Brien in *United Ireland* for as long as the three-year duration of the act. This strengthening of the government's hand was facilitated by a corresponding weakening of Nationalist determination. Parnell adhered to the decision to opt for nonviolent methods implicit in the Kilmainham treaty and had no trouble in carrying his followers with him. The problem of building up the party machine through the newly established Irish National League, tame successor to the proscribed Land League, took pride of place to Home Rule and land reform. It was left to William O'Brien to preserve the façade of advanced Nationalism in the pages of *United Ireland*. But not even his tumultuous rhetoric could disguise the fact that evictions were proceeding at a pace not experienced since 1853,[22] while the high tide of agrarian outrage during the turbulent Land League days was never

---

[22] In the four years 1882 through 1885, over 16,000 families were evicted. Of these, about 48 percent were readmitted to their holdings, the vast majority as caretakers (Carnarvon Papers, PRO 30-6/64, folio 38).

again to return. Aggression was to be replaced by exasperation— a pin-
pricking policy directed at all phases of government at home and
abroad.

Those who had supported coercion came in for special abuse. The
tone had already been set by *United Ireland*, which advised its readers on
February 18, 1882: "Metaphorically speaking, whenever you see a
Radical head, hit it . . . wherever a vote can help to kick a Radical, kick
him." And Liberal party radicals like Joseph Chamberlain and Sir
Charles Dilke were denounced as "rich bourgeois, with a grudge
against the aristocracy from which their vulgarity excludes them."
Their offenses were remembered against them three years later when
they earned similar abuse for their attempts to mediate the Home Rule
question. Sir George Trevelyan, as Chief Secretary, bore the brunt of
Nationalist invective, and, according to J. G. Shaw-Lefevre, the ordeal
visibly aged him. He was not the first, and certainly not the last, Irish
secretary to suffer from the rigors of tenure in Ireland. Throughout the
summer of 1882, *United Ireland* gloated over the imperial problems posed
by the Zulu chief, Cetawayo, and the Egyptian nationalist, Arabi
Pasha, while deploring the bravery of Irish regiments in the service of
the Queen. Gladstone's Sudan adventure came in for such scurrilous
treatment that it probably did as much to consolidate the latent preju-
dices against the Irish among the English as any hacking of a landlord's
agent. One prophetic dart is worth quoting:

We wish the Mahdi every success. For us he is no False Prophet, but a Hot
Gospeller from heaven, that, we trust, may be vouchsafed to every suffering
people. Go on, sweet Mahdi and put every infidel Giaour in Khartoum to the
edge of the sword . . . With the slaughter of its [Khartoum] garrison, no man
can tell what complications the future has in store for the Gladstone
Government.[23]

Although the flow of invective seemed endless, 1883 and 1884 were
years of demoralizing ineffectuality in Ireland. The pages of *United
Ireland* testify to the virtual self-effacement of the prominent men in Irish
politics who occupied themselves with little beyond a banquet speech,
an occasional by-election, opening a branch of the National League,
and the like. Parnell's preoccupations in this period were other than
political. The firebrand Dillon who had departed for America in October 1882, ostensibly for his health, unaccountably stayed away for
over two and a half years. Davitt shied away from League activity to in-

[23] *United Ireland*, January 26, 1884.

volve himself with Henry George's land-nationalization scheme. Justin McCarthy and T. P. O'Connor, journalists by profession, resided in England. Little was heard of Home Rule in those years despite the fact that it formed the main plank in the program of the National League. Even the land question receded into the background, palliated by an Arrears Act and ensuing good harvests. The most aggressive face presented to British rule was O'Brien's long journalistic harangue against jury-packing and malpractice by Dublin Castle officials. One celebrated case titillated the national appetite by its allusions to the "unspeakable" offences of two of those officials.[24] By comparison with this type of assault the Fenian-inspired dynamite forays seem almost patriotic.

An important personal achievement of O'Brien was his election to Parliament for his native Mallow in January 1883. The town, with an electorate of fewer than three hundred, was one of those Irish boroughs which Archbishop Croke claimed "would elect Barabbas for thirty pieces of silver": Parnell's candidate in the 1880 election had been routed. In 1883, O'Brien stood for the seat at Parnell's request and won handily from a Castle lawyer. His accession to the councils of the Parliamentary party was appreciated by the able T. M. Healy: "William O'Brien is great value. He is worth a 100 trainloads of ordinary men."[25] In his first session as a member of Parliament, O'Brien voted in 230 out of a total of 314 divisions, the average for the Irish M.P.'s being only 73.[26] One English observer, Henry Lucy, was not so impressed, finding O'Brien at this early stage of his career "repulsively uncouth."[27] But, of course, this could be the expected reaction of Victorian priggery to the rambunctious Irish member. Indeed, O'Brien twitted himself in his memoirs on his "tendency to idealise, and to weave reverential aureoles even about common things . . . the headlong, shouting, wildly gesticulating way."[28] It was a style and manner which, however amusing or boring at Westminster, never failed to arouse his Irish audiences.

[24]The officials involved were the secretary of the Post Office and the director of detectives in the constabulary. As a result of O'Brien's perseverance in the face of libel suits, both men were convicted of operating a vice ring. Another case, of a different nature, against the Crown Solicitor resulted in a defeat for O'Brien, with damages of over £3,000 being assessed against him. Ireland subscribed over £7,000 to cover his costs (*United Ireland,* August 9, 1884, and January 2, 1886).

[25]T. M. Healy, *Letters and Leaders of My Day* (New York, 1929) 1:184.

[26]*United Ireland,* September 8, 1883.

[27]H. Lucy, *Diary of the Salisbury Parliament* (London, 1892), 135.

[28]W. O'Brien, *Recollections,* 490.

Benefiting from Parnell's indulgent exercise of leadership in this period, O'Brien, Tim Healy, T. C. Harrington (secretary of the National League), and one or two others gained invaluable experience in directing and controlling the activities of the Nationalist movement. From the founding of the National League in the previous October, O'Brien, Healy, and Harrington were the chief spokesmen for the party at the small public meetings held on Sundays throughout the country. The slow work of building up the local branches of the Nationalist organization was begun by that trio, and the fruits of their labors were the compliant county conventions which ensured Parnell's hegemony for the rest of the decade. By 1885 Healy, with forgivable egoism and wishful thinking, could declare to Henry Labouchere, Liberal M.P. and friend of Home Rule: "Dillon, McCarthy, O'Brien, Harrington and I settle everything. When we agree, no one can disagree."[29]

The organizational work performed by O'Brien and his colleagues began to bear fruit about the beginning of 1885. At that time, close to 700 branches of the League existed. Within six months the total was 818 branches, excluding about 200 branches that had collapsed but that probably could be revived at election time. The membership was distributed fairly evenly throughout the twenty-eight Nationalist counties, with the exception of that area (counties Dublin and Wicklow) under the control of the Dublin Metropolitan Police (DMP) where the meager total of five branches existed.[30] The League was not successful where the clergy proved hostile, as was the case in Galway, Mayo, and Roscommon. Conversely, the League was strong in areas in Limerick and Tipperary where the priests were under the control of the Nationalist Archbishop Croke. By December the branches totaled 1,261, and more than thirty public meetings were held per month, a remarkable change from the apathy of the preceding years.[31] The meetings were almost always held on Sundays, so as to encourage the priests to appear on the platform.

[29]A. L. Thorold, *The Life of Henry Labouchere* (London, 1913), 251.

[30]Then, as later, the industrialized working class of Dublin found little attraction in the agrarian structure of the Nationalist movement.

[31]Data on the progress of the League obtained from reports of R. E. Beckerson to Inspector General RIC, dated July 15, 1885, and April 15 and July 16, 1886, in SPO, Police and Crime Records, 1848–1920, carton no. 6 (Proceedings of Irish National League, 1885–1889). The Nationalist movement was at all times closely watched by the police, who relied on information from local surveillance, from informers, and from the Nationalist press. Month-by-month detailed reports emanated from the local police stations which were passed up the chain of command to the Inspector General, who then made summary reports for the Lord Lieutenant, the Chief Secretary, and the law officers in Dublin Castle.

An unexpected fillip was given to the awakened popular interest in politics by the announcement of the visit to Ireland of the Prince of Wales and his consort. Nationalists regarded the visit as a political gimmick to detract from Parnell's influence—well they might, considering that royal visits till then had been about as rare as heavenly apparitions. William O'Brien expressed the Nationalist resentment at a huge demonstration in the Phoenix Park on March 1, 1885, and for the next six weeks he encouraged unremitting hostility to the visit in *United Ireland*. With the memory of General Gordon's death at Khartoum still exciting the English, the Prince was taunted with the assurance that "the Mahdi would get a thousand cheers in Ireland for every cheer H.R.H. could buy."[32] The April 11 issue of the paper, in an "Irish salute" for the Prince, contained a four-page supplement bearing hundreds of notices disapproving of the visit from individuals representing virtually every facet of Nationalist society. O'Brien, in a speech at Cork, declared, "it would be false delicacy and poltroonery on the part of the Irish people to hold their voices or conceal their feelings." As Croke sardonically remarked, "they are not coming to reopen the Parliament at College Green!"[33] Only at Belfast were the visitors received with any degree of enthusiasm. Elsewhere they were greeted with cheers for the Mahdi, green flags, black flags, and the inscription "We will have no Prince but Charlie." The strongest protest was made at Mallow on April 13, where O'Brien again led the demonstrators and provoked what must have been the first baton charge by police in Ireland in over three years.

It would seem that *United Ireland* was leading a charmed life in this period. Its scathing attacks on cherished English institutions, the personal insults it hurled at officials, and its ridicule of British military efforts in the Sudan—all must have sorely strained the patience of Liberal and Tory alike. Yet, there was no interference with publication. The matter did not go unnoticed in the Commons, where the government was frequently urged to action against such "incitement to crime and disaffection" in Ireland. Campbell-Bannerman, Gladstone's Chief Secretary for Ireland, was well aware, however, that the incidence of agrarian crime in Ireland was at a very low ebb. The better strategy, he believed, was to endure Irish blather in exchange for relative peace and quiet in Ireland. As he explained to his colleagues: "The point we have

---

[32]*United Ireland*, March 14, 1885.

[33]Croke Papers, NLI microfilm, p. 6012: draft of a letter to his clergy on the greeting to be accorded to HRH—"no more and no less than a courteous reception."

always to consider is whether the harm which might unfortunately be done by the circulation of such articles might not be intensified, if any legal proceedings taken against a newspaper gave it a fictitious importance in the eyes of the more ignorant classes."[34]

Nevertheless, the popular response to O'Brien's lead in the spring of 1885 was symptomatic of deeper and more immediate feelings—namely, the discontent which accompanied agricultural depression. It is unlikely that the National League would have gathered the strength it did during 1885 were it not for the fact that rents were again becoming a burden. However, concerted public agitation was largely confined to boycotting and there was no recurrence of the alarming outrages of 1881 and 1882. Nevertheless, the authorities were doubtless impressed by the perceptible increase in the murders of "grabbers" (takers of evicted farms) and in assaults on bailiffs. By August 1885, when the number of agrarian outrages was more than double what it had been in the previous January, the Lord Lieutenant was sufficiently alarmed to warn the Home Office, "We are going on well here but it is really like walking over a volcano."[35]

The worst areas for boycotting were in the southeast and southwest of the country, particularly Tipperary, Kilkenny, Wexford, Cork, and Kerry. The situation in Kerry was aggravated by the return of the "crowbar brigades" to speed the work of eviction and by the appearance of marauding bands of peasants whose only allegiance was to "Captain Moonlight." On the political scene, Parnell, now in an unedifying alliance with the Tories since Gladstone's defeat in June, shied away from supporting the agitation. His forbearance was noted with relief at Dublin Castle by E. G. Jenkinson, the assistant undersecretary for police and crime, in his report to Lord Carnarvon, the Tory Viceroy.

"Mr. Parnell and his lieutenants are doing all they can to keep down outrages, and have even condemned the indiscriminate use of boycotting . . . I do not hesitate to say that were it not for the faith which the people have in Mr. Parnell, and for the influences which he and his party exercise over them, there would be an outbreak of serious outrages in all the worst and most distressed parts of Ireland."[36]

Tim Healy, responding to Lord Randolph Churchill's request to visit Kerry and help quell the disorder it was feared would result from

---

[34]*Parliamentary Debates*, 294 (4 December 1884), 613.

[35]Carnarvon to Sir Richard Cross, August 31, 1885 (copy), in Carnarvon Papers, PRO 30-6/62.

[36]E. G. Jenkinson to Carnarvon, September 26, 1885, *ibid.*

Davitt's "extremeness," found no difficulty in enlisting the aid of O'Brien, who "backed up as willingly as myself the Tory policy of peace."[37]

But there was no peace in Ireland. At the very time Parnell and his colleagues were working so effectively to curb agrarian outrages, much greater violence was being visited on the browbeaten peasants by the minions of Dublin Castle. Throughout the country a spate of notorious evictions was in progress. On Lord Kenmare's estate in Kerry, where refusal of requests for rent reductions was followed by evictions, more than two hundred armed police and light infantry descended on the property to make sure the law was upheld. That story was repeated wherever the crowbar brigade appeared, a sure sign that the countryside was seething with unrest. A deeper political reason for the unrest did not go unobserved at Dublin Castle, where even Home Rule was not without its champions. Again, Assistant Undersecretary Jenkinson reported to his superiors:

The first thing that we must try and do is to bring our government in touch with the people. At the present moment, our administration in Ireland is isolated . . . No honest and unprejudiced man can say that our administration, whatever our intentions may be, is popular, or that under it Ireland is well governed and prosperous. If we wish to place ourselves in touch with the people, we must practically show our sympathy with them by acknowledging that our present system of administration is not suited to the country, by joining hands with their leaders, and by acknowledging the principle of Home Rule.[38]

The Home Rule Bill of 1886

The events leading to the first Home Rule Bill marked the end of that phase of the Nationalist agitation which had begun with the founding of the Land League. The agitation had been intense between 1879 and 1881, but the heavy hand of coercion had imposed an uneasy calm in the following years. During that time the Irish Nationalist party had no option but to continue the struggle in Parliament and build up the National League at home. The latter task was eminently successful,

[37]Healy, *Letters and Leaders* 1:227. In fact, Davitt was far from being extreme during his Kerry sorties. In a speech at Castleisland he deplored outrages, which only gave satisfaction to the enemy, and exhorted the people to control themselves lest public opinion in England be offended (*United Ireland*, February 27, 1886).

[38]E. G. Jenkinson Report of January 22, 1885, on "Secret Societies in Ireland and America." This document, along with Jenkinson's previously quoted report of September 26, 1885, was submitted in 1889 for use by the then existing Cabinet [PRO, Cabinet minutes, CAB/37/23, no. 5 (1889)]. These reports were also used later by A. J. Balfour to supplement his report to the Cabinet in January 1889 on the "condition of Ireland."

mainly because of the patient labors of O'Brien, Harrington, and Healy. The party was less successful in Parliament, though one should not discount the effect of suspensions there for infringing the rules of the House in whipping up resentment among the followers in Ireland. For example, the great demonstration in the Phoenix Park in March 1885, at which O'Brien had berated the royal visit, had been called in "honor" of his suspension from the House for defying the Speaker's call to order. The benefits of all this political spadework were reaped in the general election of December 1885, when the number of Irish Nationalist seats jumped to eighty-six. The election was another great personal victory for O'Brien, who, having lost his Mallow seat under redistribution, was selected to confront the Orangemen on their home ground in South Tyrone. The Loyalists had a majority of more than three hundred on the electoral register, but divisions between Liberals and Unionists over the nomination of a candidate suitable to the Orange lodges caused many Liberal voters to abstain, with the result that O'Brien scraped through with a margin of fifty-two votes.[39] The victory was sweetened by the fact that his defeated opponent, Captain the Honorable Somerset Maxwell, had distinguished himself some years before in those famous Orange forays for the relief of Captain Boycott. More important than individual successes, of course, was the solid victory in Ireland of the Parnellite forces—for the first time the Irish representation held the balance of power in the House of Commons.

There had been two attempts to solve the Irish question before Gladstone introduced his Home Rule Bill in April 1886. The first was by Joseph Chamberlain and envisaged, basically, the extension of local government under the coordination of a "central board" in Ireland. The scheme was rejected by the Cabinet in May 1885. But after the defeat of Gladstone's government in June and pending the general election, Chamberlain, aided by Sir Charles Dilke, sought to convert Parnell to his so-called central board idea. However, Chamberlain looked with finality on schemes which Parnell could obviously only accept as interim measures pending restitution of an Irish Parliament. The abuse in *United Ireland* made Chamberlain's planned tour of Ireland to popularize his program impossible. Nationalists bent on Home Rule wanted no part of any substitute local government scheme. Many also

[39] *The Times*, London, December 8, 1885. O'Brien's victory was but a temporary one. In the election the following summer the seat returned to the Unionists and never again fell to Nationalist "invaders."

distrusted the proposed visit as a ploy to conciliate Irish electors in Britain before the general election. Neither were the votes of Chamberlain and Dilke in favor of Gladstone's Crimes Act of 1882 forgotten. The second attempt was that by Lord Carnarvon, Lord Lieutenant of Ireland in the Conservative government, which had assumed office on Gladstone's defeat. Carnarvon's effort, apparently arising from personal convictions as an Imperial federationist, involved a statutory legislature with proper safeguards, but this too failed when he found that none of his Cabinet colleagues shared his convictions.[40] With this failure, Parnell withdrew his support of Lord Salisbury's government, and Gladstone took office once more in January 1886.

We have seen how O'Brien's *United Ireland* heaped abuse on Gladstone and his policies throughout most of his administration and how, latterly, O'Brien himself had backed the Tory "policy of peace." Now, however, with Gladstone's conversion to Home Rule, the time had come to lavish praise on Liberal peacemakers. The first intimation of that conversion in December 1885 had brought a rapturous acknowledgment from the member for Mallow: "Never sounded more joyous heavenly music of hope around our Isle of Destiny than fills the air this memorable Christmastide." It was followed by pleas from *United Ireland* urging the people to conform to the moderating counsels of Parnell, Sexton, Dillon, and Davitt. Dillon, lately returned from his long sojourn in Colorado, issued the most eloquent appeals for "self-restraint and abstinence from anything that could be distorted into crime." The lowest point in this unseemly timidity was reached by Tim Harrington, secretary of the National League. During the spring and summer of 1886 he threatened several branches with dismissal from the League if they persisted in the "discreditable transactions" of boycotting! Sending nonmembers of the League to Coventry he branded "stupid and pernicious," and a branch which urged members merely to boycott White Star steamers built at the Belfast Dockyards (the scene of recent anti-Catholic riots) he condemned likewise.[41]

The introduction of the Home Rule Bill in April 1886, damned by Matthew Arnold as the nadir of Liberalism,[42] was hailed by O'Brien's paper as the greatest event of the century for Ireland. This seemed high

[40]See R. B. O'Brien, *The Life of Charles Stewart Parnell* (London, 1898) 2:62–95; C. C. O'Brien, *Parnell and His Party*, 102–107.

[41]*United Ireland*, December 26, 1885, and February 6, 1886. For Harrington's activities, see his letters to various INL branches in Harrington Papers, NLI MS. 9454.

[42]Curiously enough, intellectuals were conspicuous by their opposition to this outburst of Gladstone's moral compulsion. They form an impressive galaxy of Victorian science,

praise indeed for a measure which promised to replace Dublin Castle by a two-tiered legislature but denied that body's rights to fiscal autonomy, and to immediately control the police, while also preventing it from making laws in matters ranging from the conduct of trade to the erection of navigation beacons. Nevertheless, Parnell led his followers in full acceptance of the measure, and there was no dissent from the Irish benches. So well had O'Brien and his colleagues done their organizing in the preceding years that Nationalist Ireland gave solid backing to the parliamentarians. The decision of the party was conveyed in *United Ireland* on April 10, three days after Parnell had disclosed the terms of the bill to a few of his trusted colleagues: "We have no hesitation in saying it seems to us to contain the elements of a great and durable treaty of peace and amity between the two nations."

O'Brien's contribution to the parliamentary debate was modest, though its patent appeal for trust and conciliation must have sounded strange to those who had formerly winced at his diatribes in *United Ireland*. It rankled, in particular, that doughty Ulster representative Colonel E. J. Saunderson, who, in addition to reminding the House of O'Brien's hostility to the Prince's visit in the previous year, quoted the threats made by the member for Mallow in the *Freeman's Journal:*

If the olive branch that we are holding out to England now should meet with no better response than the raving of the Cockney newspapers . . . If they do not want peace Mr. Parnell will give them war . . . such a war as eighty members can carry on in Parliament and as Irish people can carry on outside with weapons of franchise and boycott . . . or any other weapons that time and opportunity may offer us or those who come after us from generation to generation.[43]

But, of course, O'Brien was as capable as the next of speaking with two voices, and it was his parliamentary tone which revealed his true nature. Despite the timid concessions of the bill, with its powerful Upper House of Peers and its numerous restrictions on the Legislature, O'Brien recognized the measure as "a most marvellous plan for recreating society out of its ruins almost in Ireland." Details did not matter in this gigantic task, for, as he foresaw, the kernel of success lay in the union of classes. The enlargement of local government, control of

---

literature, and art: Huxley, Tyndall, Tennyson, Browning, Swinburne, Lecky, Froude, Jowett, Spencer, Martineau, and Millais [H. Paul, *Modern England* (London, 1906) 5:57].

[43] *Parliamentary Debates*, 305 (10 May 1886), 1763–64.

the purse, and settlement of the land problem were details which would naturally proceed with the good will of the mother Parliament.[44] O'Brien was firmly convinced that the future of Ireland was necessarily bound up with that of the Empire. The economic ties between the two countries—the flow of laborers in one direction and capital in the other—demanded as much. All of his colleagues felt similarly, and this accounts for the ease with which they accepted the niggardly provisions of Gladstonian Home Rule. As O'Brien had assured his English listeners earlier in the debate, "The interests are so interlaced that separation is impossible."[45]

Of course, Irish hopes were doomed from the start. The opening of the Home Rule question sparked an Orange "revolt" which hardened with the passing years. During the first half of 1886 Ulster propagandists of the Irish Loyal and Patriotic Union flooded England with scurrilous pamphlets inciting racial enmities with lurid reminders of the massacre of Ulster protestants by "Irish papists" in the insurrection of 1641. The Nationalists were being warned that two nations also existed within the geographical confines of the sister island. An England which so recently had striven, at long range, to keep intact her interests in Egypt and the Transvaal, refused to dismember her unity at home and Parliament rejected the bill on its second reading by 341 votes to 311.

In the election which followed Gladstone's defeat, O'Brien lost his seat by ninety-nine votes. The divisions among the South Tyrone Loyalists had now been smoothed over, and the Unionist majority secured the seat for T. W. Russell, a Protestant land reformer who was to join with O'Brien sixteen years later in solving the land question. Relieved of parliamentary duties, O'Brien also began to relax his grip on *United Ireland* by assigning editorial duties to his literary colleague M. McDonnell Bodkin. With the national question out of the way for the moment, attention could once more be directed to the needs of the tenants. Therefore, O'Brien prepared to plunge headlong into the agrarian agitation along with his fellow zealot Dillon. For the next five years the history of the Nationalist movement is very much the story of the exploits of these two men.

[44] *Ibid.*, 305 (10 May 1886), 622–632.
[45] *Ibid.*, 304 (13 April 1886), 1466.

TWO

The Land War
in Ireland

W ITH THE shelving of Home Rule in the wake of the Liberal
defeat, the land question became once more the paramount
issue in Irish politics. For the moment, however, the focus of Nationalist
activity was the convention of the Irish Race in America, to be held in
Chicago in August 1886. The main attraction there was the presence of
William O'Brien and Michael Davitt, members of a four-man Irish
delegation. The proceedings were mainly concerned with ensuring
American backing for Parnell's acceptance of Gladstonian Home Rule.
It was also necessary to prevent the dynamitards of Clan na Gael, the
American Fenian organization, from capitalizing on the defeat of the
Home Rule Bill to foment another bout of terrorism in England.
O'Brien, with Davitt's help, was successful in getting the Clan leaders
to withdraw the candidacy of an extremist as president of the American
National League in favor of John Fitzgerald, a "railway king" from
Nebraska. Of the seven resolutions unanimously adopted at the convention, none proposed any radical solution of the land question. But
O'Brien did give private assurances to the recalcitrant Patrick Ford,
again aligned with the constitutional movement, that the land war
would soon be waged in Ireland with all the old fervor.[1] O'Brien, who
had more or less been an observer of the mass agitation of Land League
days, was to take a leading role in the second great campaign in less
than a decade.

Ever since the previous winter there had been every indication that
Ireland was drifting toward a renewed Land War, as acute depression
in the prices of farm produce maintained high eviction rates, and the

[1]W. O'Brien, *Evening Memories* (Dublin, 1920), 143ff.

Arrest of William O'Brien and John Dillon at Loughrea, County Galway. Scene at the Plan of Campaign rent-office after the arrest in December 1886. O'Brien, in top hat and spectacles, is followed by Dillon, Matt Harris, and David Sheehy (contemporary sketch from *Illustrated London News*).

taking of evicted farms by land-grabbing tenants precipitated a wave of boycotting. One wonders what social dislocation would have occurred had not the rent-reducing provisions of the Land Act of 1881 been operating.[2] During the first half of 1886 the tenants had shown remarkable forbearance in obeying the calls of the parliamentary leaders for social peace so as not to embarrass their political negotiations or retard the concession of Home Rule.[3] With Gladstone's defeat, however, the politicians could no longer implore the tenants to suffer in silence. Moreover, since the speech of Lord Salisbury, the Conservative leader, at St. James Hall in May calling for twenty years of resolute government as the cure for "mutilating, murdering, robbery and boycotting," they had no illusions about the type of regime which would follow a Tory victory at the polls. Nor did it seem likely that a few acts of agrarian violence could be used by Parnell to coax concessions from Lord Salisbury.

With this in mind, the delegates to the Chicago convention saw their mission as an effort to replenish their dried-up financial reserves with American support in preparation for the struggle which would surely begin when rents became due in November. The return of O'Brien and the others to Ireland in early September coincided with a series of well-publicized evictions, which were notable for signs of a tenant resistance that had been lacking during previous years. There were, of course, still cases in which evicted families trudged in humble procession to the workhouse, but on the Woodford estates of Lord Clanricarde five hundred police were needed to protect bailiffs and emergency men. The tenant resistance was so great that it took one whole day to evict one family. Bailiffs dodged buckets of boiling water, gruel, and hot lime, but the tenants finally surrendered to the threat of a bayonet charge.[4] The excitement mounted during the following weeks in which bayonets, scaling ladders, and crowbars were pitted against boiling water and swarms of bees. But gruel and hot lime do not a revolution make! The resistance was invariably confined to the tenants whose homes were under attack, and they could expect little assistance from the rustic

[2]From August 1881 to August 1885 almost 170,000 rents had been fixed by court decisions or voluntary agreement at an average of 20 percent reductions [J. E. Pomfret, *The Struggle for Land in Ireland, 1800-1923* (Princeton, 1930), 201].

[3]The peasants were not the only ones from whom self-restraint was demanded. Parnell wrote to Healy shortly after the 1885 election, "I wish you would use your influence to impress upon those newly-elected Members with whom you come in contact the necessity of avoiding the use of violent, boastful and extreme language" [T. M. Healy, *Letters and Leaders of My Day* (New York, 1929), 237].

[4]*United Ireland*, August 28, 1886.

onlookers beyond groans for the "peelers." The parliamentarians shied away from counseling anything more violent, for they always hedged their more militant speeches with appeals for self-restraint and self-sacrifice.

... stick to honest combinations ... do not stain your hands with those cowardly and disgusting crimes that revolt the conscience of every civilized human being ... Demand your abatement, and if the landlord refuses to grant it, then I tell you to keep it in spite of him. (William O'Brien at Gurteen, County Sligo, October 10, 1886).[5]

The call to withhold rents was merely one of a number of utterances, usually heard in bad years, acknowledging the fact that rent reductions were necessary to avoid widespread distress. Davitt had proposed a scheme in 1882 whereby rents would be paid into a national fund for the relief of tenants.[6] No scheme was more explicit than the remedy proposed in a leading article in O'Brien's *United Ireland* in February 1885. Stressing the need for combination, unity, and cooperation in generating a national resistance to rack-renting, it explained:

Once the tenants on an estate have come to a conclusion as to what would be the fair rent for the year ... they should lodge in a bank the amount of each man's reduced rent to the credit of trustees so that it cannot be withdrawn by any individual without the consent of all ... not a penny can be touched until an arrangement has been effected with the estate as a whole ... The Fund should only be drawn upon in case of the eviction of a member of the combination.[7]

It is remarkable that such a clearly enunciated fighting policy should have passed without comment from the politicians. Perhaps it was Parnell himself who squelched the policy, which far outdistanced the moderate course he had charted for the movement, especially considering that he was then in the midst of negotiations with Chamberlain on the latter's abortive attempt to formulate a Home Rule measure. Since the level of agitation in the countryside was quite low in the beginning of 1885, tenant support for such an advanced program would require considerable urging from the leadership of the National League. The latter was not forthcoming, and soon political minds were fully exercised by royal visits and tottering administrations. Conditions were otherwise in the autumn of 1886, when the peasants, as in Land League days, were ahead of the parliamentary movement.

[5] *Ibid.*, October 16, 1886.
[6] F. Sheehy-Skeffington, *Michael Davitt* (London, 1967), 115.
[7] *United Ireland*, February 21, 1885, "A Remedy for Rack Rent."

The Plan of Campaign

The opportunity for O'Brien to enter the struggle on behalf of the tenants came at the end of September with the rejection in the House of Commons of Parnell's Relief Bill, designed to stay evictions on payment of half the rent. Soon after, on October 17, John Dillon and William O'Brien, now the two most influential leaders under Parnell, hastened to Woodford to champion the cause of tenants who had organized a rent strike on the Clanricarde estate. At the meeting there that day Dillon outlined a brave policy to counter the landlord's demands, resurrecting a remedy proffered in *United Ireland* twenty months earlier. This lead prompted a handful of members of the organizing committee of the National League in Dublin to promulgate the entire policy as "A Plan of Campaign" in O'Brien's paper on October 23, 1886, almost five years to the day since the same paper had issued the no-rent Manifesto.[8] The document, drawn up by the lawyer Timothy Harrington, was unsigned. None of the committee members, including O'Brien and Dillon, would take the responsibility of promulgating it on his authority, lest such action provoke the immediate suppression of the National League. In fact, the Plan of Campaign was published without the official authority of Parnell or the League.[9]

For the next few months O'Brien and Dillon, aided by a dozen or so fellow M.P.'s, roamed the country carrying the message of the Plan to the tenants and condemning as fools and traitors any who paid rents without getting reductions. The Plan, like the earlier manifesto, was in no sense a repudiation of rent. Rents might be paid after "a reasonable and fair reduction." Complete solidarity was called for, and there was to be no exception even for large tenants. For, as the Nationalists liked to remind the government, Sir James Caird, an agricultural economist, had stated in 1886 that "on 538,000 holdings in Ireland . . . the rent is practically irrecoverable by anybody, whether landlord, English

[8]O'Brien acknowledged Healy as the foreshadower of the plan, though obviously several other members of the party had wrestled with the strategy of rent strikes in the preceding years. We can assume, therefore, that the plan outlined in *United Ireland* in February 1885 was Healy's. See also, F. S. L. Lyons, *John Dillon* (London, 1968), 74, for a similar scheme proposed by Healy the following October. Healy himself credited Parnell's vow to him after the failure of the No-rent Manifesto that he would never again head another agrarian movement unless the tenants lodged 75 percent of their rents in a common fund, as suggesting the final plan scheme: "I [Healy] told this to Harrington who embodied the idea in the Plan of Campaign" (Healy, *Letters and Leaders* 1:266).

[9]O'Brien, *Evening Memories*, 158.

government or Irish government."[10] Conceivably, therefore, a national rent strike could involve hundreds of thousands of tenants. A hopeful sign was the adoption of the Plan by local branches of the National League, usually headed by parish priests or members of the local clergy. In November the Plan was started on the O'Grady (Limerick), Clanricarde (Galway), Ponsonby (Cork), and Dillon (Mayo) estates, comprising in all six thousand tenants. At Portumna on November 18 O'Brien and Dillon ostentatiously headed the managing committee which collected the tenants' contributions to the Clanricarde Estate Fund set up by the Plan. On December 1 Archbishop Walsh of Dublin publicly gave his approval, observing that "tenants, in fixing rents, are merely doing what the landlords have been doing for too long."[11] In the next few weeks other prominent estates were added—DeFreyne (Roscommon), Kingston (Mitchelstown), Lansdowne (Luggacurran), O'Callaghan (Bodyke), Brooke (Coolgreaney), and Massereene (Louth).

The pattern was the same on each contested estate: the landlord offered about half the reduction demanded by the tenants, whereupon the latter invoked the Plan. This involved the election of a small managing committee to accept the rents refused by the landlord. These rents were then lodged in a secret estate fund and used to fight for reductions. The struggle was to be continued as long as the majority of the tenants on an estate held out. No part of the fund was to be paid to compensate the landlord for any legal costs incurred by him, for the tenants "should remain out for ever" rather than condone their own fleecing. All possible loopholes in the law were to be employed to avoid or delay evictions. The sheriff's power of conveyance was to be thwarted by the tenant's mortgaging his goods and chattels to creditors and selling his cattle before seizure. The response of the landlords was, of course, eviction, which meant in all cases a steady drain on the resources of the Plan as huts were erected to shelter the victims and small payments were made to those in distress. In no case was any tenant to "grab" the farm of an evicted comrade and, above all, those who aided the evictors were to be

---

[10]The number of individual holdings at this time totaled about 590,000 (in the 1871 census, 592,590). This included 169,378 tenants whose rents had been fixed under the terms of the Act of 1881 plus about 100,000 or more leaseholders who were excluded from the benefits of that act. Only 1,608 purchases had been made under land-purchase schemes prior to 1885, and the Ashbourne Act of that year only added another 25,000 purchasers by 1888 (Pomfret, *The Struggle*, 201; *Irish Year Book*, 1922).

[11]*United Ireland*, December 4, 1886.

rewarded with boycotting. In the event that an estate fund should become exhausted, the support of the evicted would become the responsibility of the National League.

As the notices of speeches and branch meetings of the League make clear, O'Brien and Dillon were the embodiment of the Plan of Campaign in the minds of observers. But as far as these two themselves were concerned, they were merely functionaries who carried out the higher strategy dictated by their leader, Parnell. The latter had not yet spoken on the Plan: he had been reportedly convalescing since October and had taken no part in the original negotiations nor in the ensuing activities of the Plan of Campaign. In early December, however, came the first blow to the hopes of the campaigners. Parnell called O'Brien to London to impress upon him the bad effect his and Dillon's activities were having on the alliance with the Liberals. O'Brien wilted in the chief's presence: "You [Parnell] are the supreme judge of policy. Once your mind is made up, I should sooner annihilate myself than cross you."[12] He thereupon agreed not to extend the Plan further, though where it was already in operation it was to be prosecuted with vigor. This was a far cry from the fond hopes for "complete solidarity amongst tenants." O'Brien's tame submission probably also indicates his realization of the difficulty of attempting to persuade the mass of tenants to face arrest, eviction, and ruin at the behest of what must have seemed to them a valiant but ineffective Irish lobby. Nevertheless, he and Dillon held to what remained of the Plan and prepared to continue the fight on behalf of those tenants who were to prove a loyal though tiny minority of Irish farmers.

The opening months of the campaign had brought a small quota of successes. Undoubtedly, also, many landlords chose to avoid the inconveniences of the Plan at the outset by coming to amicable voluntary settlements. The law, of course, had to be faced on occasion, the first being at Loughrea, County Galway, where police arrested O'Brien, Dillon, and two others in December 1886 and seized £200 of the estate fund.[13] Released on bail, they returned to the agitation despite the fact that Dublin Castle had just proclaimed the Plan an unlawful and criminal conspiracy. When their case came to trial the following February, the jury disagreed, and eventually the matter was abandoned by the authorities. This, of course, further enhanced the popularity of the campaigners.

[12] O'Brien, *Evening Memories*, 179.
[13] *United Ireland*, December 18, 1886.

A welcome boost to the agitation was given by the capitulation of Lord Dillon in Mayo early in January 1887. O'Brien had been active in negotiations with the landlord's agent which had secured to the tenants a 20 percent abatement (they had requested 25 percent) and reinstatement of all those evicted.[14] As the agitation gathered pace, O'Brien began to perfect his dual role of champion of the tenants and bane of the landlords and the Irish Administration. He was certainly behaving quite recklessly at this juncture. In January 1887, we find him at Luggacurran threatening to take the war to Canada by confronting the Governor General of Canada (Lord Lansdowne) as the exterminator of his tenants in Ireland. Some days later, stirred by the resistance of the formidable Bodyke tenants in County Clare, he warned: "I tell you and I wish the Government reporter was here to listen to it, that if our people had power to meet them, man to man and rifle to rifle, I for one would cut short my speechmaking this very moment and the next speeches that the destroyers of your homes would hear would be the speeches out of the mouth of your guns."[15] No doubt, talk like this was more of an embarrassment to members of his own party than to the authorities.

At this stage, the English observer might wonder where the resolute government promised by Lord Salisbury was. Nationalists were openly defying proclamations, several groups of tenants were refusing to pay rents, support for the Plan was expressed by the Protestant Home Rule Association, and even the Archbishop of Cashel had written the *Freeman's Journal* calling for the withholding of taxes just as the Plan withheld rents.[16] In addition, there were the perennial statistics on agrarian crime to stir the coercionist impulses of the authorities. The retaliation by the government evened the score considerably and elevated the Plan to something of an epic struggle between the government and the Nationalists or, rather, between the Irish Chief Secretary and William O'Brien.

"Bloody" Balfour

One of the first acts of the Conservative ministry in the summer of 1886 had been the appointment of Major General Sir Redvers Buller, VC, as temporary special commissioner to put down moonlighting in Clare

---

[14] *Ibid.*, January 15, 1887.
[15] *Ibid.*, January 29 and February 5, 1887.
[16] *Ibid.*, February 19, 1887.

and Kerry, counties in which a third of all agrarian crimes committed
in Ireland took place. This appointment reflected the government's dis-
satisfaction with the security arrangements in Ireland. This security
depended on the Royal Irish Constabulary (RIC) and, in the last resort,
on the army. The RIC was a unique body of men, 12,000 strong, who
were dressed, drilled, accoutered, armed, and quartered like soldiers
and regarded by Irishmen as a special bodyguard to Irish landlordism.
Up to 1881, they were commanded by inspectors in each county, but
after that year reorganization eventually divided the country (exclusive
of the small Dublin Metropolitan District) into five divisions with a
Divisional Magistrate (DM) in charge of each with full powers over the
entire forces of law and order.[17] The reorganization, though sound in
theory, had not worked well in practice, and the Irish Administration
was given some rude shocks, first by the Dublin police strike in 1882
and later by the repeated expostulations of high officials about the bad
effect the debate on Home Rule had had on the efficiency of the force.[18]

The advent of a Conservative anti-Home Rule government, coupled
with Buller's firm authority, restored the situation considerably. The
reports of the DMs for December 1886 indicate the country was
generally peaceable, though discontented. In the northern and midland
sectors, comprising eighteen counties, the Plan of Campaign had made
no real headway. The southeast saw Plan activity on five estates, while
the Plan had failed entirely in Kerry. Only at Michelstown, Bodyke,
and the eastern sections of Galway was there any cause for concern.[19]
The administration was also appreciative of the manner in which the
National League, as in the past, was working to keep down crime.

Buller soon realized, however, that the remedy lay not in protecting
rapacious landlords but in securing fair and reasonable rents for the
tenants. Shortly after his appointment he had requested authority to
refuse aid to evicting sheriffs, power to stay evictions, more money for
land purchase under Ashbourne's Act, and a bill permitting leaseholders to avail themselves of the rent-fixing provisions of the land act of
1881.[20] The Cabinet, however, was more exercised by the dangers of let-

[17]C. Lloyd, *Ireland Under the Land League* (London, 1892), 227; E. G. Jenkinson to Carnarvon, July 24, 1885, Carnarvon Papers, PRO 30/6/62. The reorganization was not completed
until 1885. The five divisions then were the Western, Southwestern, Southeastern, Midland,
and Northern divisions.
[18]Jenkinson to Buller, November 27 and December 2, 1886, Buller Papers, PRO,
WO/132/4A; PRO, Cabinet Minutes, CAB(1886) 37/18, no. 46, M. Hicks Beach
Memorandum on the State of Ireland, October 4, 1886.
[19]SPO,CSO, Registered Papers, 1886/218.
[20]See M. Hicks Beach to Buller, September 18, 1886, Buller Papers, PRO,WO/132/4A.

ting O'Brien and Dillon roam free to incite the tenants to boycotting and illegality.

Under these circumstances, some summary remedy seems absolutely necessary to enable the Executive to effectively combat such a state of things as exist at present in Ireland and which might at any moment spring up in England if a class of reckless agitators were to arise there.[21]

Those cautionary words were written by Arthur J. Balfour, Hicks Beach's replacement as Chief Secretary and soon the most formidable foe O'Brien and Dillon were ever to encounter. The summary remedy was soon forthcoming in the form of an ironic Jubilee gift to the Queen's Irish subjects—a permanent Crimes Act. Some indication of Balfour's mettle had already been shown in an incident on the Ponsonby estate early in March. O'Brien had been inciting the tenants on that property after the arrest of their aggressive pastor, Father Keller of Youghal. Stone-throwing resulted in a fracas with the police in which a bystander was bayoneted to death and twenty or more police were injured. In anticipation of trouble at the funeral of the victim, the Divisional Magistrate, Captain Thomas Plunkett, issued a famous telegram—"Do not hesitate to shoot." This action was stoutly defended by Balfour in the Commons, which earned him the title (coined by O'Brien) Bloody Balfour. The Nationalists were completely unprepared for the hitherto-undetected callous streak in Balfour's nature. Their epithets for him at that time betray their unbelief—"sybarite tyrant"; "tiger lily"; "the silken aristocrat with the heart of steel"; "Balfour of the tiger's heart, wrapped in a woman's hide"! However, they should have been forewarned by Balfour's recent performance as Secretary for Scotland. He had been appointed to that newly-created post by his uncle, Lord Salisbury, after the general election in 1886. At that time he got a foretaste of what to expect in Ireland from the activities of the Scottish Land League. Crofter agitation against excessive rents was particularly rife in the island of Skye, and marines were landed there to support the sheriff in recovering rates and rents. As he was later to do in Ireland, Balfour backed the local police authorities and took firm action in nip-

See also Buller's remarkable testimony before the Cowper Commission in January 1887, in which he lauded the National League as the only friend of the Irish tenants and observed that the law, instead of looking after a poor and ignorant people, served rather the rich [H. Paul, *Modern England* (London, 1906) 5:90].

[21] PRO, Cabinet Minutes, CAB(1887) 37/19, no. 1, Memorandum of the Chief Secretary on the Plan of Campaign, January 13, 1887.

ping in the bud an attempt at boycotting cattle sales, urged by the Highlands agitators.[22]

While the Coercion Bill was being debated in Parliament, O'Brien took the opportunity to make good his threat to beard Lansdowne in his colonial den in the hope that Canadian opinion would induce Lansdowne to settle with his tenants, who were just then being evicted wholesale. It was the first of O'Brien's wild adventures. His trip across the Atlantic was not a pleasant one, since the captain, crew, and saloon passengers held aloof from the "wild Irishman" and hailed his disembarking at New York with shouts in favor of Salisbury and Balfour. Even the act of leaving the ship brought a bad omen. When the New York reception committee came to take him off the steamer lying fogbound outside the harbor, the hawser of the rope ladder he was descending snapped and almost threw him into the water. When he arrived in Montreal on May 11, all large halls were refused him, for the Catholic clergy were opposed to the visit, and French Canadians stood aloof from the Irish movement. At Toronto, an Orange stronghold, he and his companions had to run a gauntlet of sticks and stones. Hostile mob scenes were repeated in Ottawa, Kingston, and Hamilton, Ontario. Shots were fired in the latter city. In fact, his life was not safe until he crossed the Canadian border, a little the worse for wear. In the United States, of course, he was the darling of the Irish, from Boston to New York.

The adventure did nothing to soften Lord Lansdowne, but it worked wonders at home, where very few MPs were doing anything adventurous on behalf of the Plan and none was as exposed to danger and privation as those tenants who had adopted it. Not an unwelcome result of the trip was $25,000 O'Brien received from the National League in America for delivery to Parnell. His stay in New York, however, brought some embarrassment. A group of Irish Socialists invited him to attend a large labor meeting at which resolutions were to be proposed denying the right of private property in land. Fully sharing Parnell's antipathies to the theories of Henry George, O'Brien, of course, declined, though not without alienating some members of New York labor groups.[23] Championing the cause of the peasants in Ireland did not necessarily evoke in him an active concern for the plight of proletarian

[22]Balfour to Sheriff Ivory, October 12, 1886, Balfour Papers, BM Add. MS. 49871.
[23]O'Brien, *Evening Memories*, 240–254; T. N. Brown, *Irish-American Nationalism* (New York, 1966), 172.

immigrants in New York or Liverpool. There was much more to be gained from the millionaire Irish of the Hoffman House Committee.

O'Brien returned home to receive the freedom of Cork and Dublin and to find that he had been returned to Parliament for the Northeast Cork constituency in his absence. Circumstances had altered during the summer of 1887, for the Crimes Act was just coming into law. Balfour had proved himself more tiger than lily in his approach to Irish unrest. The act was directed against the National League in areas where that organization was suppressed, against the Plan of Campaign, and against conspiracies to intimidate or boycott. All this was to be facilitated by powers to abolish the jury system for certain classes of crime, and by giving resident magistrates, most of whom were former policemen or ex-army officers, jurisdiction to try cases of conspiracy, for which in England and Scotland juries were required. Furthermore, in contrast to previous practice, there was no duration fixed for the new coercion. Balfour's Crimes Act was to be permanent. The Chief Secretary's stance was patently coercive, and the police and magistrates were backed up accordingly. These new conditions prompted some reconsiderations by both tenants and exponents of the Plan.

Encouraged by the firmness of the Administration, landlords maintained the high eviction rates (see Appendix B) that had scarred the countryside since the Land League agitation eight years before. The Luggacurran evictions of March and April which left hundreds homeless were followed in May by distressing scenes on the rack-rented Bodyke estate of the intractable Colonel John O'Callaghan, to whom the authorities attributed much of the cause for the disturbed state of County Clare. The noticeable timidity of the tenants on the Coolgreaney estate in Wexford, where evictions were in progress in mid-July, prompted a scathing attack by Davitt on those who counseled self-restraint and against tenants who only resisted by calling names. John Redmond interpreted Davitt's abusive speech as a criticism of the policy of Parnell, Dillon, and O'Brien and forced him to back down in deference to Parnell's authority.[24] There could be no question that Redmond had rightly placed O'Brien with the forces of moderation, for one day later, speaking at Drogheda to the Massereene tenants, O'Brien reasoned in a manner which must have sounded strange to listeners who had lost everything.

[24] *United Ireland,* July 23, 1887 (speeches at Coolgreaney, July 15 and 16).

Irish evictions now carry English elections . . . the moment evictions now occur in Ireland the white light of publicity is turned upon them . . . the more of these scenes that occur in Ireland today, the more are the landlords and the Tory Government trembling for their effect upon English public opinion . . . [25]

As for Dillon, he too criticized Davitt for expressing difference with the policy of the organization in public and, far from looking to an extension of the Plan, called for a solid front on the crucial ten or fifteen estates where the tenants were holding out.[26] Obviously, there was to be no attempt at social revolution. Rather, the field was to be left to the sheriffs and emergency men in the expectation of parliamentary deliverance. The new, timid policy was furthered by Parnell's sealing of the Liberal alliance in his "Union of Hearts" speech at the National Liberal Club July 20, where he acknowledged the Liberal Party's achievement in bringing the Irish people "to look to the law of the Constitution and to Parliamentary methods for the redress of their grievances":

I trust the Irish people may continue to rely upon the good faith of the English Liberal party, that even where they are oppressed, where they are trampled upon, and where they are evicted that they will be slow to retaliate, that they will remember that today is not always, and the Conservative Governments cannot last for ever.[27]

The government, of course, was not immune to parliamentary criticism or the need to consider that their Liberal-Unionist allies detested coercion. Balfour had not looked forward to the inevitable landlord reaction once the Coercion Bill became law: "I should be unwilling on grounds of policy to use powers of the Coercion Bill in the first instance to crush the resistance of tenants, who, whatever be their faults, have not been well treated by their landlords."[28] He also confided to Buller a desire to delay evictions so tenants could benefit from ameliorative provisions of the Land Act, which was also to come into force soon. That measure, repeating the Gladstonian coercion-conciliation balancing act of 1881, enabled judges to halt evictions, made it easier for some tenants to pay their debts, allowed the revision of fixed rents, and, most important of all, brought the 100,000 or so

[25] *Ibid.*
[26] *Ibid.*
[27] *Ibid.*
[28] Balfour to Buller, June 11, 1887 (copy), Balfour Papers, BM Add. MS. 49826. See also Colonel Alfred Turner, DM to Buller, July 29, 1887, *ibid.*, Add. MS. 49807: "I am sorry to say I am being very heavily pressed to carry out evictions *all round*—in Clare there is a perfect sheaf of applications to the Sheriff and agents are pressing hard."

leaseholders (Protestant and Catholic) under the rent-fixing clauses of Gladstone's act.[29]

Such unexpected largesse conquered O'Brien, always alert for the slightest conciliation in the solution of the land question. Speaking to his old friends at Luggacurran on July 24, he hailed the bill as an event "of the very highest importance . . . in relation to the peace and to the happiness of the whole country . . . if there is a good spirit abroad we ought to reciprocate it."[30] This was indeed a vain hope, for Balfour's solicitude for rack-rented tenants did not extend to those who advocated boycott or intimidation. In that same month, eighteen counties were placed under the legal restrictions of the Crimes Act, even though the county assizes, with the exception of Clare, had yielded very little work for the grand juries—white gloves, symbolizing the absence of crime, having been presented to several judges. This was followed in August by the "proclaiming" of the National League as a dangerous associa-tion, enabling the Administration to suppress a considerable number of branches.

Law and Disorder

What impact, then, had the Plan of Campaign made in its first year of operation? In their public speeches of July 1888, O'Brien and Dillon claimed that 30,000 tenants on eighty estates had joined the Plan. By that date three-fourths of those tenants had allegedly got the settlements asked for, which left a score or so of estates still in the fight, about fifteen of them being considered crucial. The compilation made by the RIC during the first two years of operation (very few estates were added after the winter of 1886/87) listed 59 on which the Plan had been adopted since 1886, including 26 where the Plan was still extant as of January 1889.[31] O'Brien later claimed that the Plan had been put in force on 140

[29]L. P. Curtis, Jr., *Coercion and Conciliation in Ireland, 1880–92* (Princeton, 1963), 341. There were also advantages for the landlords: simpler and less onerous eviction processes, im-proved appeals courts for the landlord, and relief from payment of rates where no rents were received. In any event, as Balfour explained in a memorandum, "They [landlords] must feel that the sacrifice asked of them (if sacrifice it be) is absolutely required if the Union, and all that the Union means to them, is to be maintained" (Balfour Papers, BM Add. MS. 49822, undated "Memorandum on the Land Bill").

[30]*United Ireland,* July 30, 1887. Dillon, who in the past had differed from Parnell and O'Brien on the attitude to be adopted toward ameliorative land legislation and who was eventually to break with O'Brien on that issue, treated the bill with contempt (Lyons, *John Dillon,* 88).

[31]PRO, Cabinet Minutes, CAB(1889) 37/23, no. 5, A. J. Balfour on "The Political Condi-tion of Ireland," January 1889.

estates, victory having been achieved on 120. Davitt thought 101 estates
were involved. Dillon's testimony before the Evicted Tenants Commission in 1893 named a total of 116 Plan estates, and since that figure was
based on detailed records which Dillon kept throughout the agitation, it
is the best one available.[32] No source exists, however, for the total
number of Plan tenants. The leaders' initial estimate was 30,000.
However, according to police records, the total number of tenants on
the fifteen most prominent Plan estates was about 11,000, and 10,000 of
these were confined to just seven estates. And, of course, not every tenant joined the Plan. It seems fair to assume that the number of tenants
on the remaining one hundred or so smaller estates would not have exceeded one hundred per estate on the average and, again, not all would
have joined the Plan. A reasonable estimate of Plan tenants, therefore,
would probably lie between 10,000 and 20,000, some two to four percent of the half-million Irish tenant farmers. But during the four years of
the Plan, activity mainly centered on some fifteen to twenty estates. For,
as Dillon's evidence, mentioned above, revealed, sixty landlords soon
settled after friendly negotiation, twenty-four others did so after a brief
struggle, and in fifteen cases the tenants capitulated to the landlords'
demands. The differences in the figures are not crucial to estimating the
strength of the Plan, for all accounts seem to agree that fewer than 30
estates were active from 1887 onward. The most important of these
were commonly identified as Clanricarde (Galway), Coolgreaney
(Wexford), DeFreyne (Roscommon), Dillon (Mayo), Kingston (Cork),
Leader (Cork), Lewis (Galway), Luggacurran (Queens county),
Massereene (Louth), O'Callaghan (Clare), O'Grady (Limerick),
O'Kelly (Kildare), Ormsby (Mayo), Ponsonby (Cork), Stewart
(Donegal), Swiney (Donegal), Tottenham (Wexford), Vandeleur
(Clare). In 1889 the Plan-related struggle on the Smith-Barry estate in
Tipperary was added.

Therefore, as a device to bring landlordism to its knees the Plan was
hardly scratching the surface. It must have been a matter of some embarrassment to O'Brien and Dillon to have their efforts damned with
faint praise by none other than Archbishop Walsh of Dublin, who
sharply criticized the Plan's advising tenants to ask for only 30 percent
reductions when, he claimed, the Land Commission would have
granted more. In an interview with the *Freeman's Journal* the archbishop
noted that the leading organizers of the Plan of Campaign made it a

[32] *United Ireland*, October 29, 1887; M. Davitt, *The Fall of Feudalism in Ireland* (New York,
1904), 520; Lyons, *John Dillon*, 86.

point to keep the tenants' claims within the narrowest possible limits:
"The reductions they seek for are, as a rule, far short of those judicially
granted by the courts. This moderation is a very good thing in its way
. . . Very little credit is given by the landlords to men like John Dillon
for the moderating influence exercised in keeping down the tenants'
claims." The innuendo becomes clearer when it is realized that Walsh,
the hierarchy's self-appointed spokesman on the land question, never
lost an opportunity to goad Irish politicians for timidity toward the
landlords.[33] The significance of his remarks was probably not lost on
those who were deserting the League for the racier affiliations of the
Gaelic Athletic Association. The only really big success the Plan had to
show in that first year was the agreement on the Dillon estate. But part
of that success was lost when the Plan had to be restarted there in 1888.
The landlords also rated one big success—the clearing of Lord
Lansdowne's Luggacurran estate, despite O'Brien's hectic exertions. In
fact, evictions proceeded in 1887 at a rate higher than that of the
previous year despite government pressure on landlords to hold their
hand. The resistance to evictors which Davitt called for was com-
paratively rare on or off the Plan estates. And when it did occur, it
devolved entirely on the evictees, who, if they were not overwhelmed by
police and emergency men, generally submitted at length to the exhortations of their priests. The spectators generally stood by to cheer or to
groan, fully justifying Davitt's taunting outburst at Coolgreaney.[34]

Nevertheless, despite the protestations of Parnell and others that it
was reducing crime, the Plan greatly agitated the Irish officials, from
the Chief Secretary down. Hitherto, the barometer of administrative
repression had been the incidence of agrarian crime. Now, with crime
actually declining, the attention of the forces of law and order was
centered on boycotting. William O'Brien was foremost in advocating
this form of retaliation against landlords, calling it "the first duty of
honest Irishmen," though it was also usually exalted as the antithesis of
moonlighting and outrage. The National League was to be the chief

[33]*Freeman's Journal*, October 23, 1887. For an example of Walsh's "extreme" opinions, see
his running battle with the Land Conference representatives in 1903, in particular his letter
in the Dublin *Evening Telegraph*, February 12, 1903.

[34]Davitt's strong feelings were also shown in an incident at Bodyke on July 24, when he
personally presented medals and money to a score of peasants who had undergone imprisonment for their recent "pluck and patriotism" in defence of their homes—all of them women
and girls. (*United Ireland*, July 30, 1887). This fracas is confirmed by the DM Colonel Turner,
who reported to Buller that the men in most cases had skulked outside while their women
and daughters ("unsexed furies" was Turner's phrase) within threw stones and hot water
(SPO,CBS Div. Commr. Reports, SW, 1887–1889, Report for June 1887).

promoter and the taker of an evicted farm the main victim. The
League's attention did not entirely prevent the hated landgrabbing.
The prevalence of that practice is demonstrated by the details ascer-
tained by the Evicted Tenants Commission. The Commission mâde a
special study of seventeen estates, and fifteen of these were Plan estates.
The latter contained 812 holdings from which the tenants had been
evicted during the Plan years and had not been reinstated. About 22
percent of the farms had been relet to new tenants, the remainder being
used by the landlord or lying derelict. Yet the threat of boycott counted
for something, for the ratio of new-tenant holdings was over twice as
great in the case of 2,755 additional (non-Plan) evicted farms detailed
by the Commissioners.[35] Not until 1908, on the heels of the Evicted
Tenants Act of the previous year, was an official start made to heal the
wounds of the land war.

. Predictably, the boycotting of evicted farms, ostensibly a nonviolent
device, provoked a climate of violence wherever it was practiced. In
many instances, outrages perpetrated against individuals came after
denunciation of the offender by the local branch of the League. Also,
landlords occasionally provoked heightened hostility by importing
Protestant farmers from Ulster as tenants of the farms from which
Catholics had been evicted (Protestants were favored tenants for they
generally declined to join combinations against the landlord). Lord
Massereene, for example, became notorious for his "none but
Protestants need apply" advertisements for tenants in the Belfast
Northern Whig. Personal police protection had to be afforded to
landlords, caretakers, and new tenants when subjected to intimidation
or threatening letters. On one eight-acre farm in Donegal such protection was necessary for the landlord's caretaker for a four-year period. In
another case a new tenant was protected for six years by police stationed in a hut on the farm. A more extreme one was that of a caretaker in Galway who persuaded the authorities that his daring should
be rewarded by having three policemen reside in his house. And, of
course, there was the ubiquitous "Captain Moonlight," whose humor

[35]Evicted Tenants Commission: Appendix II, House of Commons (1893–94), 31. The
copious statistics supplied by the Commission cover evictions from May 1879 through 1892
and only those of tenants making application to the Commissioners for reinstatement (the
total number of evictees in Ireland probably was close to 6,000). However, since the date of
eviction is given in almost all cases, it has been possible to isolate those evictions which occurred during the period of the Plan. The estates used for the Plan figures given in the text
are: Ancketill, Brooke, Byrne, Clanricarde, Langford, Lansdowne, Lewis, Massereene,
O'Grady, O'Kelly, Olphert, Ponsonby, Smith-Barry, Stewart, Swiney.

may have been lost on those who barraged Dublin Castle with demands for action against the proponents of rent strikes.[36] Thus, it was impossible for the Irish Parliamentary party to avoid becoming identified by successive English Cabinets with the various manifestations of agrarian discontent in areas canvassed by branches of the National League. Yet, the sporadic violence posed as much of a dilemma to the Plan's leaders as it did to the Administration. We have seen how O'Brien and his colleagues took every opportunity to denounce agrarian crime. After all, they were as fervent in upholding the rights of private property as an English landlord. The difference, of course, lay in which person—landlord or tenant—possessed those rights.

Such assistance to the forces of law and order did not go unacknowledged by the officials of the Irish Administration. Nevertheless, the Administration was usually disposed to rely on the reports of police officials, who tended to ascribe to secret societies the more boisterous manifestations of rustic animal spirits. There could be no other reason for the alarm Divisional Magistrate Byrne expressed in a report concerning Mayo and Galway: "These counties have been actively worked and specially organized by Messrs. O'Brien, Davitt, Dillon, Crilly, Sheehy and Deasy and the districts which they have frequented . . . are in a state closely bordering on rebellion."[37]

Though the Plan posed but a narrowly-contained problem for Irish landlordism, the strain on the Administration was somewhat more noticeable. The climate of violence induced the authorities to provide large forces of police to protect process servers. Evictions always took place with police and military at hand, and, throughout, hundreds of people had to be protected by police patrols. For instance, on one day of the Luggacurran evictions as many as 206 police were on hand. The evictions on the Lewis estate in Galway saw 204 military in attendance on one occasion. All this entailed considerable expense and was regarded as an embarrassment by the Chief Secretary, who said, "The very

---

[36]The "Captain's" warnings were always sure of prominence in the pulp literature of the Loyal and Patriotic Union. One hilarious example has been preserved in the official papers of Sir Redvers Buller:

Notice any man pay his rent I don't care whom is he we woent spare bruck shot on him it isint a like the old time at all doent ye be afraid of bailefs sheriefs or bobies or soldiers or any man to come before ye stand up like men ye are sure to win

"Captain Moonlight will stand to ye"

(PRO, War Office, 132-4B).

[37]J. Byrne, DM to Inspector General (RIC), March 6, 1887, in SPO, CBS, Div. Commr. Reports (Western Division).

magnitude of the force required to support the law gives an impression of weakness."[38] The Administration gave so much credence to a report that Clare was in a state little short of open rebellion that a gunboat was stationed in the River Shannon after the murder of Head Constable Gerald Whelehan of Ennis by "moonlighters" in September 1887. It is true, however, that large areas of the country were in a disturbed state, especially those in which the Plan operated. The various reports received at constabulary headquarters during 1887 all stress the malign influences of the National League in that regard. Intimidation was sufficiently rife to cause the Chief Secretary to say to General Buller, "The Land League [sic] is practically ousting the established Courts of Justice." The latter's reply was equally doleful, admitting that intimidation was being carried on as defiantly as ever.[39] Sir J. West Ridgeway, scouting Ireland preparatory to replacing Buller as Under Secretary, observed: "So far as I can see, the situation in Ireland has a resemblance, almost absurd, to certain districts in India and Afghanistan."[40] The situation fully justified Balfour's fears that the Administration was in for a difficult winter.

[38]Balfour to Buller, September 26, 1887, Balfour Papers, BM Add. MS. 49807.
[39]Balfour to Buller, August 4, 1887; Buller to Balfour, August 16, 1887, *ibid.*, Add. MS. 49826. Buller backed up the case against the League by adding details of an anonymous letter urging the League's proclamation on the grounds of immorality. The writer, obviously a priest, cited the falling-away of communicants in the parish of Millstreet and the fact that "where there was one case of fornication, there are now 50."!
[40]Ridgeway to Balfour, August 20, 1887, *ibid.*, Add. MS. 49808.

THREE

The Fight Against Coercion

WILLIAM O'BRIEN was selected by Arthur Balfour to be the first victim of the new Crimes Act. The prosecution arose out of speeches O'Brien had given in August 1887 to tenants on the Kingston estate, in which he advised them to resist evictors by "every honest means in your power."[1] This could only be interpreted by the authorities as incitement to resist and obstruct bailiffs, and, according-ly, O'Brien and John Mandeville, chairman of the Mitchelstown Board of Guardians and leader of the tenants, were ordered to appear before the magistrates at Mitchelstown on September 9. Both men refused to appear, but an expectant crowd which had gathered in the town had the inevitable confrontation with the police. This time, however, the latter completely lost their wits and fired into the crowd, killing three and wounding others. The incident became famous as the Mitchels-town Massacre. The depth of feeling it aroused is evident in the lasting effectiveness of the Liberal taunt "Remember Mitchelstown!" over the next few years.[2]

Thus, when O'Brien celebrated the first anniversary of the Plan of Campaign by returning to the Clanricarde estate for a meeting which the authorities had declared illegal, he already had a three-month sentence hanging over his head. In view of the catastrophic developments at Mitchelstown a few weeks before, elaborate

[1] *United Ireland*, August 13, 1887.

[2] P. Magnus, *Gladstone* (London, 1954), 370. For details of the official investigation of the affair, see SPO, Police and RM Letter Book (1882–1889), items 8618 and 9012. The Lord Lieutenant concluded that the firing was fully justified, but two of the officials involved (Cap-tain H. Segrave, RM , and County Inspector Brownrigg) were severely reprimanded for failure to control the police and prevent riot. The District Inspector was compulsorily retired from the force.

53

precautions were taken by the organizers of the meeting to avoid another confrontation with the police. The five hundred police and two companies of soldiers who were stationed at Loughrea and Portumna, ready for action, were effectively kept out of the way by cutting telephone wires and by holding the meeting at midnight miles away at Woodford. Flanked by two of his colleagues and by English sympathizers Wilfrid Scawen Blunt and James Rowlands, M.P., O'Brien publicly burned a copy of the Lord Lieutenant's proclamation banning the meeting to the cry of "No crime and no surrender."[3]

This was the advice heard on platform after platform as O'Brien and Dillon, careful of their duty to maintain social peace for the benefit of English public opinion, advised patience as the best policy. Now, besides, O'Brien could point to visible proof of the Union of Hearts which was expected to maintain the tenants' hopes until the Liberals returned to power: "We have now upon our side that Liberal party . . . Do nothing to mar this glorious work of Gladstone and Parnell. Take his advice and shun outrage as you would shun poison."[4] In reality, such advice meant submission with or without broken heads, for in the context of passive resistance, overwhelming force could always be brought to bear on tenants. Nevertheless, the authorities did not make fine distinctions in analyzing Nationalist speeches and had already taken action against O'Brien under the Mitchelstown prosecution. O'Brien's appeal against his sentence was rejected, and thus began another one of those half-comic, half-tragic adventures which endeared O'Brien to the Irish masses and provided amusement or disgust for English observers.

O'Brien and Mandeville entered Tullamore jail on November 2. Both men had already decided to confront the Administration on the issue of wearing convict garb, performing menial duties, and associating with ordinary criminals. When the Crimes Bill had been debated in Parliament during the summer, the Irish members, with an eye to the future, had failed to carry an amendment that persons convicted of certain offences should be treated as political prisoners in order that they might avoid the usual severities of prison life. This to Balfour seemed sentimental rubbish. In fact, one of the reasons Balfour did not contemplate making the suspension of habeas corpus part of his bill was precisely that anyone imprisoned under those terms would have all the privileges (special quarters, own clothes, etc.) of a first-class mis-

---

[3]*United Ireland*, October 22, 1887.
[4]*Ibid.*, November 5, 1887 (O'Brien's speech at Kanturk, October 30).

The Plan of Campaign on the Glenbeigh estate. Police attempt to arrest a girl for assaulting "emergency men" during the evictions in January 1887 (contemporary sketch from *Illustrated London News*).

demeanant.[5] The same firmness lay behind many of the subsequent sentences under the Crimes Act for smaller offences—a sentence of less than five weeks prevented recourse to an appeal. Balfour was also determined that the government should, under no circumstances, appear weak in the face of Irish agitation. It was a course he may have regretted after his encounters with the formidable member for Northeast Cork.

The first to bear the brunt of O'Brien's planned confrontation was the prison governor, baffled by his prisoner's adamant refusal to wear prison dress. All the coaxing and threats of prison officials could not break down O'Brien's determination to make a test case of his demand to be treated as a political prisoner. Balfour was not prepared for the governor's disinclination to use force, and his sharp reaction was expressed in a letter to the Undersecretary:

I am rather dismayed at what you tell me about the Governor of Tullamore. Tullamore was originally selected on the grounds that both Doctor and the Governor were specially to be relied on. It is characteristic of Irish administration that the best Governor to be found should be, to all appearances, so exceedingly weak. It is absolutely necessary in my opinion that if possible by some means or other O'Brien should be compelled to wear Prison dress. Absurdly trifling as the matter seems, it has really now been magnified into an important incident in the struggle between the National League and the Government and I should be sorry if anything gave cause even for the smallest triumphs to the wrong side.[6]

Ridgeway did not share his superior's iron resolve to make no concession to Irish "criminals." Convinced that the government was winning the fight against the Plan, he felt that O'Brien's release would eliminate all the publicity attending the prisoner's antics and would disarm the mounting indignation of their Liberal opponents. Besides, there was the question of O'Brien's health and family medical history, which had once evoked from Balfour the comment that there must be some mysterious connection between diseased lungs and Irish patriotism. The Undersecretary conveyed his fears to Balfour:

O'Brien is being treated like any other prisoner. He has sheltered himself behind the doctor, but the fact is that his heart *is* affected and his life is by no means a certain one. His death in jail would be a disaster.[7]

[5]Balfour to Buller, March 12, 1887, PRO, War Office (Buller Papers), W.O./132/4A: "experience under Forster's Act appears to show that they [Nationalists] rather like this than otherwise."

[6]Balfour to Ridgeway, November 8, 1887, Balfour Papers, BM Add. MS. 49808. It was the same Balfour who displayed similar resolve more than thirty years later when he advised the Cabinet against releasing another tough-minded Irishman, Terence MacSwiney, as he lay dying in Brixton prison after a ten-week hunger strike.

[7]Ridgeway to Balfour, November 10, 1887, *ibid.*

O'Brien's constitution, however, was somewhat stronger than Ridgeway estimated. The prisoner did lose his clothes, which were stolen from him while asleep, and for some days he lay in his shirt. He was more fortunate than poor Mandeville, who was roughly treated by warders, fared ill under the prison punishment diet of bread and water, and succumbed to pneumonia a few months after his release. The Undersecretary was relieved when O'Brien was smuggled, through the connivance of a friendly warder, a new suit of Blarney tweed.[8] No further attempts were made to put him in the blue serge of the prison uniform. After this episode, several clothing manufacturers took up the Blarney tweed idea, and for a long time thereafter *United Ireland* carried advertisements for the "O'Brien suit," the symbolic victory of the victim of coercion over Balfour's prison rules.

O'Brien was released at the end of January 1888, after having given the less obdurate officials in the Administration some anxious moments. Much to his dismay, he found that the movement had subsided since the great affair at Woodford three months earlier. Dillon, left alone and fearing for the movement should he also be arrested, had spent most of the intervening period in England.[9] In fact, O'Brien had conveyed his disappointment at the trend of events to T. C. Harrington even before his release:

Things look decidedly *uneventful* in the country. Those who complained that D[illon] and myself were taking too much upon ourselves do not err by over-activity now that they have got the field to themselves. It seems a little absurd to find . . . members of Parliament congregated at a little wayside meeting in Co. Dublin and not a stir reported from Galway, Clare, Cork or Kerry where activity would be really embarrassing to the Government . . . mere platonic resolutions won't beat Balfour . . . What they should do is to attend meetings in suppressed districts as long as possible till arrested . . . It seems a terrible pity that P[arnell] won't come upon the scene and say something which would justify vigorous action by the party without compromising himself.[10]

Though Parnell had been "on the scene" early in January, he had only announced then that he would not attempt any public work before Parliament met. Nor were his followers overenthusiastic for the work of agitation. Of the twenty-odd members who normally supported the

[8]Ridgeway to Balfour, November 29, 1887, *ibid.*: "it is lucky those clothes were smuggled in."

[9]F. S. L. Lyons, *John Dillon* (London, 1968), 92.

[10]O'Brien to Harrington (no date), Harrington Papers, NLI MS. 8576/34.

Plan in person, only four were imprisoned for their activities, during the time O'Brien was enjoying the comforts of the plank bed.[11] The help from Davitt was of dubious worth, as in his speeches at that time he reverted to the old "National" settlement (i.e. nationalization) of the land question, which had got him into hot water with Parnell and O'Brien on many a former occasion.[12]

The recent settlements on the Burke, de Freyne, Kingston, and O'Callaghan estates, though Plan victories, gave little cause for rejoicing. There were no signs of early victory on the Lewis estate, nor on the Clanricarde estate, where a thousand arbitrary evictions could be expected at any time. It was becoming ever more difficult to hold meetings in suppressed areas, and Hussars were being freely used to disperse gatherings up and down the country. Balfour was even having street urchins arrested for selling copies of *United Ireland*. The offences prosecuted under the Crimes Act at this time also included such dangerous crimes as serenading released prisoners, grimacing at the police, lighting bonfires, blowing horns, refusing to sell bootlaces, and voicing "cheers for William O'Brien." The effectiveness of the act was also observed in a decline in the number of boycotting cases reported, which dropped from 4,835 persons being boycotted on July 31, 1887, to 2,469 at the end of the year.[13]

Indeed, there was plenty of evidence that the National League itself was in decline. In the first place, the funds available for evicted tenants were contracting as early as January 1888.[14] For the Plan to have any credibility at all, there could be no interruption in the monies voted by the central branch of the League for the support of helpless tenants. Every branch suppressed would increase the burden, and there was little hope that the Irish farmers themselves would come to the aid of the unfortunate "wounded soldiers" of the Land War. It is a sad commentary on the general level of peasant solidarity and elementary patriotism in those years that the many who profited by the agitation did little or nothing for the few who lost by it. There were always tenants who would settle privately with the landlord behind their neighbors' backs, and only the threat of secret-society vengeance prevented the taking-up of evicted farms in greater numbers. The number of such farms record-

[11]The four M.P.'s were T. D. Sullivan, W. J. Lane, John Hooper, and E. Harrington. For a list of twenty-two Irish M.P.'s imprisoned during the Plan of Campaign agitation see Law and Crime (Ireland): House of Commons no. 158 (1889), 61.

[12]*United Ireland*, January 7, 1888 (speech at Rathcormac).

[13]PRO, Irish Crimes Records, 1887–1892, C.O./903/2, Intelligence Notes, series V, p. 49.

[14]Lyons, *John Dillon*, 332.

ed as unlet on January 1, 1889, was 2,750, of which 1,405 were left derelict, the remainder being worked by the landlord. The highest number of derelict farms was reached in 1891, and then they only totaled 2,088. Thus, even before the Plan of Campaign ended in the debacle of the Parnellite Split, a mere two thousand tenants out of more than half a million were gambling their livelihoods in the fight against the landlords, and less than half of those two thousand belonged to the Plan.[15]

The constabulary reports for 1888 confirm the lessening of League activity as the Crimes Act began to take effect and police interest became increasingly concentrated on the Gaelic Athletic Association.[16] League meetings were now more likely to be held on boats or in sacristies, though they were still reported as formal meetings in *United Ireland* in order to demonstrate the movement's vitality. Though reports of hole-in-the-wall or bogus meetings might annoy the authorities, they could not conceal the fact that resistance was on the wane. The lack of vigor in fighting evictions was used by the Secretary of the Irish National League of America to castigate the Nationalist leadership:

Only for the "cause" itself Irish Americans would long ago permit your distinguished leaders to hoe their own patch . . . God help the Irish people! Between law and order, harangues, and doses of moral theology, it is a wonder there is an ounce of unemasculated manhood left in the country.[17]

Despite its fears, therefore, the Administration had not had a bad winter, after all. The individual most responsible for this was, of course, the Chief Secretary himself. While O'Brien had been building his reputation as an aggressive Nationalist agitator, Balfour had been equally displaying his own tough-mindedness in dealing with Irish affairs. Lord Salisbury, much to the general surprise, had found the ideal protagonist of "resolute government" in the person of his own nephew. Officers of the law found that they were supported when they overstepped the bounds of duty, and their morale increased considerably. Balfour had stopped the Plan in its tracks and forced the

[15]SPO, CBS, Intelligence Notes 1895–1900 (carton no. 1), B series no. XLI.

[16]The Irish Administration believed the GAA was infiltrated by elements of the Irish Republican Brotherhood, secret-society heirs to the Fenian tradition. The police, in particular, were apt to overestimate the military potential of hurley sticks; see, for example, Ridgeway's letter to Balfour, December 10, 1887, Balfour Papers, BM Add. MS. 49808: "These hurlers—drilled, armed [*sic*] and headed by bands—are becoming dangerous at meetings. The A.G. [Attorney General] is considering the possibility of prosecuting them. It would take a very strong force of police to disperse them."

[17]John P. Sutton to T. A. Lynch (dated 1888), Harrington Papers, NLI MS. 8577/4.

HOLD YOUR GROUND

Men of Mitchelstown,

The Plan still holds the field, despite the treachery of a few traitors and the wavering of a dastard or two. Be loyal to your fight and remember your cause is just and must triumph. You have centred your all in this battle, and do not allow the coward or poltroon to cross your path. Are your homesteads and your children to suffer ruin by the action of any sordid wretch who would basely betray even his God? Woe to the man or men on the Kingston Estate who will betray their fellow tenants as their treachery will be as Cain's brand on their children and children's children and it were better that they were never born.

The children of those who sold their country in former times now curse the bones of their vile ancestors in dishonored graves and which of you will leave a similar legacy to your children?

WOE TO SUCH A TRAITOR ! ! !

BOYCOTT ! BOYCOTT ! BOYCOTT !

Down with ANNA KINGSTON, the usurper; FREND, the tyrant; JIM. NEILL, POWER, the Exterminator; Judas Iscariot O'GRADY, who out Herod's Herod in his baseness and villany, and who will yet use the thirty pieces of silver; His Cook and Mistress, MARIA; JOHNNY COUGHLAN, the renegade, his Dairymen and Workmen the "Cuckold" and English Bastard DAVIS; and the shopkeepers who will be named in next list.

COURAGE WINS THE FIGHT.

Plan of Campaign boycott notice . A warning posted at Mitchelstown, County Cork, by the Vigilance Committee of the Kingston tenants.

campaigners into a narrow corner, which made the struggle more of a personal contest between individual leaders (himself and O'Brien) than a manifestation of Irish unrest against landlord domination.

Yet, the success of the Plan at this stage cannot be measured only in terms of rents withheld and farms derelict. To a repressed people, words and gestures acquire a symbolic value out of all proportion to their worth. O'Brien knew this, and hence he was an even more effective agitator in prison than without. The Administration erred if it calculated that coercion would intimidate men like O'Brien and Dillon. Both seemed quite prepared to fight to the death if that should be necessary. This is what made the headlines in Ireland, not the paucity of participants in the Plan. Thus, the National League prospered and retained the confidence of the peasants despite (or because of) official suppression. Likewise, the Irish M.P.'s excelled in the Commons, taunting the Tories for their administrative failures in Ireland to Liberal cries of "remember Mitchelstown!"[18] Nor did English radicals overlook the parallel between exploitation by landlords in Ireland and the capitalist abuse of the freeborn Englishman. O'Brien's imprisonment happened to coincide with a series of working-class demonstrations held in Trafalgar Square in the first half of November, one of which was called in sympathy for O'Brien and developed into a riot between 50,000 demonstrators and 2,000 police.[19]

Balfour, though tough and unrelenting, was never able (and would have been unwilling in any case) to flout English public opinion by imposing a reign of terror in Ireland. He hesitated before deciding to suppress branches of the League because of the reservations of law officers in Dublin Castle. Nor could he bring himself to muzzle the Nationalist press, despite the urgings of his Undersecretary.[20] These limitations on the action of the Chief Secretary reveal that Ireland was as ungovernable under Balfourian coercion as it had been in the days of Earl Spencer's viceroyalty. Something of Balfour's dilemma is seen in the following letter to his Undersecretary:

[18]St. John Brodrick recalled many years later the total domination of English politics by Irish issues at this time: "The Session of 1887 . . . was the greatest test to which any P.M. has been subjected in modern times . . . During practically the whole period, Irish measures were debated night after night" [Lord Midleton, *Ireland—Dupe or Heroine* (London, 1932), 69].

[19]United Ireland, November 19, 1887; L. P. Curtis, Jr., *Coercion and Conciliation in Ireland, 1880–92* (Princeton, 1963), 201.

[20]See Balfour to Sir Peter O'Brien, April 5, 1888, Balfour Papers, BM Add. MS. 49814; Balfour to Ridgeway, April 9, and May 19, 1888, *ibid.*, Add. MS. 49826.

As you know, Morley has asked me for a Return giving particulars of persons prosecuted under the [Crimes] Act. I am afraid that the fact which you brought under my notice the other day (i.e. that a great many offences which, in ordinary course, would be tried before Petty Sessions are now being tried before the Crimes Court), however desirable, will greatly swell our statistics in comparison with those of Lord Spencer; and I am further rather alarmed at the inaccuracies that have been discovered in the number of persons proceeded against.[21]

On the Defensive

William O'Brien did not wait long after his release from prison before he began again to defy the authorities and invite arrest. A meeting held on the Ponsonby estate at Youghal in March 1888 developed into a bloody riot, in which the people were batoned while O'Brien was left studiously alone—apparent evidence of the Administration's dislike of another "Blarney tweed" episode. Ridgeway expressed both relief and caution concerning the action of his divisional magistrates in a letter to his chief: "Plunkett did very well at Youghal yesterday . . . I really shudder to think what Byrne would have done—he could not have resisted the temptation of arresting O'Brien . . . If O'Brien does not succeed on the Ponsonby Estate the P of C is doomed and he knows it."[22] The Administration knew that Dillon and O'Brien were the very backbone of the Plan of Campaign, but they could not feel much comfort at the thought of incarcerating either man—both so prone to tuberculosis that prison hardship could easily prove fatal. However, humanitarian and political considerations were usually overcome, for a time at least, by Balfour's desire never to appear weak in the face of Irish agitation. As he was soon to remark privately in defending himself on the death of Mandeville, "We cannot hope that everybody sent to an Irish prison will prove immortal."[23] For, as long as rents remained unpaid, evicted farms went unlet, and retribution from boycotters was to be feared, men like Ridgeway and Balfour were unlikely to agree with their magistrates that the National League was mastered.

Therefore, the agitators were arrested on April 8, O'Brien for attending the outlawed meeting at Loughrea, Dillon for a speech to the

---

[21] Balfour to Ridgeway, May 16, 1888, ibid., Add. MS. 49826.

[22] Ridgeway to Balfour, March 26, 1888, ibid., Add. MS. 49808. The Youghal riot had tragic consequences for Captain Plunkett. He was felled by a blow from a stick and developed a brain tumor which the medical specialists attributed to the attack. He died after a long and painful illness in December 1889.

[23] Balfour to Ridgeway, July 13, 1888, ibid., Add. MS. 49827.

The Papal rescript condemning the Plan of Campaign was issued in April 1888.

Massereene tenants. Only the success of O'Brien's appeal of his sentence of three months with hard labor prevented their joint imprisonment. This deliverance, however, was but temporary. Soon the Plan was subjected to two hammer-blows in quick succession—the Papal rescript and Parnell's Eighty Club speech.

The story of the rescript is well known.[24] Issued as a circular to the Irish bishops on April 20 by Cardinal Monaco on behalf of the Pope, it condemned both the Plan and boycotting. It was less of a blow in many ways than Parnell's speech two weeks later. The tenants had long been used to clerical involvement in the Nationalist movement and in the Plan. The work of priests like McFadden (Donegal), Humphries (Tipperary), "General" Matt Ryan (Limerick), and Keller (Youghal) were an inspiration to Plan tenants throughout Ireland, while the Nationalist proclivities of Archbishops Walsh and Croke were a byword in Irish politics.[25] In fact, Balfour and Ridgeway were much exercised by the involvement of priests in the Plan of Campaign. The former had investigated how pressure might be brought to bear by the Pope via the Duke of Norfolk, the latter having been anxious to put refractory priests into prison clothes.[26]

The Nationalist reaction to the rescript was swift and hostile. The agrarians, especially Davitt, Dillon and O'Brien, were quick to point out that Irishmen would not take their politics from Rome. The private opinions of the two archbishops were not too different, both being as eager as anyone to preserve the Nationalist movement.[27] *United Ireland,* still edited by O'Brien, sensed the provenance of the rescript and allowed that the Pope "is like ordinary mortals, at the mercy of malignant, false witnesses."[28] The furor was maintained throughout May, with O'Brien pronouncing his own finale to the debate in a speech at Cork: "I think we are in a position here today to bury and to obliterate this whole wretched business of the Rescript . . . we mean to stick to the Plan of Campaign and we mean to stick to boycotting."[29]

[24] See C. C. O'Brien, *Parnell and His Party, 1880-90* (Oxford, 1957), 214–216.

[25] If the Cabinet had adhered to a peculiarly dim-witted decision made in February 1887, Croke would have found himself under prosecution for a letter published in the press advising people to withhold taxes, which were being used "not for the public good but against the people." For details of the Cabinet discussion, see Lord Salisbury to the Queen, February 26, 1887, in PRO Cabinet Minutes, CAB(1887) 41/20. Croke's letter is in *United Ireland,* February 19, 1887.

[26] Ridgeway to Balfour, November 27, 1887, Balfour Papers, BM Add. MS 49808; Ridgeway to Balfour, October 5, 1888, *ibid.*, Add. MS. 49809.

[27] Archbishop Walsh to Archbishop Croke, May 8, 1888, Croke Papers, NLI microfilm, p. 6012.

[28] *United Ireland,* May 5, 1888.   [29] *Ibid.,* June 9, 1888.

No pronouncement, however, excited more comment than Parnell's speech on May 8. It was not noted for the fact that he acknowledged the Plan had saved thousands from eviction, but rather for his public reminder that neither the National League nor the Irish Parliamentary party had ever had anything to do with the Plan of Campaign, that he would have advised against it had he known about it in October (in fact, he had known about it), and that in any event it merely gave the Tories an excuse for introducing coercion and probably lessened English Liberal sympathy for the victims of eviction.[30]

The speech was a traumatic shock for O'Brien, who actually wrote an article for *United Ireland* announcing his own resignation. This extreme action was fortunately prevented by one of his colleagues on the paper. Similarly, it took arbitrary action by Dillon and Harrington to prevent O'Brien from annihilating the Plan by an act of public submission to Parnell's authority.[31] Actually, such submissive action in public or private would not have been surprising in any of Parnell's followers, especially O'Brien, who had earlier offered his own "annihilation" rather than cross his chief. For the past six years Parnell had been the dictator whose eminence they all shared. He had decreed the course adopted in the cases of the no-rent manifesto, the Kilmainham treaty, and the Home Rule negotiations. He had even exacted a promise from O'Brien in 1886 to confine the Plan of Campaign within narrow limits. Now, despite two years of aloofness from the Nationalist movement, his mere word was enough to squelch the slightest protest from men who had virtually risked their lives for the tenants. Parnell accomplished with a whisper what the thunder of Rome had failed to do. It was unlikely that henceforth the Plan would continue along the same lines.

These critical events of May 1888, brought a noticeable lull in the agitation. The Vandeleur evictions which began in July saw an impressive show of force from the Administration: more than two hundred police, Hussars, and infantry were there to observe the work of Balfour's new toy—the battering ram.[32] Twenty-four evictions were carried out

[30]It may be noted in passing that their Plan of Campaign activities did not prevent Dillon's friendship with the younger Liberals [Lyons, *John Dillon* (London, 1968), 90–92], nor O'Brien's dining with their leader, William Gladstone (O'Brien to Herbert Gladstone, November 21, 1888, Viscount Gladstone Papers, BM Add. MS. 46053).

[31]T. M. Healy, *Letters and Leaders of My Day* (New York, 1929) 1:269; C. C. O'Brien, *Parnell and His Party*, 220.

[32]Ridgeway had succeeded in having the use of this ancient weapon adopted at Balfour's suggestion and related with obvious satisfaction and to Balfour's "delight" how Captain

in that month "quietly and without sensation." There would have been considerably more, were it not for the restraints Ridgeway put on the DM, Colonel Alfred Turner.[33] With Dillon in jail for the summer, O'Brien, having recovered his composure, was left with the impossible task of clinging to the Plan and yet not giving offence to Parnell or the Liberals, whose Union of Hearts was—for the Nationalists at least—fast becoming a shirt of Nessus. Indeed, O'Brien could have given up the struggle with honor only a few days after Parnell's speech. E. Dwyer Gray, managing editor of the *Freeman's Journal,* had just died, and Mrs. Gray offered O'Brien the prestigious post. Rather than abandon the cause of the tenants, however, he refused the attractive offer.[34]

More than ever before, the Plan was on the defensive. Evictions were begun again on the Clanricarde estate, and landlord violence was met by appeals from Nationalist leaders to the people for restraint. O'Brien was attuned to the new moderation or, rather, the old moderation writ large: "We must be true to our faithful friends and allies in England, Scotland and Wales . . . We must remember never to do anything that we cannot defend to our consciences and that we can't stand up and defend before any honest assembly of Englishmen."[35] Dillon, just out of prison, admitted the scaling-down of the campaign at a League meeting in Dublin: "The plan which we have put forward with much diffidence [sic] is one for which we struggled at great cost. Yet, we will not hesitate for one moment to follow the new course." The new course was in effect Dillon's written promise to Archbishop Croke that "no reference to, or approval of, the 'plan' should in future be made by him or O'Brien."[36]

Parnell's strictures, the attractions of the Liberal alliance, and Dillon's realistic appraisal of their financial difficulties may have moderated O'Brien's proselytizing for the Plan, but they could not stop him from baiting the Administration. In this he was indomitable. He led his few supporters in Parliament in making "illegal" speeches and

---

Owen Slacke had evicted in eight minutes a Wexford family which had barricaded itself with food and water for a ten-day siege (Ridgeway to Balfour, November 29, 1887; Balfour to Ridgeway, December 1, 1887, Balfour Papers, BM Add. MS. 49808). Balfour was surprised to learn that the device was the result of police ingenuity and not the invention of the landlords (Balfour to Ridgeway, April 18, 1889, *ibid.* Add. MS. 49827).

[33]Ridgeway to Balfour, July 18, 1888, *ibid.,* Add. MS. 49808: "It [the Vandeleur evictions] is not a case of which we can be proud."

[34]W. O'Brien, *Evening Memories* (Dublin, 1920), 353.

[35]*United Ireland,* September 15, 1888 (speech at Waterford).

[36]Croke to Cardinal Manning, November 26, 1888, Croke Papers, NLI microfilm, p. 6012.

Foiling an eviction in County Clare. An enchained Father Little of Rossmanagher belies his name in frustrating police and bailiffs on the Desterre estate (contemporary sketch from *Illustrated London News*).

in endeavoring to bring Balfour's regime into contempt. Boycotting, as always, was advanced as the main weapon in the struggle, though it did not appear to be working too well. Only 130 cases of boycotting were recorded by the police in December 1888, probably involving about 800 persons, compared to 427 and 909 cases for the same dates in 1887 and 1886, respectively.[37] Little did O'Brien know that his plans for a series of demonstrations throughout Ireland "to show Balfour that his troubles in Ireland are only beginning" were known in advance by the authorities, having been communicated to them by the M.P. for East Kerry to whom O'Brien had written.[38] Actually, Balfour had put the Plan very much in retreat by the autumn of 1888. Confined to aiding the victims of the past struggle out of fast-diminishing funds, O'Brien and Dillon acknowledged the crisis as they desperately turned to Parnell for help. Father Keller, leader of the Plan on the Ponsonby estate, dolefully wrote O'Brien of the crisis there and throughout the country in general, exclaiming, "Where are the fire and eloquence that roused England in the days of the . . . Bulgarian atrocities?"[39] It very likely would have required an invasion by the Turks to evoke that kind of response for Ireland's woes.

The field was largely left to the coercionists. The individual reports of sixty-four of Ireland's seventy-five Resident Magistrates (RMs) painted a rosy picture of the state of the country. Almost without exception, the reports stressed the dormancy or decline of the League, and the absence or virtual cessation of boycotting. The only trouble spots were the Galway and Clare Plan areas and the wild Kenmare region, where O'Brien had attempted to spread the Plan—"all disturbed there since then." Clare upheld its tradition of being the toughest county in Ireland, the threat of invoking the Plan there generally being sufficient to bring landlords to their knees—"The general demoralization of the people is terrible, hard work is almost unknown and the only trade holding its own is the publican's."[40] With evictions proceeding on all sides and the heavy burden of agitation falling almost solely on O'Brien, it must have seemed something of a deliverance to him when he was

[37]MacGiolla Choille, *Intelligence Notes* (Dublin, 1966), 251.
[38]Ridgeway to Balfour, September 8, 1888, Balfour Papers, BM Add. MS. 49808.
[39]Father Keller to O'Brien, September 12, 1888, William O'Brien Papers, UCC, Box AB.
[40]SPO, CSO, Registered Papers 1889/3200, Quarterly Report of RMs, November 1888. For data on Clare and Kerry, see Reports of F. Welch and R. MacDermott. The missing reports of the remaining eleven RMs, covering the normally quiet southeastern counties, would not change the general picture.

arrested on January 24, 1889, for a typical "illegal" speech delivered four months earlier to the DeFreyne tenants. Something of his exasperation had been betrayed in a speech only a few weeks earlier in his native Mallow when he explained the struggle as one to turn "a race of crawling slaves into owners and rulers of this land." He had never before described the tenants in such terms.[41]

The Plan at Bay

O'Brien's new brush with the law was not without that element of farce so often associated with the fiery agitator. Having escaped from the courtroom on the day of his arrest, he was sentenced to four months *in absentia*. For the next five days he dodged the police, eventually turning up at Manchester to keep a Union of Hearts engagement with Jacob Bright. Arrested again on the platform after successfully insisting on delivering his speech, he was conveyed through the streets of Manchester to the sympathetic cheers of the onlookers. These events set off another wave of appeals against coercion, while his treatment in jail sparked a series of antigovernment meetings from London to Glasgow. In Ireland twenty-six bishops signed a petition for his release, and meetings were held in almost every town in Ireland.[42] When he was finally lodged in Clonmel prison on January 31, he presented the governor with the same baffling problem he had presented the Tullamore officials in November 1887—"how to act if he remains in his shirt."

O'Brien was as firm as ever on the question of convict dress, but this time there was to be no Blarney tweed. Instead, his clothes were forcibly removed by three warders, and after a wild struggle he finally ended up clad in the hated garb with his hair and beard cut in convict style. Back in his cell, he removed all his clothing except the calico shirt and lay in that manner on a plank bed until his clothes were returned a few days later, the governor having taken care at all times to keep up good fires to increase the temperature in the prisoner's cell. Meanwhile, the news was flashed to the world that O'Brien lay "blind, naked and cropped in an Irish jail." In point of fact, he was never naked, and his spectacles "restored" his sight after they were returned within a few hours. The furor following his tribulations achieved a major victory for

---

[41] *United Ireland*, December 22, 1888.

[42] *United Ireland*, February 9, 1889. Among prominent English petitioners for O'Brien's release were: C. P. Scott, W. T. Stead, H. M. Hyndman, the Reverend Price Hughes, F. E. Harrison, Professor E. S. Beesly, George Meredith, and Oscar Wilde.

Irish political prisoners, however, for it finally forced Balfour to relax prison rules regarding the "sentimental grievances." The plank bed, of course, stayed—it was a deterrent which Ridgeway maintained kept the prisons free of Nationalist M.P.'s (twenty-two had in fact served prison terms ranging from 14 days to six months between July 1887 and May 1889).[43] As further evidence of capitulation by the authorities, O'Brien was transferred to the more congenial atmosphere of Galway jail on February 21 to serve out the remaining three months of his sentence. The prison governor, warders, and the medical officer could not have been sorry to see their prisoner transferred. As long as he lay in Clonmel jail, these individuals were virtually prisoners too, afraid to walk the town because of threats and intimidation from the townspeople. It would appear, indeed, that O'Brien had given the lie to the famous Swiftian quip that twelve men well armed were more than a match for one man in his shirt!

His treatment in Galway was decidedly lenient. According to the medical officer's examination, the thirty-seven-year-old prisoner (5 feet, 11½ inches tall, weighing 137 pounds) was in fair health, in good mental condition, but "of a decidedly emotional and excitable temperament." To obviate the tendency to phthisis, he was given special quarters, long exercise, and a supplemented diet of quite exceptional proportions, as well as writing material and books "as essential to the prisoner of cultivated mind."[44]

Cut off from outside activity, O'Brien performed the unusual feat of writing his first full-length novel. *When We Were Boys* was published the following year and made him friends and enemies. Written to expose the evil effects of the clergy's aloofness from Nationalist politics under the firm hand of Cardinal Cullen in the 1860s, when, as the author put it, Dublin Castle ruled Ireland by canon law instead of martial law, O'Brien's clerical portraits were used against him in the Healyite "wars" of the 1890s. The book's hero, Ken, was based on O'Brien's Fe-

---

[43]Details of O'Brien's treatment in Clonmel prison are in SPO, CSO, Registered Papers 1889/4492, 5537, 6796. For Ridgeway's and Balfour's soul-searching on the prison rules during 1889, see Ridgeway to Balfour, February 25 and March 2, 6, 7; Balfour to Ridgeway, March 8, 9 in Balfour Papers, BM Add. MS. 49809. The official enquiry into O'Brien's prison treatment was published as House of Commons paper C.5698 (1889)61.

[44]SPO, CSO, Registered Papers 1889/4401, 6543. His treatment and diet were in stark contrast to the rigor undergone in the previous year in Holloway prison by John Burns and R. Cunningham Graham for their involvement in the Trafalgar Square riots of November 1887. The prison arrow, solitary confinement, picking oakum, and association with ordinary criminals was their lot and skilly, brown bread, and suet pudding their diet (*Pall Mall Gazette,* January 19, 1888).

nian brother, and the novel sheds light on social, religious, and national aspects of Irish life in the Fenian era. Though the novel is marred by a highly effusive style, O'Brien deserved credit for adding to the literature of the Nationalist movement at a time when that output was singularly meager. The novel was unsuited to English audiences, but it was a success in Ireland, and, in the opinion of at least one Sinn Feiner, it probably had a healthy influence in inducing patriotism among readers of the younger generation. Maunsel, the publisher, brought out a cheap edition of the work in 1919 which was sold out. It was O'Brien's intention to write a sequel redeeming the clergy for their support of the tenants during the Land War. Such a work might well have spared him the imputations of anticlericalism, but the intervention of the Parnellite Split put an end to that project.[45]

Another fateful aspect of his imprisonment in Galway jail was a personal drama involving himself and a young French woman, the daughter of wealthy Jewish parents resident in Paris. Madame Raffalovich and her daughter, Sophie, had become interested in O'Brien through newspaper accounts of his sufferings in jail. A correspondence was struck up which led to his marriage to Sophie one year later.

Meanwhile, however, the battle against the coercionists was winding down, what with O'Brien's being in prison and Dillon's being off on a thirteen-month tour of the Antipodes in search of funds for the evicted tenants. Significantly, Dillon did not go to the United States, from which source there had been a great falling-off of funds and, presumably, of interest in the previous two years.[46] Thus, for about four months in the spring and early summer of 1889, the Plan was without the physical inspiration of its two greatest exponents. John Redmond and T.P. Gill, their Parliamentary colleagues, appear to have kept the flag flying as best they could in their absence. A notable victory had been won on the Vandeleur estate in Clare. In the previous July police, hussars, and magistrate had seen the battering ram do its devastating work on the thatched cottages of helpless tenants. Now, nine months later, the landlord agreed to a 40 percent reduction in rents and the commutation of all arrears up to March 1887. Also, the Plan was kept in the public eye somewhat through the meetings of the central branch of the League, at which an average of £350 was voted each fortnight to

[45]O'Brien to Father Moloney (New York), January 8, 1897, UCC William O'Brien Papers, Box AH; J. M. Kennedy (Thurles) to O'Brien, October 1, 1916, *ibid.*, Box AS.
[46]*United Ireland*, January 26, 1889 (Parnell interview).

cover the tenant stipends.[47] But costs mounted as evictions took place in June on the Massereene and Ponsonby estates.

The gloomy picture O'Brien faced on his release in May 1889 was worsened by a sudden resurgence of landlord resistance. Plans were set afoot by a diehard Southern Unionist landlord, Arthur Smith-Barry, for a landlord syndicate to take over the hard-pressed Ponsonby estate to prevent its capitulation to the Plan of Campaign. Defense of this nature by landlords was an idea close to Balfour's heart. As early as November 1887 he had written to his colleague Colonel Edward King-Harman recommending it as "elementary wisdom for the landlords to combine together to help owners in the test cases where the Plan is being attempted . . . as a mere speculation I do not believe the landlords in Ireland could invest their money better."[48] It was also a crisis in the affairs of C. Talbot Ponsonby that sparked Balfour's intervention on that occasion, but, fortunately, Smith-Barry was unable to persuade his fellow landlords to avert what seemed like imminent surrender to the Plan of Campaign. In the two years which followed, Balfour made several other attempts to enlist the landlords in combination against the Plan, but he did not succeed until the summer of 1889.[49]

Of course, the landlords had not been entirely helpless against the Plan over the years. The Property Defence Association formed in 1880 was one of several organizations which defended landlord rights by serving writs, combating boycott, and providing caretakers for evicted farms. Among its list of subscribers were several people who were O'Brien's friends in his later All-for-Ireland days—Earl Dunraven, Lord Castletown, Lord Rossmore, Colonel Nugent Everard, and Smith-Barry himself. The Association also hired civilian storm troopers (emergency men), who wielded the crowbar and battering ram.[50]

O'Brien was not one to take this new attack on the Plan by landlords lying down. His retaliation took the form of urging Smith-Barry's own Tipperary tenants to combine against their landlord as a mark of solidarity with the Ponsonby tenants, some of whom were just then be-

---

[47]That amount was computed from figures published in *United Ireland*. However, for the second half of the year the average was only a little above £200 every two weeks.

[48]Balfour to King-Harman, November 19, 1887, Balfour Papers, BM Add. MS. 49840.

[49]Balfour to Lord Courtown, May 2, 1888, *ibid.*, Add. MS. 49826; Balfour to Lord Northbrook, January 21, 1889, *ibid.*, Add. MS. 49827; Balfour to Lord Pembroke, February 8, 1889, *ibid.*

[50]These so-called emergency men were generally considered to have been of Protestant and Unionist stock from Ulster or from Dublin. However, the appearance of some Hibernian names on the few occasions on which they were identified in the press reveal that these formidable characters were not all of undiluted Saxon blood.

ing evicted. His speech on this occasion contains hints of a more formal scheme in the offing.[51] In fact, he was in contact with Parnell at this time, attempting to force the chief once and for all to publicly endorse the crushing need for funds if all was not to be lost.[52] Having convinced himself that Parnell intended to aid the proposed tenant coalition, he went ahead quickly, racing against the time when his rearrest on June 30 for yet another "illegal" speech would again land him in jail. Indeed, his association might never have gotten off the ground had not a suit (eventually unsuccessful) by O'Brien against Salisbury for slander been pending. This delayed O'Brien's imprisonment for almost two months, the period of crucial negotiations with Parnell.

On July 10, again at Tipperary, O'Brien announced the formation of a new Defence League "to be established by Mr. Parnell and the Irish party." The leader in *United Ireland* on July 13 announcing the details also indicated that the new tenant defense scheme was authorized by Parnell. In fact, though the rules of the Tenants Defence Association were established at a party meeting in London on July 22, Parnell was far from happy at the events O'Brien had set in motion. When the rules appeared in *United Ireland* on July 27, they were hidden away on one of the lesser news pages with none of the fanfare which had accompanied the announcement of the Plan of Campaign—symbolic of the cloud under which the whole affair transpired. Parnell absolutely refused direct personal support of his lieutenant's efforts as late as August 13, and it required unusually sharp words from O'Brien to arouse Parnell to commit the party to a substantial involvement in the work of the conventions later in the year. "I think you will find," O'Brien angrily assured Parnell, "that you are mistaken in supposing that you have tied us to the stake and that you can leave us all the responsibility on our hands, while you take all the advantages and none of the labour."[53] Parnell's attitude on the Tipperary scheme remained unchanged, however, as is evident from J. J. Clancy's letter to a colleague:

I saw the Chief by the merest accident at the House today . . . I told him a deputation had come over expressly from Tipperary to wait on him. He inquired what about and I told him briefly their object. He replied there was no use in his seeing them as he would not undertake the responsibility of advising tenants to give up their interests in their holdings . . . [54]

[51] *United Ireland*, June 29, 1889 (Speech at Tipperary, June 23).

[52] F. S. L. Lyons, "John Dillon and the Plan of Campaign, 1886–90" *Irish Historical Studies* 14 (September, 1965): 335–337.

[53] *Ibid.*

[54] J. J. Clancy, M.P., to Dr. (Kenny?), September 2, 1889, Gill Papers, NLI MSS. 13478–526 (Plan of Campaign/Box no. 2).

These events put a severe strain on the allegiance of Parnell's most loyal colleague, who confided his disillusion to his henchman T. P. Gill:

The more I think of it, the more I am convinced it would be utterly impossible for me to attempt to explain the position in which P[arnell] has placed himself to myself. "The rest is silence."[55]

The Tenants Association was finally inaugurated at the Nationalist convention on October 28, 1889, with only fifteen M.P.'s present and with Parnell being represented by one of his colleagues—the final affront to O'Brien.[56] Of course, the new body was not intended to supplant the Plan. It was founded to facilitate tenant combination against landlord syndicates and as such was ancillary to the Plan. Tenants were invited to contribute to the Defence Fund in a fixed proportion to the Poor Law valuation of their holdings. There were then to be three Nationalist organizations in "friendly rivalry"—the National League, with its national character; the Plan of Campaign, limited to particular estates; the Tenants Defence Association, against landlord combination wherever that should occur.

O'Brien was in jail for the last four months of the year—further proof of the Administration's tenacity in pursuing him. However, he caused almost as much trouble in jail as out and was a particular trial to Ridgeway, who was never sure whether to be firm or lenient with him. At any rate, O'Brien took up where he had left off seven months earlier: "O'Brien is trying to give trouble. He won't eat mutton chops—his health I fear will give way, and we shall have to release him before his time is up."[57] Next O'Brien's voluntary constipation over ten or eleven days tested Ridgeway's endurance: "Our first duty is to keep the man alive and in order to attain that end we must regard him as insane . . . It goes greatly against my grain having to yield to O'Brien, but considering the political implications which would follow his suicide, I am sure that I have done the right thing." Fortunately, a pill had been successfully administered to O'Brien in his food which enabled Ridgeway to report exultantly to Balfour, "William O'Brien has had a motion!!" The battle of the bowels filled the Under Secretary with disgust: "Really, between O'Brien and Coneybeare [an English M.P. who

---

[55]O'Brien to T. P. Gill, M.P., August 20, 1889, *ibid.*
[56]*United Ireland*, November 2, 1889.
[57]Ridgeway to Balfour, September 3, 1889, Balfour Papers, BM Add. MS. 49810.

had complained of having picked up crab lice in an Irish jail] Irish administration is becoming unfit for gentlemen to engage in."[58]

As before, O'Brien's constitution triumphed over the Administration's nerve, and the remaining three months of his stay in prison were without incident. Heartened by his developing romantic correspondence with Sophie Raffalovich, O'Brien recovered his optimism. He also wanted to finish the novel begun earlier in the year. More important, he had heard from Dillon that £30,000 could be expected as the result of his Australian tour, and even though that amount would hardly enable the movement to be profligate, O'Brien also expected the forthcoming convention to realize £30,000. Gill and Redmond were taking care of things on the outside, and the only damage to be feared within the movement was that "Davitt's fads" might be aired at the convention. Evidence of a revived spirit in the movement, at least in Tipperary, was also heartening. There, as a result of O'Brien's earlier remonstrations, the Smith-Barry tenants demanded a 25 percent abatement of rent to alleviate the burden they had assumed in supporting the Ponsonby tenants. Their landlord naturally declined to indulge this attempt to rob Peter to pay Paul. Notices of eviction were served in September 1889 and these became effective at the end of the year. Town and rural tenants on the Smith-Barry Tipperary properties numbered 253, but 107 of them had refused to join the Association.[59] In the next two years the remaining 146 were evicted, many of them tenants and shopkeeping lessees who moved their belongings to the fringe of town to launch a minor epic of the Plan of Campaign—New Tipperary.

New Tipperary

The struggle in Tipperary during 1890 marked the final phase in the Plan agitation, before that and much more besides fell victim to the Nonconformist conscience in December of that year. Some of the optimism O'Brien had gained in prison soon evaporated on his release. He bared his soul to Gill: "Dillon did more service in a few months than the whole of us put together has done for years. As for work in Parliament, it may be more useful this season, but for the past three sessions it has been an utter fraud and waste of breath."[60] It was the old story of a

[58]These events are described in Ridgeway's letters to Balfour of September 3 and 4, 1889, *ibid.* The epic struggle is also recounted in L. P. Curtis, Jr., *Coericion and Conciliation,* 227–228.

[59]SPO, CBS–DICS Reports (Southeast Division), Report for November 1890.

[60]O'Brien to Gill, January 16, 1890, Gill Papers, NLI MSS. 13478–526 (Box 1871–92/folder 6).

lack of continuous financial support and aloofness from the agitation by
too many of the Nationalist representatives of the people. The Tenants
Defence Association, set up to combat landlord combination wherever
it appeared, was soon strained to the utmost by a vain attempt to
pauperize Smith-Barry in defense of the Ponsonby tenants, all of whom
were evicted during 1890. Many, indeed, must have wondered whether
the Association had in fact supplanted the Plan instead of being an ad-
junct to it. Most of the money collected as a result of the recent conventions went toward the erection of a "town" in which the shopkeepers
evicted by Smith-Barry might carry on their business. Thus, the evicted
tenants loyal to the Plan remained largely dependent on the funds
brought by Dillon from Australia, money which at best might last a
year.[61]

O'Brien's enthusiasm for New Tipperary did not relieve his gloom
over the "absolute quietude" which left the field to the coercionists.
Again he shared his burden with Gill, who was then one of the more
energetic members of the Nationalist second string: "I tell you candidly
I wish some less useful people would ruffle the surface of affairs a little
more vigorously, in the way of forcing the ruffians into suppression,
prosecutions, etc."[62] Significantly, he did not wish for the evictions
which he had earlier held up as terrifying the government for their effect
on English public opinion. Now the tables had been turned, and the
threat of evictions could mean a rush of tenants to join the Plan for
whom there would be no support. Laurence Ginnell, who described
himself as the "sole office worker of the P of C from the beginning and
still [December 1890] have the accounts in my charge" reported at the
end of the year that 1,600 familes then depended for their daily bread
on the Plan and that the bank accounts were in a desperate condition."[63] O'Brien himself was reduced to refusing the shelter of the
Plan to Donegal tenants who had paid their rents to the local priest. As
he explained to Gill:

It is a question of £ S.D. It would be a pity for us to abandon any fight in that
district—on the other hand, we must take care not to flood our books with
bodies of pauper tenants. I think on the whole our best plan would be to

[61]Lyons, *John Dillon*, 109.
[62]O'Brien to Gill, January 7, 1890, Gill Papers, NLI MSS. 13478–526 (Box
1871–92/folder 5).
[63]Ginnell to McDonnell Bodkin, December 28, 1890, *ibid.* (Plan of Campaign/Box no. 2).

arrange with him [Father McFadden of Gweedore] that *our liabilities should not be on Plan lines*, but should be limited to such occasional grants as the state of our funds . . . might enable us to make.[64]

All attention was now centered on the grand opening of New Tipperary April 12. O'Brien was the hero of the hour and led the procession into the town on an open carriage along with Davitt (again *persona grata*), two Irish and six English M.P.'s, and representative bodies from all over the south of Ireland. Ridgeway visited it a month later and reported to Balfour:

New Tipperary is a more substantial reality than I expected it to be. It is very creditable to the Nationalists . . . The shops are bright, clean and large but there are no dwellings attached and no storage room. They will be bitterly cold in winter. So will the wooden double-storied houses outside, between the arcade and the market place. They are pleasant enough now. A few brick houses are now being built.

The shops in the arcade are occupied but there seems to be little or no trade . . .

It is worth noting that the labouring class, who inhabit particularly good cottages, have all been allowed to pay rent to Mr. Smith-Barry.[65]

Priests and people joined in the work of creating a rival to the important butter mart on nearby Main Street in the old town. The Nationalist priests, Father Humphries and Canon Cahill, aided by the Irish members, Sheehy and Gill, together with a few town stalwarts, held weekly meetings to regulate the affairs of the new town, dispose of houses, and solicit the custom of merchants for the rival mart.[66] O'Brien and Dillon (back in Ireland since the end of April) could indeed be grateful to Smith-Barry for the retaliatory spirit he had engendered in a moribund agitation. True, the effect was mainly felt in Tipperary, but this was better than "absolute quietude." Even the old riotous at-

[64]O'Brien to T. P. Gill, January 19, 1890, *ibid.* (Box 1871–92/folder 5). The italics are mine.

[65]Ridgeway to Balfour, June 1, 1890, Balfour Papers, BM Add. MS. 49811. John O'Leary, the erstwhile revolutionary of 1867 and a considerable "middle tenant" in Tipperary town, called New Tipperary "a piece of cowardly cruelty on the part of Mr. William O'Brien, with no intelligent reason behind it save that of lying to England" (*Freeman's Journal*, June 8, 1891). The O'Leary of the Yeats poem is the cultural Nationalist, not the harsh landlord remembered by his fellow townsmen [see M. Bourke, *John O'Leary* (Tralee, 1967), 198].

[66]Royal Irish Academy, MS. 24/D/37, Notebook of W. F. D'Alton.

mosphere of recent years returned as the two agitators attempted to hold meetings in the face of rigid government prohibition (no public speeches had been allowed at the festivities April 12). At Cashel, for instance, the Nationalists were almost handed another Mitchelstown Massacre, as Ridgeway confided to Balfour:

We were very nearly let in by the C.I. [Stephens] who lost his head and twice ordered his men to load and fire. They were only just stopped in time . . . He is a fine specimen of an overfed Bull—most of the C.I.'s are cows—fine pluck and physique but *no* brains. Apparently the Nationalists have no idea as to the escape they have had.[67]

As an indication of the Administration's continuing concern with the Nationalist agitation, the prospect of papal intervention was apparently canvassed once more. Colonel Ross of Bladensburg, a Catholic Unionist, was the intermediary.[68] The objections were to the chapel-door collections for the Tenants Association and the obvious sympathies of some of the bishops. Archbishop Croke had publicly sided with O'Brien's suggestion of a combination when it was first aired in the summer of 1889, and the "contempt of the Pope's Rescript" which Ridgeway discerned in the public statements of Archbishop Walsh prompted his desire for "open war" with that cleric.[69] Such allies more than compensated for the alleged proclivities of Bishops O'Dwyer and Healy toward Dublin Castle. The agitators were also blamed for more serious developments—the lack of discipline in the RIC and its indifference to boycotting in the southeast counties. Ridgeway's rage at the "impotent and spineless creatures" who filled the posts of county inspectors exploded in letters to Balfour.

Meanwhile, building operations continued at New Tipperary. By September, two streets, appropriately named for Dillon and Parnell, had been completed. The former contained twenty-three small houses and nine shops which showed signs of hasty construction and seemed to present a fire hazard. Parnell Street boasted thirteen shops in front of two-story brick houses. In all, about forty shopkeepers had vacated the

[67]Ridgeway to Balfour, May 27, 1890, Balfour Papers, BM Add. MS. 49811.

[68]Balfour to Ross of Bladensburg, January 22, 1890, *ibid.*, Add. MS. 49828: "I hope there is no chance of the Malta mission coming to untimely end. I should very profoundly regret it." Ross, then a captain, had accompanied the Duke of Norfolk to Rome in December 1887 to negotiate the famous rescript. Ridgeway had also hoped Ross would be instrumental in having papal pressure exerted on Canon Keller of Youghal, so as to dissociate him from O'Brien in the interests of a settlement on the Ponsonby estate (Ridgeway to Balfour, December 11, 1888, *ibid.*, Add. MS. 49809).

[69]Ridgeway to Balfour, March 16, 1890, *ibid.*, Add. MS. 49810.

old town to relocate in the streets and Mart of New Tipperary. However, the Mart was running into difficulties as the merchants preferred their old haunts. Moreover, it was doubtful, as one observer noted, whether the venture would survive at all in the absence of the liquor licenses tactically withheld by the magistrates. At any rate, by October Balfour was wondering whether it was good strategy for Smith-Barry to go on evicting rent defaulters in the old town "for fear of sending all to New Tipperary which . . . is now a much more substantial affair than at one time it promised to be."[70] Actually, it was the very success of O'Brien and Dillon in keeping the agitation going that determined Balfour to arrest them at all costs. Their speeches always gave him plenty of opportunity, and, accordingly, the pair was arrested on September 18, granted bail, and subsequently found to have absconded to the United States—evidence enough of the importance they gave funds over prison heroics in keeping alive a faltering and greatly circumscribed agitation.

Indeed, the idea of an American tour had been discussed as early as August 1890, and the two Redmond brothers, T. D. Sullivan, Tim Healy, and T. P. O'Connor had all been considered as emissaries. John Redmond refused to go, while his brother, Willie, was considered too much of a lightweight. It was felt that Healy, though apparently willing to travel, would not get the sanction of Parnell. The delegation finally consisted of O'Brien, Dillon, Sullivan, O'Connor, T. P. Gill, and T. C. Harrington.[71] Thus did it transpire that six important members of the party were abroad during the climactic events in Committee Room 15 of the House of Commons the following December.

It was O'Brien's intention to use the proceeds of the tour entirely for the support of Plan tenants. Parnell quickly disabused him of this notion for, as he explained in a letter to O'Brien shortly before his escape to America, the Paris securities were being depleted at the rate of £12,000 per year to sustain the party's expenses in England. Therefore, it would be necessary to use some of the American money to defray election expenses in Ireland and to support the evicted tenants of Land League days, a time when Parnell was much closer to the hearts of the people than he had been for several years.[72] These hopes were, alas, not

[70]Ridgeway to Balfour, October 13, 1890, *ibid.*, Add. MS. 49829. A description of the new "town" is given in *The Times*, London, September 12, 1890.

[71]O'Brien to Gill, August 14, 1890, Gill Papers, NLI MSS. 13478–526 (Box 1871–92/folder 8).

[72]Parnell to O'Brien, October 3, 1890, *ibid.* (Letters and Telegrams, 1889–92/folder 3).

to be realized. The next month saw the work of O'Brien and Dillon and the hopes of the thousands of tenants swept away in disintegration and defeat with the revelations of the Parnell-O'Shea divorce case.

Less than Victory

Thus ended the so-called Land War. It had not been a war to abolish landlordism but rather one to win rent reductions for the half-million tenants whom Nationalists held up as being rack-rented by insatiable landlords. Instead, the vast majority had to wait until 1896 to earn the reductions guaranteed by the judicial fixing of second-term rents under the Land Act of 1881. In reality the war was a weak resistance put up by a few small and vulnerable redoubts dependent on the sporadic foraging of Nationalist sympathizers. William O'Brien and John Dillon generaled the campaign, and its failure is largely theirs, though not all theirs. Parnell himself, the people's leader in the fight against English supremacy, shrank from lending his great authority to a movement that might well have been transformed from a selective struggle against the landlords to a mass movement drawing its strength from the land hunger of the peasants and from an instinctual patriotism that could be tapped and channeled into a general assault on the multifarious aspects of British rule. The task that was taken up by a handful of party members should have been a duty followed by eighty. Instead, the aloofness of one was the cue for the many, and what remained was stunted from the beginning.

The beneficiary of "constitutional revolution" was the Liberal party, the alliance with which had been carefully nursed by Parnell and supported by his lieutenants since his speech at the National Liberal Club in July 1887. At home, political education in Nationalism consisted of reciting the malignities of one English party, the Conservative, and magnifying the goodness of the other, the Liberal. The casualty was the independence of the Irish party and eventually, also, the integrity of Home Rule.[73] Lacking the authority and force of Parnell, O'Brien and Dillon meekly consented to their assigned roles and bravely accepted the hardships—the batons, the jails, the incessant round of outdoor meetings in a climate particularly unsuited to platform comforts. They were activists and managers, not leaders, as the history of the Irish party after Parnell's death painfully attests.

As for "the people," that great imponderable whose role is too often

[73]The one important voice raised against the Liberal alliance was Davitt's in September

to follow or endure, they were never short of advice to do the latter. Parnell's call for a kind of national immolation of the spirit on behalf of English public opinion was a refrain that could almost always be discerned amid the bluster of O'Brien and Dillon. Little wonder that evictions were in general very easily accomplished or that the British army and the RIC were never short of recruits in Ireland.[74] Yet, compared to the dullness of the period between 1882 and 1885, the years of the Plan seem ones of spirited defiance. Many paid for their defiance with a stint on the plank bed. Between July 1887 and December 1890, almost 3,500 persons were proceeded against under the Crimes Act, over 1,800 of them suffering imprisonment, usually up to two months with hard labor, for offenses ranging from unlawful assembly, to intimidation, assault, conspiracy, or defending their homes against the evictors. But a rent strike on a small scale, a peaceful meeting held in a proclaimed district, or the concerted effort to defeat a syndicate of landlords did not betoken any revival of the purely nationalist spirit manifested in Fenian days. Colonel Turner, who had a penchant for lacing his official reports with dire prophecies of the future of Ireland, thought that that spirit was being nurtured elsewhere:

The present system of National Education instils sedition and hatred of England into the rising generation from their earliest years, the younger priests are with few exceptions disaffected, and I fear it is idle to hope that with these elements and with the continued going and coming of Irish Americans, finality to agitation can ever be secured.[75]

1888, when he blamed it for most of the evils inflicted by the Tory coercionists since 1886 (C. C. O'Brien, *Parnell and His Party*, 227).

[74]The army in Ireland totaled about 30,000 men throughout the 1880s. During the Plan of Campaign years, six cavalry units and twenty-five or twenty-six infantry battalions were maintained at all times. Of the ten "Irish" regiments (thirty-one battalions) in the British army never more than three battalions were quartered in Ireland during this period, and from 1888 on at least one of those was a detachment from a regiment recruited in the Protestant North (see Hart's *Army List*, London, 1887–1890). The Nationalists never made any concerted effort to discourage recruiting and certainly never thought in terms of capitalizing on the potential "disloyalty" of Irish troops. That such an element was not entirely lacking is evident from a letter of Ridgeway on the Fenian sympathies of the Leinster Regiment stationed at Limerick in 1887: "We shall have a disaster some day if these Irish Regiments are sent here" (Ridgeway to Balfour, November 27, 1887, Balfour Papers, BM Add. MS. 49808). Needless to say, the Leinster Regiment was sent packing.

The RIC lower ranks were about 80 percent Roman Catholic. Intimidation or Nationalist sympathies appear to have been the reason for a spate of resignations in County Kerry in 1887. Yet, Balfour was able to report to the Cabinet that in 1888 there were more candidates for admission to the ranks than in any year previously [PRO, Cabinet Minutes, CAB(1889) 37/23 no. 5: A. J. Balfour on the Political Condition of Ireland in January 1889].

[75]SPO, CBS, Divisional Commissioner Reports (Southwest), Report for May 1889.

The spirit did, indeed, eventually revive, though not until the groundwork of the constitutional revolutionists had all but emasculated the separatist tradition of their predecessors.

Toward the end the advocates of boycotting were even deserted by the bishops, who had for so long given passive approval to their efforts on behalf of the tenants. Speaking for the Irish Episcopacy, Michael Logue, Archbishop of Armagh, warned Parnell of the grave political, social, and moral consequences deriving from the activities of O'Brien and Dillon. Such action taken on individual responsibility could no longer have the cooperation of the clergy, and it was only out of regard for the unity and strength of the Nationalist movement, explained Logue, that the bishops had not spoken out earlier.[76] This episcopal admonishing came suspiciously on the heels of Balfour's congratulations to Colonel Ross on the results of his recent dealings in Rome as secretary of a mission designed largely to advise the Vatican of violations of the Papal rescript by Irish priests. Balfour's tendentious moralizing scarcely conceals his animus against O'Brien and Dillon:

You have done very great service to the cause of public morality by keeping your friends in Italy acquainted with what is really going on . . . I think even those who most obstinately shut their eyes to the governing tendencies which are shaping the future of Irish history must have realised that no more dangerous ally for religion could exist than the so-called "Constitutional Revolutionists."[77]

The Plan of Campaign was, as we have seen, of small dimensions. Its last stand at New Tipperary was ridden by defeats and disappointments before it fell victim to the collapse of the Evicted Tenants Fund after the party split in December 1890.[78] That it was invested with a notoriety out of all proportion to its actual effects was due to the propagandizing genius and pugnacity of William O'Brien. He and Dillon were the perfect complement to each other: the former ebullient, romantic, adventurous; the latter austere, calculating, and pragmatic.

It is hard to imagine how such a beleagured movement could have

[76]Cardinal Logue to Parnell, October 15, 1890, Gill Papers, NLI MSS. 13478–526 (Letters and Telegrams, 1889–92/folder 3). Archbishop Croke later assured O'Brien that he was no party to the Logue letter [Croke to O'Brien, March 22, 1891, *ibid.* (folder 31)].

[77]Balfour to Colonel Ross, September 12, 1890, Balfour Papers, BM Add. MS. 49829.

[78]By mid-1891 many of the evicted tenants and shopkeepers had returned to their old homes on Smith-Barry's terms, i.e., at the former rent and on payment of all arrears and costs of eviction. As late as 1893, eighty-three tenants were still awaiting reinstatement. Significantly, no "planter" could ever be found to take up an evicted tenancy in Tipperary. As for New Tipperary, the site eventually reverted to Smith-Barry and was levelled to the ground.

THE NEW AND THE TRUE ST. PATRICK.

Arthur Balfour, bearing light railways for the depressed western counties, vanquishes O'Brien's New Tipperary and Dillon's National League.

kept going for so long without O'Brien's inspiration, sacrifices, and es-
capades. No member of the party, including Davitt, had been the
champion of or risked more for the tenants so consistently and for so
long. There was no hiatus in O'Brien's activity like Dillon's two-and-a-
half-year voluntary absence from Ireland and his one-year trip, admittedly for funds, to Australia and New Zealand. O'Brien's prison
companion in Kilmainham days, Andrew Kettle (one who had few
kind words for the Plan) paid compliment to an otherwise "dangerous
personality": "The work undertaken by Mr. O'Brien and his personal
sacrifices were astounding and they seemed to actually fascinate the
Irish people . . . John Dillon was associated with Mr. O'Brien in this
rent strike . . . but Mr. O'Brien was the ruling if not the guiding
spirit."[79] O'Brien's colleagues, even those who were later to differ
violently with him, all attest to the great qualities he possessed during
the 1880s—his fearless and unselfish nature, disdain for personal gain,
unfailing optimism, journalistic flair, organizing ability, and passionate
oratorical style that made him the greatest platform speaker in Ireland
since Daniel O'Connell. Perhaps the greatest commendation for his
fighting qualities was that of his great antagonist, Arthur Balfour, who
was not above assessing his worth over that of would-be Liberal supporters: "One speech of O'Brien's against land-grabbing does more
mischief than it is in the power of all these English busy bodies to accomplish in a twelvemonth."[80]

The Administration could feel satisfied that it had both outlasted and
prevented a complete victory for the Plan of Campaign. True, there had
been many smaller settlements of varying degrees of satisfaction in the
beginning, and many landlords probably conceded reductions rather
than risk a fight, but the great Plan confrontations saw but two
settlements of any satisfaction to the tenants—on the Kingston and
Vandeleur estates. In May 1891 seventeen prominent cases were still
unsettled.[81] The Nationalists could not claim any government conces-

[79]A. J. Kettle, *Material for Victory* (Dublin, 1958), 75. For a view contrary to Kettle's last
observation, see Lyons, "John Dillon and the Plan," 345–346.

[80]Balfour to Colonel Turner, DM, September 9, 1889, Balfour Papers, BM Add. MS.
49828. For assessments of O'Brien's qualities by contemporaries, see J. McCarthy,
Reminiscences (New York, 1899), 2:348; M. Davitt, *The Fall of Feudalism in Ireland* (New York,
1904), 694–695; Healy, *Letters and Leaders* 1:170; J. J. Horgan, *Parnell to Pearse* (Dublin, 1948),
40, 165.

[81]SPO, CBS Files (1891) 3408/S. These were, listed by counties: Cork (Langford, Leader,
Marmion, Ponsonby); Donegal (Olphert); Galway (Clanricarde, Lewis); Kildare
(O'Kelly); Limerick (Delnege, Lloyd, O'Grady); Louth (Massereene); Queens
(Lansdowne); Tipperary (Smith-Barry); Wexford (Brooke, Byrne, Tottenham).

sion as great as Gladstone's Land Act of 1881. Far from being frightened by the Plan into concessions, Balfour fought it relentlessly. One instance of the vindictive feeling he held toward Plan tenants was the glee
with which he hailed the news that the small railways he was
promoting in the West would not pass through Plan estates. Seldom did
he fail to take the side of the landlords, and, at times—as in the syndicate—he led them. Besides, like many Chief Secretaries before him,
his solutions to the distress of Irish tenants included state-aided
emigration.[82]

Finally, it cannot be said that the Plan originated any revolutionary
steps to advance land purchase. The first meaningful step in land
purchase was made by the Conservatives with Ashbourne's Act in 1885.
Under that act and amending legislation three years later over 25,000
tenants became purchasers of their holdings. Even though only
£10,000,000 was provided for advances (about six percent of the
amount needed to abolish landlordism), the measure dwarfed the
paltry land transfer (a mere 1,608 holdings) effected by the Gladstonian
legislation of 1870 and 1881. Of course, the real revolution in land
ownership awaited the attractive financial inducements of the Land Act
of 1903. By then, the landlords had ceased to play any effective role in
Irish political life, a further inducement to sell. This loss of their former
primacy had begun with the secret-ballot act of 1872, was accelerated
by the dual-ownership theory of the Land Act of 1881 and the extended
franchise of the reform legislation of 1884, and finally sealed by the
Local Government Act of 1898. Perhaps we may also allow that the
long years of boycott, agitation, and litigation visited on the landlords
by agitators like O'Brien, widened immeasurably the social gulf
between Protestant owners and Catholic tenants and helped to hasten
the day of reckoning. In his later conciliationist years, O'Brien may well
have regretted this phase of his career. As may be expected, the implications of it at the time were not lost on one of the guardians of
landlord interests, the redoubtable Colonel Turner:

Much remains to be done and it is very doubtful whether the evil caused by
Mr. Parnell and his allies can ever be undone. Their agitation has swept across

---

[82]Balfour to Ridgeway, October 1, 1890, Balfour Papers, BM Add. MS. 49829. For
Balfour's novel views on emigration, see Balfour to Sir Henry Robinson, September 5, 1890;
Balfour to Eric Barrington, September 17, 1890, *ibid.*; also, Balfour to Buller, May 12, 1887
in PRO, War Office (Buller Papers), W.O./132/4A.

the country like the plague of locusts, leaving ruin, desolation and crime in its tracks and having successfully engendered a feeling of intense hatred between the "classes and the masses" which it will require more than one generation to eradicate.[83]

[83]SPO, CBS, Divisional Commissioner Reports (Southwest), Report for February 1888.

FOUR

In the Wilderness

O'BRIEN was in America making speeches and collecting money for the evicted tenants when the news of the decision against Parnell as corespondent in the O'Shea divorce suit was made public on November 17, 1890. Within the next few weeks, O'Brien's leading position in Irish politics was swept away in the bitterness of party strife, and both the evicted tenants and the victims of mounting economic distress in the western coastal districts were left to the tender mercies of bankrupt Poor Law Unions and grudging government relief projects. The rancor and vilification that for years had been spewed out by Irish politicians against successive coercionist regimes were now turned inward against comrades-in-arms. It was a situation for which O'Brien, torn between genuine affection for Parnell and fearful concern for Home Rule, was ill-suited.

The story of Parnell's love affair with the wife of Captain William O'Shea, the thunderbolt of the uncontested divorce suit, Parnell's own death within a year, and the aftermath of division and rancor in Ireland mark one of the most tragic personal and political episodes in Irish politics.[1] Parnell's relationship with the charming and vivacious Kitty had begun as far back as 1880, when she and her husband were already estranged. Though the affair was carried on with the utmost secrecy and discretion, the implications of Parnell's forcing the captain on the Galway electorate in 1886 were not lost on his closest colleagues. O'Shea's subsequent relations with Parnell and the Irish party were

[1]The events of November 1890 to February 1891 are treated in elaborate detail in C. C. O'Brien, *Parnell and His Party, 1880–90* (Oxford, 1957), chapter 9; and F. S. L. Lyons, *The Fall of Parnell, 1890–91* (Toronto, 1962). The role of the hierarchy in the crisis is discussed in E. Larkin, "Mounting the Counter-Attack: The Roman Catholic Hierarchy and the Destruction of Parnellism," *Review of Politics* 25 (April 1963):157–182. For the impact of the crisis on the Liberal party, see J. F. Glaser, "Parnell's Fall and the Nonconformist Conscience," *Irish Historical Studies* 12 (September 1960):119–138.

stormy—he had abstained in the vote on the Home Rule Bill and had appeared as a witness against Parnell in the special commission set up in 1888 to investigate *The* (London) *Times*'s allegations of Parnell's complicity in Irish terrorism. Few of Parnell's closest colleagues were surprised, therefore, when the cuckolded captain, for reasons not necessary to go into here, chose to file his divorce petition in December 1889. Yet, O'Brien and Dillon, the two most powerful figures in the party after Parnell, appear to have accomplished nothing beforehand (if actually they tried at all) to force Parnell or the party to assess the contingencies of the suit. As one historian has noted, "The nationalist movement as a whole simply drifted towards the catastrophe, with a dumb confidence in its leader's ambiguous assurances."[2]

Immediately upon receiving the news of the decision from London, O'Brien and four other members of the delegation to America expressed their confidence in Parnell by reaffirming his leadership in a joint telegram to the hastily convened National League meeting in Dublin on November 20. O'Brien wrote resignedly to Gill, who was separated from him by their fund-raising schedule, "Prospects are looking very gloomy. What is certain is that we have done the only possible thing open to us."[3] The publication of Gladstone's letter to Morley on November 26 intimating the consequences for Home Rule if Parnell were retained as leader induced a veritable panic among the delegates in America. The flurry of telegrams received and sent by them over the next two weeks testify to their wild disarray. O'Brien's ominous reaction was to regard Parnell's defiance of Gladstone's call to resign as "insanity," and he cabled the party in London that "in view of our obligation to Gladstone and of our responsibilities to Irish tenantry on faith of a General Election fought in cordial alliance with Liberal party would earnestly recommend party to open immediate friendly communication

[2]C. C. O'Brien, *Parnell and His Party*, 282.
[3]O'Brien to Gill, (postmarked) November 24, 1890, Gill Papers, NLI MSS. 13478–526 (Letters and Telegrams, 1889–92/folder 3). The lone, silent dissenter in the six-man delegation was T. D. Sullivan. But the most prominent and outspoken critic of Parnell's remaining party leader at home was Davitt, both in *Labour World* and in a letter to Croke:

> If Parnell appears in Parliament next week, or even this Session, as the *newly elected* leader of the Irish Party, it is all up with the Home Rule cause . . . The tone and temper of the British organ of Liberal and Nonconformist opinion say this in the most decided manner possible . . . Are we going to allow Parnell to wreck the Irish cause in the interests of the strumpet for whom he has all but sacrificed us already?

(Davitt to Croke, November 20, 1890, Croke Papers, NLI microfilm, p. 6012). This was a strange turnabout indeed for the man who little more than a year before had blamed all Ireland's ills on the Liberal alliance.

with Gladstone."[4] The next day, November 27, brought the news that Parnell had absolutely refused to reconsider his position and would only be deprived of the chairmanship by a vote of the party.

O'Brien abhorred the headlong rush to condemn that was fast becoming evident on both sides of the Atlantic, but it was impossible for him to remain entirely neutral, for he was being ineluctably drawn to the position that what was paramount in the issue was not Parnell's successful defiance of Liberal dictation, but rather the dangers in such a stance to the cause of Home Rule. Letters and telegrams began to pour in on O'Brien from American partisans, denouncing Parnell and requesting him to address anti-Parnellite meetings. Though O'Brien reserved his judgment in public, in private he, Dillon, and the others, excepting Harrington, had decided that the only course was for Parnell to resign and have Justin McCarthy nominated as chairman of the party.[5] O'Brien's hand was stayed for only a few hours by Parnell's telegram asking Dillon and himself "to suspend judgment until you see my statement to be issued tonight." The statement was the famous manifesto made public on November 29 against the "wirepullers of the English Liberal party"—those "English wolves" howling for his destruction.

It is almost impossible to believe that Parnell could expect that his mordant harangue would have any effect other than to force Dillon and O'Brien to yield even more quickly to their Liberal inclinations. A note written in O'Brien's hand of a telegram apparently sent to Parnell on the evening of November 28 clearly indicates his unalterable decision: "Would earnestly beseech you not to embitter situation by issuing manifesto. Opinion here overwhelming and universal in favour of retirement."[6] For the past five years the maintenance of the Liberal alliance had been the common denominator in the political makeup of Parnell's lieutenants. They would not now repudiate it for what must have seemed to them the personal vendetta of Parnell against Gladstone. Accordingly, all the delegates, again with the exception of Harrington, wired McCarthy (the anti-Parnellite chairman) that Parnell's continued leadership was impossible. While the manifesto cer-

---

[4] O'Brien to Gill (telegram), November 26, 1890, Gill Papers, NLI MSS. 13478–526 (Letters and Telegrams, 1889–92/folder 3).

[5] O'Brien and American delegation to Parnell (telegram), November 28, 1890, *ibid.* (folder 6).

[6] *Ibid.* As it turned out, Harrington alone refused to associate himself with his colleagues' abandonment of their leader.

tainly embittered the situation, the actual parting of the ways had been reached on November 26. This was a fact which O'Brien was to be the last to admit.

Efforts to retrieve the situation were taken first by John Redmond and Dr. Joseph Kenny, two of Parnell's staunchest supporters. Redmond wired Gill requesting that the delegation strongly urge the party to hold their decision on the leadership until all the delegates arrived in Paris for consultation. O'Brien, because of the mutual regard and confidence that existed between him and Parnell, was eventually selected as peacemaker, but two precious weeks had gone by, and the formal secession of the anti-Parnellites had taken place before O'Brien set sail with Gill on December 13. Some of the despair that enveloped the onlookers was conveyed to O'Brien by Kenny: "Had you and John listened to us you would both stand today in the position of peacemakers who were outside the whirlpool of strife . . . Without the moral support your adhesion gave them [the anti-Parnellites] they would never have persevered . . . The cause was to me all in all and that lost, all is lost."[7]

There was no denying that O'Brien's and Dillon's endorsement of the anti-Parnellite stand had brought immense prestige to the seceders. O'Brien, who had once vowed that he would sooner annihilate himself than cross Parnell, denied his leader at the first cockcrow of Liberal moral revulsion. Of course, his faith in Parnell had been greatly weakened since 1886 by the latter's demoralizing inactivity and by the damper which he had thrown over the agrarian agitation, the New Tipperary episode being a recent bitter memory. Nor were Parnell's experiences with the rank and file of the party during the Plan days such as to entice O'Brien to place party unity above all other considerations. Significantly, most of the Plan of Campaign members were anti-Parnellites.[8] Still, old loyalties died hard, and O'Brien clung to the hope that Parnell could be persuaded to withdraw on terms as yet undefined as he prepared to meet his shattered idol in Boulogne. Something of the mental travail he was undergoing comes through in the following rather bathetic poetic flight, composed on the S.S. *Obdam*, which was carrying him to France:

[7]Kenny to O'Brien, December 17, 1890, *ibid.* (folder 8).
[8]C. C. O'Brien, *Parnell and His Party*, 332. For an instance of one campaigner's utter disillusion with Parnell because of his lack of support of the Plan of Campaign, see W. J. Lane to Gill, September 7, 1889, Gill Papers, NLI MSS. 13478–526 (Plan of Campaign, Box no. 2).

Over the desolate water the wind howls stormingly
And the heart in my breast it breaks as I think of thee
We are coming Chief and the billows break against our good ship's side
But is it weal or is it woe for thee that we betide
Oh why did you ever . . . [9]

Meanwhile, dismay set in on all sides. Dillon, also anxious for the safety of the Liberal alliance and as much a pessimist as O'Brien was an optimist, became convinced that the bitterness of the preceding weeks coupled with the amount of support in Ireland for Parnell, had rendered the situation hopeless for the party. He wrote to O'Brien from America: "Since you left no resolutions of support, and very few letters in support have reached me, and this in view of the fact that my address is so well known, convinces me that we have not a body of opinion behind us [in Ireland] to be relied on in a fight."[10] T. P. O'Connor, still in America, also wrote, though his intention was clearly to pressure O'Brien into not surrendering to Parnell:

No bitterness can be too great in resentment of the wrong he has done Ireland. I fear very much that all this anger will be turned against you if you counsel surrender . . . if Parnell wins at Kilkenny I fear the evicted tenants are ruined: none of the well-to-do classes here will give him a dollar.[11]

Urgent appeals poured in on O'Brien from priest and bishop, including particularly trenchant denunciations of Parnell from O'Brien's old friends Archbishop Croke and Father Keller. The situation in Ireland, as described for him by the amiable Harrington, who had hastened home, was such as to make the most sanguine despair of conciliation:

How can I describe to you the position in Ireland? The change since you and I left home is such as you could scarcely have expected to take place in a century. Old friends pass one another without speaking, members of the same family have quarrelled and fallen out and in the mad zeal of partizanship no man's former services are remembered . . . Kilkenny was the saddest scene I ever witnessed in Ireland. In every polling booth in the division a priest sat at the table as personation agent. The people were instructed to declare they could not read and the voters came in in bodies with the priest . . . The magic war cry everywhere to be heard, and used even by the priests and young children was "Kitty O'Shea's petticoat."[12]

[9]See Gill Papers, NLI MSS. 13478–526 (Parnell Crisis/folder 10). Fortunately for O'Brien, the poem never fell into the hands of the anti-Parnellite press.

[10]Dillon to O'Brien, December 18, 1890, *ibid.* (Letters and Telegrams, 1889–92/folder 10).

[11]O'Connor to O'Brien, December 19, 1890, *ibid.* (American Delegation/folder 15). Familiarity with the well-to-do was one of O'Connor's chief assets to the party.

[12]Harrington to O'Brien, December 27, 1890, *ibid.* (folder 15). This evidence of electoral

Not the least of O'Brien's worries was that his name was being used in connection with the anti-Parnellite successor to *United Ireland*, McDonnell Bodkin's *Insuppressible*. Though the tone of this paper was designed to inflame passions and vilify Parnell, O'Brien could not bring himself to repudiate it during the negotiations, feeling that to "disarm" himself so would lessen his power for good with Parnell—a strange decision, indeed, for one who was ostensibly wholly engaged as the sole conciliating voice in all those dramatic proceedings.

Much to his credit, O'Brien persevered in the face of mounting hostility and misrepresentation and duly met Parnell at Boulogne on December 30, after having first apprised McCarthy and Sexton of the tentative proposals for vacating the chairmanship which he and his fellow delegates had agreed on in New York. This was the first of several meetings that were to end in defeat for O'Brien's aim of preserving the Nationalist movement from ruin. He was not overly confident, realizing there was only a very slender hope that Parnell could be brought to assent to withdraw in such a manner that greater evils would not ensue. It is not necessary to go into the almost interminable round of proposals and counterproposals of the next few weeks other than to state that O'Brien went as far as it was possible to go to satisfy Parnell, whose unalterable stand involved deposing McCarthy (elected to the chair by the anti-Parnellite majority) and obtaining Liberal guarantees on the land question and on the control of the police in any future Home Rule Ireland.

From the outset, Parnell wanted O'Brien to become chairman in succession to McCarthy, an offer O'Brien forcefully declined. He had to break off negotiations before Parnell would accept Dillon in his place.[13] The latter, who had not arrived in France until January 18, had not been of great help to O'Brien and cast a melancholy gloom over the proceedings from the start. His communications are full of complaints

---

intimidation is corroborated by Dr. Brownrigg, Bishop of Ossory, in a letter to Archbishop Croke: "The battle has been a dreadfully tough one. No doubt the sympathy of the people was entirely with Parnell and it had to be broken through as a wall of brass. If victory crown our banner, it is due not to politics, not to morality, not to the Irish Party, but purely and simply to the influence, family, personal and ministerial, of the priesthood of Ossory" (Brownrigg to Croke, December 19, 1890, Croke Papers, NLI microfilm p. 6012). For Archbishop Croke's and Father Keller's denunciations of Parnell, see Croke to O'Brien, December 19, 1890 and Keller to O'Brien, December 19, 1890 in Gill Papers, NLI MSS. 13478–526 (Letters and Telegrams, 1889–92/folder 10).

[13]O'Brien to Croke, January 12, 1891, Croke Papers, NLI microfilm p. 6012.

"La Rixe." The split in the Irish Parliamentary party: archenemies Parnell (restrained by O'Brien and Dillon) and Healy (held by Justin McCarthy) with Gladstone as onlooker. From *Punch, or the London Charivari,* March 7, 1891.

of the "cruel unfair position" in which he was being placed, the un-
wisdom of O'Brien's concessions, and the mischievous nature of
Parnell's terms. But Parnell, as O'Brien saw, had to be conciliated if
irretrievable damage was not to be done to the constitutional movement, a point also not lost on the Liberals, who eventually gave the requested guarantees—though, alas, not in a manner satisfactory to
Parnell. The negotiations thereupon were abruptly broken off by
Parnell on February 10, and two days later O'Brien and Dillon crossed
over to England, probably welcoming their pending six-month imprisonment which would remove them from the bitter mudslinging
quarrels they had come to detest. As Gladstone observed in a letter to
Archbishop Croke during the crisis: "one is tempted to say there never
was anything like it since the War in Heaven."[14]

O'Brien's role as negotiator earned him the abuse and distrust of the
anti-Parnellites. They—the clergy, Davitt, Healy, and his followers—could not get rid of Parnell fast enough, whereas O'Brien had
been working to oust McCarthy and save Parnell for the Nationalist
party.[15] His efforts won faint praise from the Parnellites, and Parnell
himself made no secret of his regard for O'Brien's qualities. Harrington
had written O'Brien of Parnell's regard for him:

When I met Parnell . . . he was most anxious for the meeting with you. It
appears that all through he has expressed to his supporters the utmost faith in
your affection for him. I am sorry to learn that he made a wide distinction
between yourself and Dillon in this respect.[16]

Thus, it was not unusual to have "cheers for O'Brien" voiced at the
various Parnellite meetings throughout January. For these reasons
O'Brien was generally, though mistakenly, regarded by the general
public to be on Parnell's side and it was expected that O'Brien's release
in July would confirm this view. Dillon, on the other hand, had had a
severe clash with Parnell at Calais on February 3, and it was felt that he
would turn up on the opposite side. Archbishop Croke, as eager as

[14]Gladstone to Croke, December 2, 1890, *ibid.*

[15]The rank and file of the secessionist (anti-Parnellite) faction were not asked for their approval of the proposals agreed between O'Brien and McCarthy, which were intended to lead
to the latter's stepping down and the elevation of Dillon to the chair. But one old member, at
least, made his opinion known privately: "Is it not extraordinary that Dillon and O'Brien
could have ever persuaded themselves that we (at least most of us) would ever have consented to the terms they offered Parnell" (Alfred Webb to J. F. X. O'Brien, November 5,
1891, J. F. X. O'Brien Papers, NLI MSS. 13418–477/folder 13).

[16]Harrington to O'Brien, December 27, 1890, Gill Papers, NLI MSS. 13478–526 (Plan of
Campaign/Box no. 2).

anyone to find out O'Brien's political views, wrote to him in March, and O'Brien gave a most reassuring reply. He and Dillon had already discussed the course to be taken: "As to our action on our release, do not be uneasy. We will be quite clear as to the impossibility of Parnell's leadership." Nor were the two prisoners content to let things drift:

I would implore your Grace [Archbishop Croke] to ponder well whether you or the Archbishop of Dublin might not make some move, private or public, to intimate your feelings in favour of letting bygones be bygones in his [Gray, editor of the Parnellite *Freeman's Journal*] case and in the case of other men like Redmond, Clancy . . . etc. who are, evidently, in the balance.[17]

This was advice O'Brien repeated to Gill before his release as he urged him to contact Redmond in the hope that the latter could be induced to throw over Parnell and force reunion with the McCarthyites.[18] O'Brien, who had exchanged loyalty for dependence, was apparently unable to perceive that men like Redmond and Harrington would put loyalty above political expediency.

O'Brien's disavowal of Parnell was not, as Healy's was, a personal vendetta, but rather the measure of his response to the needs of the Liberal alliance. He was above all anxious to preserve some kind of unity in the political movement by capturing Parnell's "best men" and, last but not least, he was alarmed at how disunity was affecting the plight of the evicted tenants. O'Brien had been quite prepared to return to America after his release in a further attempt to collect funds for the evicted, but there was no encouragement from Dillon for a venture Dillon claimed would simply make them scapegoats for the party.[19] Dillon lacked the selfless regard and compromising spirit that infected O'Brien and thought much more in terms of political results and his

[17]O'Brien to Croke, Tuesday (apparently March 24, 1891), Croke Papers, NLI microfilm p. 6012. Despite Archbishop Croke's repeated expressions of disinterest in this unhappy phase of Irish politics ("I wish I could get back again to New Zealand") he nevertheless kept doggedly after O'Brien to make sure he held to his promise to speak against Parnell [see Croke to O'Brien, July 29, 1891, Gill Papers, NLI MSS. 13478–526 (Letters and Telegrams 1889–92/folder 32)].

[18]O'Brien to Gill, no date (July 1891), Gill Papers, NLI MSS. 13478–526 (Letters and Telegrams 1889–92/folder 37).

[19]F. S. L. Lyons, *John Dillon* (London, 1968), 139. Plan expenditure, which had been almost £84,000 in 1890, fell to £48,000 in the following year and declined catastrophically thereafter. As of December 1891, the total number of families on the grants list was 1,495. By 1893, reinstatement of tenants had brought the total down to 884 (see Expenditure List in UCC William O'Brien Papers, Box AD; Evicted Tenants Commission: Minutes of Evidence, House of Commons (1893–94), 31, Q. 15018 (evidence of John Dillon). For total amount of annual grants 1887–1893, see M. Davitt, *The Fall of Feudalism in Ireland* (New York, 1904), 529.

own place in them. Likewise, he discouraged O'Brien from attempting, while in prison, to influence events on the outside.[20] Shortly before their release in July, Dillon finally persuaded him to abandon his policy of neutrality in the search for reunion with moderate Parnellites and instead to join with the majority faction (renamed the Irish National Federation) in order to negotiate as necessary from a position of strength. For Dillon, who had politics in his bones, this was the politically correct decision, but for O'Brien, primarily a man of the people and agrarian above all else, agreement to this course was a disaster. Worn out in exercising his fighter's instincts against the Irish Administration, he was at a loss amid the verbal battles of intraparty strife. He had not yet acquired that fatal Irish propensity to factionalism which was to make him the focus of that corrosive tendency almost twenty years later.

Factions

O'Brien had spent his time in prison working on his second novel, *A Queen of Men,* an Irish historical romance which did not see publication until many years later. The peace of mind which allowed him this literary pursuit was rudely shattered on his release. O'Brien, like Dillon, now suffered abuse from both sides—from Parnellites for his "betrayal" of the leader and from anti-Parnellites for his efforts to mediate the conflict at Boulogne. Dillon had induced him to opt for the anti-Parnellite side rather than remaining neutral, but that did nothing to lessen the hostility of Tim Healy, a powerful force in the Irish National Federation, the breakaway rival of Parnell's National League. O'Brien was early given an example of the force of public hostility when he was forced to withdraw his name from nomination for the presidency of the Cork Young Ireland Society because of Parnellite opposition.[21] More ominous was Healy's revelation that the police were on constant watch at the residences of O'Brien, Dillon, T. D. Sullivan, and himself.[22]

However, Parnell's death in October 1891 took some of the edge off the extremeness that had characterized the Parnellite position. John Redmond assumed the leadership of the Parnellites and was soon in correspondence with his opponents in a less diehard approach to

[20]Dillon to O'Brien, no date (probably July 1891), NLI William O'Brien Papers, MS. 8555/1.
[21]W. McMahan (Cork Young Ireland Society) to W. O'Brien, November 14 and 23, 1891, UCC William O'Brien Papers, Box AD.
[22]T. M. Healy, *Letters and Leaders of My Day* (New York, 1929), 2:369.

politics. The Waterford by-election in December was the first opportunity for détente, and Redmond wrote to no less bitter an anti-
Parnellite than Davitt, who was contesting the seat, indicating he
"would welcome a truce upon reasonable terms so as to avoid electoral
contests before the General Election." Alas, Davitt could wish his opponent nothing better than defeat in the coming struggle, so the
bitterness was sustained.[23] The new year brought attempts by Gill and
O'Brien to get Dillon to treat with Redmond, followed in April by more
suggestions from the latter, but all such schemes foundered largely on
the implacable hostility of Healy—no small testimony to his power base
within the Federation.[24] Attempts to forge reunion before the return of
the Liberals to power were even made by the Irish National League of
America. A three-man delegation visited Ireland in the summer of 1892,
having written in advance to both Redmond and McCarthy on their
scheme. Redmond, out of deference to the Americans, went so far as to
set up a committee to meet with the anti-Parnellites. The latter,
however, declined the suggestion and the matter was dropped.[25]

To O'Brien, however, the issue was not merely the apportionment of
Parliamentary seats, but the danger to the constitutional movement
resulting from the alienation of the younger generation. He commended
to Archbishop Croke the work of giving the Gaelic Athletic Association
a new lease of life:

The idea is not to give the Association any special political tinge, but to make
certain that our friends should have the supreme power and that the poisonous
influences which crept into the Association before should be kept out. Dillon
and other friends agree that the prospect is one of the utmost importance if we
are to hold our ground with the young men of the country. It is impossible to
interest the young men actively in the working of the Federation branches . . .
Besides the importance of saving the young men from being led astray, it is also
of the utmost importance for us that we should be able to command bodies of
men physically capable of defending themselves against organised intimidation
on the other side. We are very helpless in that way at present . . . I cannot but
think it would be a splendid thing for our chances of keeping our hold on the
young men if your Grace would lend a hand.[26]

[23]Redmond to Davitt, December 7, 1891; Davitt to Redmond, December 8 and 11, 1891,
Redmond Papers, NLI MS. 15179.
[24]Redmond to Gill, April 8, 1892, Gill Papers, NLI MSS. 13478–526 (Box 1871–92/folder
15); Lyons, *John Dillon*, 145. For Healy's opposition, see Walsh to Croke, May 13, 1892,
Croke Papers, NLI microfilm p. 6013.
[25]O'Neill Ryan to Redmond, July 2 and August 11, 1892; Redmond to O'Neill Ryan, July
23, 1892, Redmond Papers, NLI MS. 15236/23.
[26]O'Brien to Croke, August 21, 1892, Croke Papers, NLI microfilm 6013. By this time
Archbishop Croke's days of aiding the Nationalist movement were over. Disillusioned by the

This statement is a contemporary endorsement of Healy's remark during the struggle against Parnell: "It appears as if we had the voters, and Parnell had their sons."[27]

The Nationalist movement was certainly in deep trouble at this time. The trouble was not merely the alienation of the younger generation but also a public apathy not experienced since 1884. The decreasing interest in the work of the National League (Parnellite) and the National Federation resulted in a loss of about 70 percent of their combined membership by 1894. Boycotting was a thing of the past, and agrarian crime, insofar as that indicated peasant unrest, was now hardly more than an occasional shooting of a horse or a cutting of a bullock's tail! The only new groups that seemed to be making any headway were the nonpolitical Trades and Labour Associations, 70 percent of whose strength was concentrated in the industrial center of Belfast.[28] The Irish party could at most take consolation in the fact that the decline in its fortunes threw up no body of Nationalists prepared to fight the "official" constitutionalists on the issue of the Irish representation. Thus, the party, though divided, returned to Westminster in the elections of 1892 and 1895 in almost undiminished strength.

O'Brien stood for election in 1892 and won a seat for Parnell's old constituency, Cork City. This ensured him a place on the Parliamentary committee, the select, decision-making group of the anti-Parnellite faction. The presence of O'Brien, Dillon, and Davitt in the councils of the party meant that some attention would be given to the evicted tenants. Accordingly, the committee decided to raise an Irish subscription in the fall of 1892 to alleviate the burden of the tenants on the party finances. The sum subscribed amounted only to £16,000, and this barely continued the reduced tenant stipends through the following summer. Little could be expected from further appeals to Irish sources,

---

Split and exempted from further involvement by the death of Parnell, it was only with the greatest difficulty that he could be induced to give even small monetary assistance to the party.

[27]Healy, *Letters and Leaders*, 1:355.

[28]Police estimates of the strength of the various Nationalist associations, including secret societies, for the years 1889–1893 are outlined in SPO, CBS Files: 1893/6317; 1894/7828. The membership figures listed below indicate the progressive decline in the fortunes of the Constitutionalists:

	Oct. 1889	Dec. 1890	Dec. 1891	Dec. 1892	Dec. 1893
National Federation	—	—	82,943	56,874	47,080
National League	160,966	138,061	13,108	8,076	6,514

and the Americans had already made it clear that contributions from Federation sources in the States were to be applied to purely political expenses.[29] In fact, the party's own financial status was so dire that the 'wounded soldiers' of the Land War, abandoned by the ingratitude of other Irish farmers, were entirely dependent for the next ten years on the diminishing reserves of the old Land League funds. Some years later, the party treasurer Alfred Webb summarized what was in effect the failure of the Plan of Campaign in these words:

> . . . you cannot imagine the heartrending stories that come into us concerning the condition of many of the evicted tenants . . . In the course of history I know of nothing more shamefully callous than the conduct of our Irish farmers. Men who have by their sacrifices gained £50 a year, refusing a penny.[30]

Under these circumstances there seemed little reason for O'Brien to persevere in Parliamentary work. He had been a member of Parliament almost without interruption since 1883. But he was never comfortable in that arena, and the oratorical style that thrilled his Irish listeners often bored members of the House. He lacked the command of detail of a Healy or a Sexton to make a lasting Parliamentary contribution, though one should not underrate the emotional effect of his eloquent appeals on behalf of Irish tenants or his lurid assaults on the "resolute government" of Lord Salisbury. Even the Home Rule session of 1893 found O'Brien to be "the ghost of his former self." Henry Lucy found it impossible to connect him with the eager, passionate personality that a few years earlier used to dominate the House.[31] Parnell's man-of-war was now more ridiculed for the comic associations of his Blarney tweeds and tear-stained Boulogne handkerchief than admired for his former control of the House. In a speech at Stratford, in the midst of the Home Rule debate, he anticipated the rejection of the bill by the Lords but warned prophetically of the strife which would ensue, whereby not Home Rule but rather "these same noble dukes, marquises, and lords" would be on trial.[32]

---

[29]These and many other details regarding the financial status of the party in the three years since the Split are contained in a lengthy memorandum from Edward Blake to Justin McCarthy, dated November 2, 1893, in NLI, F. S. Bourke Collection, MS. 10702/1.

[30]Alfred Webb to J. F. X. O'Brien, February 26, 1898, J. F. X. O'Brien Papers, NLI MSS. 13418–477/folder 13. The paltry response to the Nationalists' appeals for the Evicted Tenants Fund is highlighted by the result of the 1897 appeal. Barely more than £3,000 was collected, of which about £1,700 was distributed among almost five hundred families dependent on the fund (*ibid.*).

[31]H. W. Lucy, *A Diary of the Home Rule Parliament, 1892–95* (London, 1896), 369.

[32]*The Times*, London, July 2, 1893.

It is a sad reflection on the Irish party that for the next five years its energies were largely consumed by the mean squabbles provoked by the political incompatibility of Healy and Dillon. As O'Brien aptly stated, "one-man power was replaced for Ireland by eighty-man powerlessness." The public quarrels resulting from this rivalry did nothing to retrieve the party's waning popularity in Ireland. Moreover, the lack of funds was an ever-increasing problem over the years.[33] O'Brien was as helpless as any of his colleagues to resolve the conflict. In 1894, when Dillon veered toward confrontation with Healy, he was held back by O'Brien and Davitt. In the following year, however, it was O'Brien who urged a frontal attack on Healy and Dillon who wavered.[34]

The bitter effect of faction on their organizations was privately admitted by Parnellite and anti-Parnellite, alike. Nor could much help be expected from the Liberal party. Incessant demands from the National Liberal Federation for Irish speakers in English constituencies exasperated J. F. X. O'Brien, M.P., head of the Irish National League of Great Britain. Neither did Davitt, who had some influence in the British Labor movement, hold much brief for these Liberal intrusions, astutely perceiving the real object in their request for him to stand for a Liberal seat: "These invitations come from where Labour candidates are spoken of. The object in asking me to stand is to either bluff the Labour men or divide their following. It is not, I assure you, out of an excessive love of Home Rule but as a counter-move to the growing demands for more direct Labour representation."[35] The stature of Parnell as a man and leader is nowhere more evident than in comparison with the abysmal ineffectuality of the elected representatives of Irish Nationalism in those years. Little wonder that O'Brien should conclude in a letter to his wife, "I can easily see my way to being far more useful outside Parliament . . . Davitt is a hundred times a more powerful man outside the House than he could ever be within."[36] For-

[33]H. Ausubel, *In Hard Times* (New York, 1960), 310–311; F. S. L. Lyons, "The Machinery of the Irish Parliamentary Party in the General Election of 1895," *Irish Historical Studies*, 8 (September, 1952): 115–139.

[34]Davitt to O'Brien, September 21, 1894, Davitt Letters, NLI MS. 913; Dillon to O'Brien, September 28, 1895, NLI William O'Brien Papers, NLI MS. 8555/5; Dillon to O'Brien, no date (probably October 1895), *ibid.* (folder 8).

[35]See the envelope of letters from F. Schnadhorst to J. F. X. O'Brien during years 1892–1895 in J. F. X. O'Brien Papers, NLI MSS. 13418–477. Also, J. F. X. O'Brien to Herbert Gladstone, July 17, 1893, Viscount Gladstone Papers, BM Add. MS. 46054, Vol. LXX. For Davitt's complaints against the Liberals, see Davitt to W. O'Brien, February 28, 1894, Davitt Letters, NLI MS. 913.

[36]W. O'Brien to Sophie (February? 1893), Sophie O'Brien Papers, NLI MSS. 4213–17.

tunately for O'Brien's future role in Irish politics, he chose the occasion of the 1895 election to desert the sinking ship of the Irish National Federation.

The Kernel of Conciliation

The romance between O'Brien and Sophie Raffalovich, which, as we have seen, developed while William was in Galway jail, had culminated in their marriage in June 1890. That affair was a great Irish event in London, with Archbishop Croke officiating and Dillon as best man, in the presence of Parnell and more than eighty Irish M.P.'s—the last amicable gathering of what was the great Irish Parliamentary party. Sophie came from a Parisian family of Russian Jews who had made their fortune in an Odessa trading concern. Her brother Arthur was for many years a powerful figure in the Tsarist financial world in Paris. The father had opposed the union, especially since the devout O'Brien made Sophie's adoption of the Catholic religion an indispensable condition of their marriage. Strangely enough, however, that religion was no stranger to the Raffalovich family. Sophie's grandfather, aunt, and two cousins on her mother's side had converted to Catholicism, one of the cousins becoming a priest who was eventually elevated to a bishopric in Paris. Sophie's own conversion was followed by that of her favorite brother, André.[37]

Since his marriage, O'Brien's lifestyle had taken a decided turn for the better. The very handsome income his wife obtained from her wealthy parents ensured him a degree of financial independence which his own modest income as journalist and writer would never have afforded him. Without this backing he would not have been able to carry through the projects which gave him a prominent place in the Nationalist movement until the collapse of his influence during World War I.

Soon after the Parnell Split, the O'Briens took up residence in Mayo, the first battleground of the old Land League agitation, and came to learn at first hand about the hard lot of the peasants in the West of Ireland. O'Brien himself soon discovered a role which was much more

---

[37]For brief details of the family history of the Raffalovichs, see Sophie O'Brien Papers, MSS. 4210, 5924; S. O'Brien, *Golden Memories* (Dublin, 1929) 1:68, 175.

congenial to him, at least at this stage of his career, than being a partici-
pant in the endless bickering of party factions. He made the western
peasants the object of his humanitarian concerns and of his undoubted
generosity. There is a certain irony in the fact that at this time the great
benefactor of these same peasants was none other than his recent antagonist Bloody Balfour. For Balfour, in a genuine burst of constructive
Unionism, had created the Congested Districts Board (CDB) in 1891 to
ameliorate the lot of the distressed inhabitants of some of the western
counties. The name "congested" was an example of official
irony—"poor and miserable" would have been less euphemistic and
more correct. There was no denying that a mountain of land agitation
during the past decade had produced a molehill of alleviation for the
half-million persons of the congested districts. As the secretary of the
CDB explained:

In some districts the cash value of the produce of the "farm," together with the
earnings and receipts of the family from every source, did not, in 1891, exceed a
total of £15 p.a. . . . But even in the most prosperous of the congested districts
the standard of living was low, the diet being altogether vegetable . . . The
houses, furniture and bedding were too often unhealthy, mean and comfortless,
and the weekday clothing was frequently ragged and scanty. More than 90 percent of the familes were on the same low level.[38]

It was with this agency of Tory conciliation that O'Brien now chose
to work. One of his first acts on settling down in Mayo was to donate
£500 to the CDB to set up a revolving loan fund for the benefit of the
fishing industry in a depressed coastal village. Another project in which
he played a decisive part was the purchase of Clare Island by the board
for resale and distribution among the ninety-five tenants who had been
carrying on a lonely struggle against eviction and rack-renting. He and
Archbishop McEvilly of Tuam were the guarantors for the advances
that were made to the tenants on terms that prefigured the vast land-
purchase scheme of the 1903 act. The alacrity with which O'Brien
became actively involved in measures initiated by the mortal enemy of
the Nationalist movement is a distinguishing mark of his open-minded
approach to Irish legislation. He hailed the board as a boon for the
peasants and a justifiable triumph for Arthur Balfour. Later, in 1895,

---

[38]W. L. Micks, *History of the Congested Districts Board* (Dublin, 1925), 10. These were the
peasants who were forgotten by the Nationalists when the potato crop failure in 1890
produced conditions of semistarvation. Support for the peasants in that winter came from
one most unexpected source: £1,400 being collected by men of the RIC toward relief (Balfour
to Inspector General A. Reed, February 26, 1891, Balfour Papers, BM Add. MS. 49829).

when Balfour's brother Gerald became Irish Chief Secretary, similar progressive measures were welcomed by O'Brien: "Some of us had sufficient faith in the indestructibility of the national sentiment to see in every fresh accession of popular power and prosperity, no matter whence it came, a new argument for completing the fabric of constitutional liberty.[39]

Here lay the kernel of the conciliation policy O'Brien was to advocate in the next decade as the land question receded into the background. It would be wrong to see in this apparent about-face merely one more instance of his erratic behavior. Tacking their sails to the wind of party politics had long been part of the political training of Irish M.P.'s—in Parnell's time they had learned to vilify Gladstone in 1882, vote Tory in 1885, and effect the Union of Hearts with the Liberals in 1887. During the Parnell crisis in 1890 the majority of them had deserted their chief rather than defy Gladstone. Nor was O'Brien at this juncture doing anything substantially different from certain Irish politicians (T. C. Harrington, John Redmond, and his Parnellite followers) who were sitting down with the Grand Master of Belfast Orangemen and with Southern Unionist peers in Horace Plunkett's 1895 Recess Committee to promote legislation which eventuated in the creation of the Department of Agriculture and Technical Instruction, yet another piece of Tory legislation to aid agriculture and distract the Irish farmers from politics. But there is something else to be said for O'Brien, for more than any other follower of the Irish party he put the interests of Ireland's rural poor in the forefront of the national program. With him, measures geared toward immediate social reform and tenant relief would always take precedence over the will-o'-the-wisp of Home Rule. It was this genuine and progressive social outlook which set him apart from the doctrinaire Dillon, who instinctively shrank from the Unionist do-gooders. But the rift inherent in these opposing attitudes was not to occur for almost a decade. Meanwhile, O'Brien's flirting with the Tory policy of "killing Home Rule with kindness" did not bring him into open conflict with the party. Though he had virtually ceased contact with the party after 1895, he had as yet no organization or political following to impose an alternative policy. Moreover, the party was in reality not one body but rather three warring factions of Redmondites, Healyites, and Dillonites (Dillon had assumed the chairmanship of the anti-Parnellite wing in February 1896). And with Gladstone retired

[39]W. O'Brien, *An Olive Branch in Ireland* (London, 1910), 95.

from politics and the Tories still enjoying their long years of resolute government, any threat to Home Rule was hardly increased by the private efforts of O'Brien in the backwoods of County Mayo.

Therefore, the more O'Brien became absorbed with the needs of the western peasants, the less he recognized the existing Irish party as the motive force of the constitutional struggle to improve the lot of the Irish people. Attempts by former colleagues to revive his interest in the affairs of the party were politely rebuffed: "I have undertaken as much as it is possible for me to do without again raising the Dillon and O'Brien cry, and I am determined not to do any more until the people take more effective steps either to support the Party manfully or to kill it."[40] The continuing deterioration in party finances, now almost wholly maintained by the herculean fund-raising efforts in his native Canada of Edward Blake, a former leader of the Liberal party in the Canadian House of Commons and an Irish M.P. since 1892, was clear proof that the country had indeed chosen by default to kill the party. This evidence of public apathy was something that O'Brien, no less than Dillon, would have to conquer if there was to be any hope for the constitutional movement. At least one member of the party felt that that hope was all but lost already:

What is going on is *talk* about the past, and inactivity regarding the present. We went to war for Home Rule and should continue that war each in our own way as best we may . . . we have the evicted with us and we are letting them starve . . . in fact Horse Racing, cycling and other amusements is what the country is most eager about at present.[41]

---

[40]W. O'Brien to J. F. X. O'Brien, May 17, 1896, J. F. X. O'Brien Papers, NLI MSS. 13418–477/folder 3.
[41]A. Webb to J. F. X. O'Brien, no date (1897), *ibid.* (folder 13).

FIVE

The Return to Politics

O'BRIEN operated only on the periphery of politics between 1893 and 1898. He maintained his contacts with Dillon and other close friends in the party, but his interest in party affairs declined when he found himself helpless to resolve the unending quarrels between Healyites and Dillonites. Besides, he had become disillusioned with the party membership for its obvious failure to rouse the people to a new sense of involvement with national goals. While the American-sponsored Irish Race Convention of 1896, in which O'Brien shared, produced no end of dithyrambs for dead heroes, it did nothing to stir the country to meaningful social or political activity.

By 1897, however, O'Brien was astute enough to perceive that the opportunity had arrived for a new start in Nationalist agitation. Indeed, it occurred to too few at this time of mounting economic distress in certain parts of Ireland that what the country needed was not more of the endless politics but a rethinking of social and economic needs. One such individual was the Anglo-Irish reformer and apostle of cooperative schemes Sir Horace Plunkett. However, Plunkett retained too high a regard for the capacity of local effort and self-help to handle distress of crisis proportions in the congested districts of the West. O'Brien was also prepared to employ self-help, but it was to be the self-help of an aroused peasantry combining against callous landlords and legislators.

Though O'Brien had to start from scratch, he possessed one vital asset that was sorely wanting in the leadership of any of the Parliamentary factions—the willingness to throw himself heart and soul into agrarian agitation. Moreover, the cause was right at hand in Mayo, itself: the existence of vast grasslands side by side with the scattered plots of poor land or reclaimed bog on which the mass of agricultural tenants eked out a bare existence. The grasslands, let to private individuals (graziers) by the landlord owners, were a relic of the system of consolidation adopted during the Famine clearances. These were the grazing ranches in the rich plains and pastures of Mayo, Roscommon, and Galway. The graziers themselves appear to have been local town shopkeepers, retired policemen, and other middle-class Irish elements. At least it was these who figured most prominently in the agrarian litany of "infernal evils" in the next few years. Small farmers were obliged to rent grazing space for their cattle from these so-called grass-grabbers. What O'Brien wanted was a redistribution of the grasslands and their conversion to tillage farming for the benefit of the poverty-stricken, land-starved inhabitants. In 1898 economic conditions were so bad that tens of thousands of persons in Mayo and Galway were saved from starvation only by charitable relief, while thousands more survived only by emigrating to England and Scotland for seasonal work.

The old cry of "land-grabber" was now supplemented by "grass-grabber" as O'Brien took the first small steps in his campaign to establish peasant proprietary in Ireland. In fact, the evils of land-grabbing were brought to O'Brien's notice in two separate incidents early in 1897. In one case, a local Mayo priest invited O'Brien and Davitt to address a meeting denouncing certain glaring cases of land-grabbing. In another, the formidable Widow Sammon, who had been evicted for nonpayment of rent along with her eight children, turned to O'Brien for help when her tract of mountain land in Mayo was "grabbed" by a former evicted tenant. The widow's case, more than any other, provided the impetus for O'Brien's new involvement with agrarian agitation.[1]

The idea of tackling the owners of grazing ranches was not new. As early as 1895 some Federation branches in the West of Ireland had called attention to the taking of grass farms by local worthies. In the following year the introduction of the Land Bill prompted O'Brien to call publicly for the insertion in the bill of a provision giving the Congested Districts Board power to purchase compulsorily some grazing ranches for distribution among the tenants. Of course, anything in the nature of compulsory purchase was anathema to good Conservatives. Their solution for the relief of distress in Ireland generally envisaged another Seed Supply Act or a niggardly extension of the puny

---

[1] The case of the Widow Sammon was a minor saga of the struggle in the West of Ireland. Between February and July 1897 she was arrested and imprisoned on five different occasions for her spirited defense of her property. The family was maintained by a fund started by O'Brien (*Freeman's Journal*, September 8, 1897). As late as 1911 (four years after passage of the Evicted Tenants Act), the tenant was still neither reinstated in her holding nor provided with alternative property.

funds available for public works projects.[2] The failure to extend compulsory powers to the CDB finally convinced O'Brien that something more than Parliamentary oratory was necessary to encourage official attention to the needs of the people.

O'Brien relied on the support of Davitt and T. C. Harrington, the active cooperation of local Nationalists, and the newspaper reports of imminent famine in the congested districts to prepare the ground for the project germinating in his fertile mind. On January 23, 1898, all the planning culminated in the establishment of the United Irish League, with its motto "The Land for the People," at a meeting in Westport, the very spot where Parnell had given his blessing to the infant Land League in June 1879. The new League did not pass unnoticed by the guardians of law and order because of the growing unrest that both the League and the celebrations of the centenary of the 1798 Rebellion were creating "amongst those who have a stake in the country." Officials lost no time in notifying the special branch officers of the RIC to keep a watch on the new agrarian agitation, especially the attitude of the clergy.[3] Thus began the campaign which Healy tartly described as "the efforts of a single individual to rescue himself from oblivion."

The United Irish League

The League had as its declared object breaking up the large grass farms by compelling the graziers to surrender their lands to the Congested Districts Board for redistribution among the tenants of small agricultural holdings. The tactic of setting the have-nots against the haves naturally appealed to the self-interest of the poorer peasants and was the main reason for the rapid spread of the movement in Mayo, where the first branch was organized February 6, 1898. Since the cry against graziers applied only in districts having large grass areas, the agitation was rendered universal by going against that archtraitor the land-grabber in other counties. The League received a welcome initial boost from the Archbishop of Tuam, O'Brien's ally in the Clare Island purchase scheme of a few years earlier. There was some opposition from Healyite priests as well as from those who feared that the revived

---

[2]The Conservative approach in this matter is starkly outlined in Chief Secretary Gerald Balfour's memorandum of November 2, 1897, in PRO Cabinet Minutes, CAB(1889) 37/45 no. 41.

[3]For the police reports on the founding of the League, see SPO Divisional Commissioner (Precis) Reports, "State of the Country Report" for January 1898; Also CBS Files 1898/15311/S.

agitation would alienate the CDB from entering into purchase transactions. This opposition was gradually overcome by the effective work of a score of local organizers, several of whom were to enter Parliament in 1900 as "O'Brien's young men."

Despite the apprehensions of the local police, there was no increase in agrarian outrage with the advent of the League. Some boycotting did occur, but this was negligible compared to the intimidation of the early days of the Plan of Campaign. Besides, the immediate draft of extra police to Mayo kept a tight rein on potential disturbances, while their instructions to sit tight and act against deeds instead of words dampened the hopes of O'Brien and his organizers for mass arrests. Indeed, O'Brien himself was under surveillance at this time by none other than Major Nicholas Gosselin, RM, Dublin Castle's expert on secret societies. Gosselin saw fit to report to the Inspector General of the RIC the Mayo county inspector's news that O'Brien had ordered 1798 pikes (for the centenary celebrations) from a London manufacturer "but whether for decorative purposes or not he is unable to say, and requests inquiry in London"![4] However, by October 1898 the League could boast a total of 53 branches, most of them in Mayo, and footholds in six other counties. This was quite remarkable, considering the moribund condition of the National Federation and the National League, with their 221 and 6 mostly dormant branches, respectively.[5]

Though O'Brien claimed that his organization had no political objective, it is a fact that he looked to the possibility of the League's uniting the Nationalist movement, still hopelessly divided into Redmondite, Healyite, and Dillonite factions. He was, of course, as anxious as Dillon to preserve the constitutional movement and a voice at Westminster. He was not prepared to use the League, however, to bring strength to his friend Dillon and thereby perpetuate animosities. The inability or unwillingness of the three factions to unite made it vital that reunion, if it came, be forced on them by the people. This was why O'Brien made it a central point in his program for individual League branches to be self-

[4]Gosselin to Inspector General, March 7, 1898 in SPO, CBS Home Office/carton no. 2. The County Inspector's fears, though unnecessary in O'Brien's case, do not seem so childish in retrospect, however. Robert Brennan relates that when his Republican group began to prepare for the 1916 Rising in Wexford, some of the items in their armory were pikes! R. Brennan, *Allegiance* (Dublin, 1950), 36.

[5]SPO Intelligence Notes 1895–1900, B series XXXVII. For details of the growth of the League in the first nine months of its existence, see SPO, CBS Files 1898/17425a/S (A. Cameron to Inspector General, October 10, 1898); CBS, I. G. Reports 1898–99 (Reports for February to October 1898).

governing within each constituency and open to anti-Parnellites and Parnellites alike. The wisdom of this novel tactic would be realized when the time to nominate candidates for Parliament arrived. Meanwhile, however, the party had its uses, and O'Brien endeavored to wean Dillon from his obsession with party maneuverings and threats to his leadership, to active involvement in the work of the League. The endorsement of Dillon, coupled with the visible support of Irish M.P.'s would at least lend an aura of dignity to O'Brien's rustic following, some of whom were not noted for sobriety.

Dillon had, in fact, attended the very first League meeting with Harrington, who for some time had been waging a one-man campaign to reunite the party. Apparently the experience did not imbue Dillon with any enthusiasm for entrusting the fortunes of the constitutional movement to the United Irish League. Further requests from O'Brien to appear with him at meetings were met by frank avowal by Dillon of his intention to avoid giving the Administration the chance of resurrecting the Thirty-fourth of Edward III—that old instrument of coercion which had dogged their steps during the years of the Plan.[6] To Dillon, still, the party was everything, despite the embarrassing evidence that it was rapidly grinding to a halt. However, in view of O'Brien's utter refusal to help the party, it could only be a matter of time before events would make Dillon's own calculations for survival as party leader irrelevant. Besides, he was under constant pressure from Blake to resign from that untenable, divisive position.

O'Brien was receiving considerable encouragement from eminent party figures not to endorse any of the existing party leaders. Edward Blake's disillusion at the state of party affairs is vividly conveyed in a letter to O'Brien at a time when Blake was actually contemplating withdrawal from the movement: "I own to you I see but little prospect of Irish Nationalism being effectively exhibited at Westminster . . . For my part, I would willingly and loyally serve under anyone—however personally distasteful—who could hold together even our own body." Of greater weight were the characteristically incisive observations of Michael Davitt, eager again to take up the cudgels on behalf of the

---

[6]Dillon to O'Brien, March 7, 1898, NLI William O'Brien Papers, NLI MS. 8555/15. The English act of 1361 establishing justices of the peace was constantly applied in Ireland. It empowered the magistrates "to take and arrest all those that they may by indictment, or by suspicion, and to put them in prison; and to take of all them that be not of good fame where they shall be found sufficient surety . . . of their good behaviour towards the king and his people." No right of appeal existed under this act.

tenants: "I have no hope of any kind for the Party so long as it is at the mercy of a gang of worthless creatures who would openly go over to Healy tomorrow if he would promise them secure seats and monthly allowances."[7]

For Dillon the writing was on the wall. Within weeks he was forced to confess to O'Brien that he was but the "nominal leader of a demoralised and discontented Party without funds," and he also conveyed his intention to resign after the end of that session of Parliament, leaving the question of reunion to a convention to be called by a nonpartisan body.[8] There was no doubt in O'Brien's mind what body that should be. But the struggle to break down Dillon's resistance was an arduous task, lasting the entire year and in the end not entirely successful. Dillon, of course, might be forgiven for resisting O'Brien's obvious intention to consign the party, as he knew it, to the scrapheap. His condescending acknowledgment of O'Brien's efforts to bestir the tenants once more indicated not only Dillon's own helplessness but also how far he had strayed along the path from agitator to parliamentarian:

He [O'Brien] has certainly worked almost a miracle in the districts to which his League has spread, and is unquestionably the one man in Ireland who has at the same time sufficient hold on the people and money to work up a National organisation—and if he could have taken a national view of the necessities of the Parliamentary situation and given a fair amount of help in keeping the Federation alive . . . his United Irish League would undoubtedly have been an exceedingly useful movement.[9]

While O'Brien certainly displayed arrogance in his brusque dismissal of Dillon's appeals for support during 1897 and 1898, it is difficult not to conclude that his stand was more justifiable than the inordinate claims Dillon was making for a party which seemed to be actually doing what he most wanted to avoid—bringing the constitutional movement into contempt in the eyes of the public. Actually, O'Brien had put more life in the country in six months than the Nationalist party had been able to arouse in years. Dillon could not even plead the attractions of the Liberal alliance as an excuse for exalting the merits of Parliamentary activity, for not only were the Conservatives in power,

[7]Blake to O'Brien, December 20, 1897, UCC William O'Brien Papers, Box AH; Davitt to O'Brien, December 9, 1897, Davitt Letters, NLI MS. 913.

[8]Dillon to O'Brien, April 4, 1898, NLI William O'Brien Papers, NLI MS. 8555/15. Even in the depth of despair Dillon could not resist the temptation to keep his irons in the fire: "I find on reading over my letter that I omitted to say that I would be prepared to resume and retain the leadership if the country unmistakably requested me to do so."

[9]Dillon to Blake, August 29, 1898, Blake Papers, NLI microfilm p. 4682.

but, as he had confessed to O'Brien a year before, "the Radicals are not in *strict* alliance with us at present."[10]

Davitt, by contrast, was of great help in the crucial first year of the League's existence. He, like Dillon, was a member for a Mayo constituency, but this does not account for his involvement, as Davitt, in this case like O'Brien, needed no excuse to fight the tenants' battle. Davitt, however, may not have been pleased by the sobriquet of Captain Moonlight, which the English Catholic newspaper the *Tablet* had conferred on him. It was through Davitt that Patrick Ford, attracted by the League slogan "Land for the People," reentered the list of subscribers to the old cause. By October 1898 the sum of £600 was received from him, but money from Ford never came on easy terms, and both Davitt and O'Brien had to fight hard for every penny. "Evidently, what we are expected to do," Davitt ribbed O'Brien, "is to invite the Constabulary to shoot the people down in an eviction campaign which we are to inaugurate for that purpose."[11]

The immediate task, however, was to expand the League, and this burden continued to be O'Briens's—organizing branches, answering thirty or so letters a day, collecting funds, arranging meetings, and supplying the oratory. By the end of the year Sligo and Galway were added to Mayo as League strongholds, which enabled the formal establishment of a provincial governing body (Directory) for Connaught in the early part of 1899 with Davitt as president and J. J. O'Kelly, the old Fenian and Parnellite M.P., as vice-president. Though these developments were largely ignored by the Nationalists, Irish Unionists were apprehensive about the League's success, and with good reason. Horace Plunkett, whose own cooperative movement might well be threatened by the League, was apprised of these fears: "This new League . . . is taking too much hold in the West of Ireland . . . This arch-schemer William O'Brien is starting it for his own purposes and to try to get power under the new Local Government Bill."[12]

For this reason alone, the founding of O'Brien's League was quite fortuitous. Without the organization he afforded the tenant farmers and laborers, Unionist landlords might well have consolidated their political

[10]Dillon to O'Brien, March 4, 1897, NLI William O'Brien Papers, NLI MS. 8555/8.

[11]Davitt to O'Brien, May 27, 1899, Davitt Letters, NLI MS. 913.

[12]See Gill Papers, NLI MSS. 13478–526/folder 11, for copy of a letter (D. J. Kiernan to J. H. Kemmis, September 30, 1898) sent to Plunkett for perusal. The Unionists, however, had more to fear than O'Brien. In Cork, where the League had no influence, Nationalists were returned for all 102 seats on the District Council, whereas the late Board of Guardians had included 48 Unionists.

hold in Connaught when the first local government elections following the Local Government Act of 1898 were held in the spring of 1899. Instead, the League candidates swept the field, and Nationalist county and district councillors began to conduct the local administrative functions hitherto performed by landlord-dominated grand juries. This success promised good results in the forthcoming general election also, for the League was expanding, though slowly, into all four provinces. In a speech at Claremorris on January 30, 1899, O'Brien claimed over 180 branches of the League in Connaught with over 35,000 members. The number of branches recorded by the constabulary increased from 175 in February to 279 in August 1899. Over 46,000 persons were presumed to be active members by the end of that year. By January 1900 the League's own listing showed 393 branches, and three months later this number had jumped to 462, representing perhaps between 60,000 and 80,000 members.[13] The organization was now represented in twenty-five counties, though in some (Dublin and the Protestant northern counties, for example) its existence was only nominal. Mayo, Galway, Roscommon, Westmeath, and Clare—the grasslands—were well represented, as were six or seven other counties. However, when one looks at the results, the League's appeal to combat appears to have had little actual force. A total of eight persons suffered boycotting at this stage, and the number of grazing farms unlet in Mayo, Roscommon, and Galway as a result of League activity amounted to only twenty-one, accounting for a bare 2 percent of the available grazing acreage! That an organization which showed such meager results from agitation should excite the minds of police officials is not remarkable in Ireland: the burning of a hayrick was apt to be interpreted by RIC inspectors as the first act in all-out agrarian war. Such close attention serves to remind us that Ireland was perhaps the most effectively policed country in Europe in the nineteenth century.

Obviously, therefore, the League even at this early stage was beginning to drift into that timid, constitutional mold of Parnell's National League—yet another electioneering agency to sustain a brand of politics that seemed fair to etherealize the national sentiment for Home

[13]*Connaught Telegraph*, February 4, 1899; SPO, CBS Files: 1899/19237a/S; 1902/26268/S. The growth of the United Irish League was considerably slower than that of the earlier National League, which boasted 371 branches within a year of its establishment (*United Ireland*, March 24, 1883). The National League press, however, generally made extravagant claims as to its strength, at one point claiming 500,000 members in about 1,800 branches (*United Ireland*, October 23, 1886).

Rule into a poetic shadow. The League's real importance lay in the fact that its members represented the active wing of the constitutional movement. The League, of course, was not the only emanation of national resurgence in the late 1890s. The Gaelic League and the GAA, leavened by the active interest of the IRB, were building a cultural nationalism which was to nurture a new generation of separatists. In the slums of Dublin the working class was being given its own historic mission in the Socialist Republican doctrine of James Connolly. Sinn Fein, the policy of national self-reliance initiated by Arthur Griffith, was soon to become the watchword that made the demands of Parliamentarians increasingly irrelevant, and the new Imperialism of the Boer War was to give a fillip to an anti-British propaganda that sought its target in the recruiting tactics of the British army. But these currents were for the moment no threat to the ascendancy of the United Irish League.

The success of the organization, as measured by its electoral victories, brought it respectability. No longer was it "Mr. O'Brien's West Mayo League." In the summer of 1899 offices were set up in Dublin, a National Directory was established, and there was talk of a newspaper. The latter idea had cropped up soon after the League was founded, and an opportunity presented itself in the form of Harrington's *United Ireland* (O'Brien's old paper), which was in financial difficulties. O'Brien, as he told Harrington, would use his wife's money to finance it. Dillon strongly urged him to take over the paper or start a new one, not only to promote unity but to spike the *Freeman's Journal* for its neglect of the party. O'Brien himself could appreciate that point, for he had already written to Brayden, the editor, threatening to start his own paper if the *Freeman* did not "show some courage" in supporting the League.[14]

The project fell through, however, as O'Brien yielded to legal advice not to touch it. The newspaper idea was resurrected by Davitt in March 1899. This time the reason was the "treachery to the National cause" posed by the priests' efforts to have their own nominees returned at the County Council elections. Without a paper to fight both the enemies of the League and the apathy of party members, Davitt said, all prospects of reunion would be destroyed.[15] The pressure was maintained by

[14]Dillon to O'Brien, March 30, 1898, NLI William O'Brien Papers, NLI MS. 8555/15; Dillon to O'Brien, May 15, 1898, *ibid.* (folder 14); O'Brien to Brayden, no date (1898), UCC William O'Brien Papers, Box AIB.

[15]Davitt to O'Brien, March 11, 1899, Davitt Letters, NLI MS. 913. Davitt was the fiercest opponent of the "priest in politics," and his letters to O'Brien abound with references to the clerical "traitors," especially the bishops who sustained Healy but ignored the tenants.

Davitt and other League colleagues until O'Brien finally took the plunge in May. The name chosen for the paper was "United Irishman," but as an unknown journalist, Arthur Griffith, had just begun a venture using that name, the equally evocative old Fenian *Irish People* was selected. The managing editor, T. McCarthy, was lured from the Freeman's Journal Company, and the first issue appeared September 16, 1899. In calling for a remedy for Ireland, O'Brien did not as yet envisage the cooperation of all classes and creeds, for that first issue advocated a public movement "wide enough to give free play to every school of honest Nationalist conviction from the believers in a Gladstonian Parliament to the believers in an Irish Republic." This left precious little inducement to moderate Unionist opinion and no doubt pleased Dillon, who in the following months campaigned strongly on behalf of the League.

Agrarians and Politicians

Despite O'Brien's success in reconstructing the semblance of a national organization, the initiative for reuniting the Irish party did not lie with him. Of course, there was always the indirect pressure of his influence as the leader of the only active, broad-based political organization of the movement for Home Rule, even though in its early stages the League looked more like a lobby for the congested districts than a lever for the Nationalist sentiment. It was O'Brien's and Davitt's hope that reunion could be forced on the party from outside, by organizing the country and transforming the Irish representation in Parliament through the election of "good men." That was why O'Brien chose to confine his movement at first to the discussion of the congested districts question and the capture of the County Councils by his own men. He was resolved to have nothing to do with the Parliamentary wing of the Nationalist movement. "All I do feel and know," he wrote Davitt, "is that any attempt at this stage to identify the League with our section in Parliament would mean the collapse of the movement." As far as O'Brien was concerned, "the one service the Party could do was by never meeting again."[16] Both O'Brien and Davitt, therefore, were inclined to view with alarm any maneuverings of the leaders of the three factions to foist a patched-up political watchdog on the League. No one could have spoken more violently against the party than Davitt in a

[16]O'Brien to Davitt, January 2, 1899, UCC William O'Brien Papers, Box AJA; Dillon to Blake, October 2, 1899, Blake Papers, NLI microfilm p. 4682.

speech to his South Mayo constituents on November 5, just after he had resigned his seat in protest against the war on the Boers. He bluntly accused the Irish members of failing the Nationalist cause by their pathetic attendance record in the 1899 session of Parliament, branded some of them as "moderate West Britons," and warned that their reelection would only return to Westminster "a party of weakness and incompetence." It was Dillon who had made the first public effort to promote unity within the party by offering a conference with the Parnellites in his Glasgow speech of October 1898.[17] This had sparked a series of events which culminated in the abortive unity conference of April 1899. Redmond next took a hand, but Dillon's refusal of his request for a conference showed that the latter had finally been brought around to O'Brien's views: "It . . . appears to me that at the period at which we have now arrived we can best promote the reconstruction of a United Irish Party in the House of Commons by cooperating individually with the people in the task which they are now taking upon themselves."[18] Two days later, Blake wrote to O'Brien in fulsome terms justifying everything O'Brien had been repeating to Dillon for almost two years:

. . . I have ceased to hope for reunion through the exertions of Parliamentary leaders. The long-continued efforts from within have failed beyond remedy and the people must work out their own salvation . . . the United Irish League is founded on a principle so comprehensive and has already done so much by reunion that it seems to me the duty of every lover of the Country to give it a helping hand.[19]

Such support, however, brought no rush of M.P.'s eager to spread the O'Brien message in the constituencies. In fact, the initiative had already passed from Dillon also, and for the next several months he was continually outflanked by the machinations of Healy and Redmond to bring about reunion by the parliamentary route. It was all very well for O'Brien to consider that the maneuverings of the party leaders were irrelevant to the goals he had set for his movement, but he was really ex-

[17]A more secretive approach to the Parnellites had been made in 1894, apparently at Healy's instigation and at a time when Healy's power in the majority faction was considerable. Labouchere, Healy's friend, paid a visit to Redmond in April to find out for "certain parties" whether Redmond would reunite with the majority on condition of his assuming the leadership and having his friends fill half of the Parliamentary committee. Showing more principle than ambition, Redmond recorded that "the whole thing was impossible" (Redmond Papers, MS. 15201/3, Notes of Interview, April 9, 1894).

[18]Dillon to Redmond, July 26, 1899, Redmond Papers, NLI MS. 15182/2.

[19]Blake to O'Brien, July 28, 1899, Blake Papers, NLI microfilm p. 4683.

pecting too much if he thought that the mere adoption of League membership would bring a new generation of pure-souled patriots to Irish politics. His agrarian message (Arthur Griffith dubbed it "a squalid class movement") was directed at those who in the past had shown little capacity for either politics or patriotism. Besides, for a movement that looked entirely to Parliamentary activity for the redress of grievances, it was somewhat chimerical to expect that men who had accepted years of hardship in what they considered the best interests of their country would be ejected from Parliament *en bloc* by the complaisant electorate which had put them there.

By November, Davitt and O'Brien began to view with alarm the apparent success with which Redmond and Healy were negotiating reunion. The strain was beginning to tell on O'Brien, who Dillon observed was "looking very ill and broken." Relations between O'Brien and Dillon had again become strained, O'Brien criticizing him for his constant attendance in Parliament and his prominent part in debates, making it seem as if Dillon was still angling for the party chairmanship, a course certain to perpetuate the eternal wrangling with Healy.[20] In December, O'Brien sent for publication in the *Irish People* a stinging criticism of Dillon couched in such offensive terms that it evoked from Davitt, who modified the paragraph, an equally stinging retort:

We must surely be prepared to pass over small mistakes made by friends and honest Nationalists in face of a growing combination of rogues and humbugs against us, or where is this thing going to end?

For my part a quarrel or the semblance of a quarrel between yourself and Dillon would compel me not alone to leave the movement but to leave Ireland. To continue on forever with no prospect but endless wranglings would be an act of insanity which I am resolved not to commit.[21]

O'Brien's outburst was probably the result of nervous exhaustion caused by overwork, which forced him to leave for the south of France to recuperate at the end of November. The police were pleased to note a "distinct lull" in League activity during his brief absence.[22] The strain was also evident on Davitt, who was driving himself relentlessly to expand the League against fierce clerical opposition. He gave the discouraging news to O'Brien in the unmistakable Davitt style:

I am suffering under a bad attack of the political blues. The country is either in a mood of craven political cowardice or in a state of political imbecility.

[20]Dillon to Blake, November 16, 1899, *ibid.*, p. 4682.
[21]Davitt to O'Brien, December 14, 1899, Davitt Letters, NLI MS. 914.
[22]SPO Inspector General Reports 1899–1902 (Report for December 1899).

Nothing will be done anywhere after 20 years of education and agitation unless a big meeting is held and some of the sick men will go and pull the people by the hair of the head to a sense of their duty. As to organisers, this is a real work that is wanted for the movement. We cannot find two in the whole country! In face of this condition of things you and O'Kelly and myself will be in Glasnevin [cemetery] by the time this wretched country will have made up its mind to help itself.[23]

The events of the next few weeks were not calculated to dispel Davitt's blues or aid O'Brien's recovery. Ignoring Dillon, Redmond and Healy had set the day of reckoning, asking all members to meet in London on January 30, 1900, to elect a new leader. O'Brien, not being a member of Parliament, would be absent, as he hoped Dillon and his friends would also. Dillon knew perfectly well, however, that to stick with O'Brien would be to court political suicide, for he probably guessed that his followers, whom he had earlier described as demoralised and discontented, would rally to the meeting. With a general election only months away, events were imposing their own logic on the situation. Blake was the first to crack, publicly announcing his decision to be present on January 30. Dillon, thankful for the stimulus of his friend's submission, also bowed to the inevitable.[24]

O'Brien could not ignore events which, whether he liked it or not, would have immediate repercussions in the League. In a letter to J. F. X. O'Brien he condemned the meeting which at last was to bring about the reunion from within, which he and Davitt had feared:

I am astonished to hear that some of our friends are thinking of giving some importance to Tuesday's meeting by attending it . . . after the filthy and diabolical attacks on poor Blake and Healy's accusations day after day against Davitt and Dillon of embezzlement and swindling . . . does not every man in the Party know in his heart that this is a thoroughly dishonest attempt, under terror of the popular movement, to tide over the General Elections, and befool the country with an utterly unreal mockery of Unity?[25]

Unable to control the direction of events, O'Brien nevertheless resolved to gain what advantage he could from his influence. He still had enough prestige and friends within the party to offer advice on the choice between the acceptable candidates, Harrington and Redmond.

[23]Davitt to O'Brien, January 18, 1900, Davitt Letters, NLI MS. 914.
[24]F. S. L. Lyons, *John Dillon* (London, 1968), 205.
[25]W. O'Brien to J. F.X. O'Brien, January 28, 1900, J. F. X. O'Brien Papers, NLI MSS. 13418–477/folder 3.

Harrington, who had long since tired of the League, was stressing the primacy of the party, a tactic not calculated to endear him to O'Brien. Haviland-Burke, one of O'Brien's chief organizers and soon to be a member of Parliament, wrote to his employer as the meeting opened, "Strictly between ourselves, T. H[arrington] has been openly blurting out all over the place, up here in Dublin, that 'The Party' is to arrange and decide everything, especially candidature questions, *in absolute independence of the United Irish League.*"[26] With Davitt pressing Dillon to vote against Harrington, O'Brien wired his other friends to plump for Redmond in the crucial vote. No one was more surprised than Redmond himself. "My unanimous election," he wrote to Gill, "astonished me and especially when I heard William O'Brien had wired strongly to all his henchmen to support me!"[27] It was a suitably squalid ending to a depressing ten-year segment of Irish history.

The League and the Party

The settlement of the party question now focused the political spotlight on the two most important men in Irish politics—O'Brien and Redmond. The initiative seemed to lie with O'Brien. Redmond needed O'Brien's organization as a backing for effective work at Westminster and for the funds it could bring to a starved party exchequer. His task, however, was to secure the League on terms which would ensure domination for the party. While O'Brien was prepared to welcome formal recognition from the party, he was not prepared to accept it on conditions which would make his movement a tool of the party, as the National League had been in Parnell's time. Yet Redmond had several points in his favor. He had the prestige of being party leader, acknowledged as such even by his former enemies. Besides, the leader's right to control and direct Nationalist opinion was implicitly accepted by that section of the population, still the overwhelming majority, which continued to be dazzled by the alleged panacea of Home Rule. And, above all, Redmond was what O'Brien was not—a politician. O'Brien indeed had great popular gifts, but he lacked that will to power which is the hallmark of the politician.

The first blast against the party came from O'Brien and Davitt at a meeting at Mallow on February 4. They claimed that the United Irish League had frightened the factions into coming together and that re-

[26]Haviland-Burke to O'Brien, January 31, 1900, UCC William O'Brien Papers, Box AKA.
[27]Redmond to T. P. Gill, February 6, 1900, Gill Papers (Letters 1900–05/folder 5).

union should not be blessed until the party showed the people what it was capable of and willing to do in Westminster.[28] This veiled hostility was hardly allayed by Redmond's public announcement a week later that reunion had been brought about "by the wise and patriotic action of the Irish [Parliamentary] representation," without a mention of the League. He coupled this with a call for subscriptions to the Parliamentary Fund. To O'Brien this seemed like an attempt to supersede, or at best ignore, his movement, and he warned Redmond that any attempt to discourage the spread of the League would lose Redmond the support of himself and his friends.[29] Nevertheless, O'Brien's letter was conciliatory in tone and left open the question of modifying the League's constitution to accommodate the new political circumstances. But, of course, there would have to be some concrete acknowledgment of O'Brien's organization and that would best come by the cooperation of individual M.P.'s in promoting the organization.

So far the League could only boast the accession of three M.P.'s, J. J. O'Kelly, David Sheehy, and P. A. McHugh, to its ranks. Harrington, in interpreting the constitution and rules of the League for Redmond, noted their elasticity and made the ominous suggestion that they could be worked to "prevent us from antagonizing any section of feeling from us in Meath, Dublin and Kildare where they look with suspicion upon the grazing agitation conducted by the League."[30] A letter Redmond sent to Harrington around this time shows that there would be no provoking of O'Brien. It would be far easier to outsmart him:

I . . . am of opinion that our best course is to do everything in our power to prevent any break before the Convention and I am in hopes we may succeed in this. As for the League we can make it *our* organisation and I certainly would be glad to see Dublin organised before the Convention. You don't imagine that if we had branches of the League in the wards of the City that they would be the creatures of anyone.[31]

Such dealings boded ill not only for O'Brien but also for the vigorous prosecution of a forward agrarian movement.

O'Brien now lost the services of Davitt, who left for South Africa at the end of February, worn out and ill. Since J. J. O'Kelly's ailing health limited his usefulness, O'Brien was left once more to bear the burden of the maneuverings and negotiations. The strain on his mind and body at this time was as great as any he had had to endure in the days of the

[28]*Irish People*, February 10, 1900.
[29]O'Brien to Redmond, February 15, 1900, Redmond Papers, NLI MS. 15212/5.
[30]Harrington to Redmond, March 3, 1900, *ibid.*, MS. 15194.
[31]Redmond to Harrington, no date (probably March/April 1900), Harrington Papers, NLI MS. 8576/45.

Plan of Campaign. Not only did he have the worry of avoiding tactical errors in bringing along his fledgling organization, but he also had to cater to the strategic needs of his policy vis-à-vis the ostensibly powerful Parliamentary forces outside it. One example of the pitfalls he faced was the South Mayo by-election in February 1900 for the seat Davitt had vacated. The contest pitted pro-Boer sentiment against the exigencies of party politics. O'Brien's candidate was his protégé John O'Donnell; the opponent was the separatist Major John McBride of the pro-Boer Irish Brigade. O'Brien regarded the candidacy of McBride as a Healyite trick (these were apparently endless). O'Donnell, who had been with the United Irish League from the beginning, suffered some abuse from opponents for his earlier youthful application to join the RIC. However, out of 7,000 electors only 2,828 voted, 427 of them for McBride, hardly a strident endorsement of either Republican or Boer sentiment. Curiously enough, Davitt, a staunch pro-Boer, had also worked for O'Donnell's candidacy, but a committed constitutionalist like Davitt certainly would have regarded McBride more as a threat to the National movement than as a supporter of the Boer cause.

Two events now occurred in rapid succession which threatened to destroy any chance of détente. The first was an instance of that West Briton mentality that would have been better hidden in the leader of what purported to be *the* Nationalist movement for attaining self-government. This was Redmond's announcement in the Commons on March 8 welcoming the proposed visit to Ireland of the Queen and adding that the "Irish people will receive with gratification the announcement that her Majesty has directed that for the future the shamrock shall be worn by Irish regiments on March 17 to commemorate the gallantry of Irish soldiers in South Africa."[32] That an Irish Nationalist leader could survive such dutiful expression of loyalty to the Queen, with its implied insult to that other struggling nationality, the Boers, perhaps explains as well as anything else why later separatists like Pearse, Connolly, and McDonagh had to pass through abuse and ridicule to martyrdom before the Irish people were to be infused with a cleansed national spirit. O'Brien, in the tone of his old *United Ireland* tirades, exploded in a letter to Jerry McVeagh, M.P., the Ulster Nationalist:

Redmond's statement in the House of Commons last night revolutionises the whole situation. Unless we are to throw up the national cause altogether it is

[32] *Parliamentary Debates* 80 (8 March 1900): 402.

impossible for any nationalist to cooperate any longer with a gentleman who uses his situation as a leader to express his gratitude for the Shamrock . . . and puts in for a slavish reception for a lady who comes to typify all that is most hateful in English rule.

Unless we are to abandon any pretence of nationality for this generation, no good Irishman ought to be a party to the glorification of a man who has used his position in such a manner . . . [33]

This verbal attack and those of other party figures like Dillon were all made in private, a curious way to instruct the people in Irish Nationalism. Perhaps the wonder of it all is that Davitt came back to Ireland after his recovery.

The second threat to party unity was more immediate and involved the calling of a national convention of the party, a traditional device for rallying the Nationalist movement. Again the announcement was made in a manner that rankled O'Brien. Redmond, in declining a request to appear on a local Tipperary League platform, acknowledged the League as the strong organization the party needed. But, he said, "a National organisation requires a National authority," and this he claimed the United Irish League (UIL) did not have. Only a convention "composed of the elements that have hitherto customarily made up our great National gatherings" would give this authority to the national movement.[34] This and the Whitsuntide (June) date set for the convention were an obvious ploy to provide room for Healyite elements at the convention, as well as to deny O'Brien the time he needed to make the League as strong elsewhere as it was in Connaught.

Redmond and O'Brien had already agreed that no convention date be set until after the Provincial Conference of the Munster UIL at the end of April (O'Brien would have preferred no convention before the general election was held in September). Now, insult had been added to injury by a date's being fixed without consulting O'Brien. Furthermore, Redmond had still not arranged the direct personal help of the M.P.'s which O'Brien had requested in order to fully organize the country in time for the election—or, as it now turned out, the convention. Little wonder, then, that he should be suspicious of Redmond. His letter to Redmond attempted to counter this turn of events by insisting that he

[33]W. O'Brien to J. McVeagh (copy), March 9, 1900; W. O'Brien to J. F. X. O'Brien, March 15, 1900, J. F. X. O'Brien Papers, NLI MSS. 13418-477/folder 21; F. S. L. Lyons, *John Dillon* (London, 1968), 208.
[34]*Irish People*, March 17, 1900.

postpone the convention until Davitt's return from South Africa: "It would be idle to conceal that what has happened since we met has seriously increased my own anxiety as to the attitude of the Party towards the UIL."[35]

His suspicions were shared by Dillon and Devlin, the latter soon to be one of the most indispensable (to the party) of Irish politicians and a staunch follower of Redmond. Dillon's fears of Healy's tricks were even more finely developed than O'Brien's, and Dillon wrote O'Brien that the country could much better face an election with an organization and without a convention than it could after a convention with an organization dominated by a combination of Redmond and Healy. "If the Convention is postponed and either you [O'Brien] or Davitt elected President of the League, I should gladly give the Organisation my warmest support." Devlin, fearing that the convention would be packed by councillors from Dublin and adjoining districts (not UIL territory) as well as by Healyite priests, also urged that either O'Brien or Davitt retain the presidency of the League, so as to keep the control of the organization in Ireland and not in London.[36]

It was obvious to all, however, that Redmond, like Parnell, would choose to control both the party and the organization, and, in truth, none of his opponents could feel very hopeful about denying him that honor. The rift which had opened up with O'Brien was masterfully closed by Redmond's simple explanation, true or not, that the Whitsuntide date given in his letter to the Tipperary UIL had been inserted in the press release by J. J. Clancy, M.P., without his knowledge.[37] O'Brien was promised also that the convention would be summoned and invitations issued by a joint committee of the party and the League and that speakers would be sent over to help his League work.

Considerable pressure not to oppose the convention now began to be exerted on O'Brien by his own friends and sympathizers. Blake, T. P. O'Connor, J. F. X. O'Brien, and O'Kelly, his own League vice-president, all pushed for conciliation.[38] After all, Redmond had conced-

[35]O'Brien to Redmond, March 27, 1900, Redmond Papers, NLI MS. 15212/5.

[36]Dillon to O'Brien, April 5, 1900, NLI William O'Brien Papers, NLI MS. 8555/10; Devlin to O'Brien, March 28, 1900, UCC William O'Brien Papers, Box AKA.

[37]Redmond to O'Brien, March 29, 1900, NLI William O'Brien Papers, NLI MS. 10496/3.

[38]O'Kelly to O'Brien, March 29, 1900, UCC William O'Brien Papers, Box AKA. O'Kelly assured O'Brien that Redmond had told O'Kelly he was wholeheartedly with the political aims of the UIL and that Dillon, Blake, and O'Connor condemned O'Brien's insistence on delaying the convention until Davitt's return. The inclusion of Dillon in this does not square with the letters Dillon was writing to O'Brien at this time.

ed everything except the disavowal of Healy, and, anyway, the recognition of the League as the national organization would weaken Healy's influence beyond repair. O'Brien, therefore, found it impossible to hold back from Redmond's concessions and by early April was pleading with Dillon to give up his aloofness (which was playing into Healy's hands) and his fears of a Redmond dictatorship, confident that the League would be capable of protecting itself from party domination:

With the powers we will now have and the additional powers from friendly members of the Party in the Committee, there is absolutely nothing to fear as to the overwhelming preponderence of the Convention and to shirk the issue would be to confess the country is not with us.

As to the question who shall be Chairman of the League, it seems to me a most horrible mistake to frame men's action on so small an issue. If Redmond behaves really well ... I see no very killing difficulty about his getting the honour, if he cares for it ... I have not myself the smallest notion of accepting the position.[39]

Outmaneuvered, O'Brien bowed to the inevitable and returned the initiative to the man who a few weeks before had disgusted O'Brien and humiliated Dillon by his abasement of Irish nationality before the Queen. O'Brien concluded his agreement with Redmond on April 11 and two weeks later declared at the Munster Conference of the League, presumably with more sense of obligation than conviction, that he was proud to call himself Redmond's follower.[40] Dillon's accustomed suspicions made him hold off from endorsing the convention until June 10, but a few days later he indicated to O'Brien that he was even prepared to second Redmond's nomination to the chair.[41]

As the date of the convention approached, the question of Healy's influence was the only problem remaining to be solved. Redmond had successfully held out against dissociating himself from Healy, who, after all, had been instrumental in outwitting Dillon and engineering the successful reunion conference in January 1900. Redmond had also resisted O'Brien's request to accept an official position on the Munster Directory of the UIL (Redmond sat for a Munster constituency), fearing that this would provoke Healy, who also boasted his own organization.[42] He wrote to O'Brien: "Remember *I* want Healy and his friends

[39]O'Brien to Dillon, April 6, 1900, NLI William O'Brien Papers, MS. 8555/10.
[40]*Irish People*, May 5, 1900; Redmond to J. F. X. O'Brien, April 12, 1900, J. F. X. O'Brien Papers, NLI MSS. 13418–477/folder 2.
[41]*Irish People*, June 16, 1900; Lyons, *John Dillon*, 213.
[42]This was the People's Rights Association, founded by Healy in 1897 to promote the in-

to come to the Convention and I am most anxious therefore to deprive them of any plausible excuse for abstention."[43] It is a tribute to Healy's great talents and a measure of his opponents' weakness that they should have persisted in mortal fear of the leader of what had become virtually a one-man organization. The party committee in charge of issuing invitations to the convention even went so far as to cite Healy's influence in America as a reason for his inclusion (it is a fair guess that if ever Healy went to America after Parnell's death, he would have been wise to travel incognito). All these suggestions brought a violent response and blunt refusal from O'Brien, still convinced that Healy and his "gang" were bent only on crushing both reunion and the movement.[44]

The crucial problem, however, was not being seriously faced. This was the question of who should be president of the League. O'Brien's self-effacement where leadership was concerned was no small impediment to ensuring the primacy of his basic aim, the abolition of landlordism. He had created the UIL primarily to promote land purchase through vigorous agitation. But the last time such a campaign had been waged it had been crippled from the start by Parnell, then the leader of the UIL's predecessor, the Irish National League. The only way such a situation could be avoided for the future was by retaining control of the UIL in the hands of individuals who were, above all else, agrarian agitators. Only three men in Ireland were entitled to assume this role—Davitt, Dillon, and O'Brien. Of the three, O'Brien would obviously have been the best choice. Davitt, though of the first rank, had never been on good terms with the party and would sooner or later have come into conflict with it. As indicated earlier, Davitt had a certain standing in the British labor movement, which had just laid down a political challenge to the English parties in creating the Labour

---

fluence of the constituencies within the party (one of the central planks, also, of the UIL). O'Brien, when estimating the strength of this effete body in 1900, thought there could not be more than twenty branches in all of Ireland. The police were less generous, their records showing 228 *members* in all, 200 of whom were in Belfast alone and who were probably only the members of the local Belfast Catholic Association (SPO, CBS Files, 1902/26268/S).

[43]Redmond to O'Brien, May 23, 1900, NLI William O'Brien Papers, NLI MS. 10496/2.

[44]J. F. X. O'Brien, W. Abraham, and Captain Donelan, to W. O'Brien, May 25, 1900, UCC William O'Brien Papers, Box AKB; W. O'Brien to J. F. X. O'Brien, May 28, 1900, J. F. X. O'Brien Papers, NLI MSS. 13418–477/folder 21. O'Brien was bolstered at this point by a welcome telegram from Patrick Ford in New York: "Stand firm—preserve League's integrity—Ireland's only hope" (telegram dated June 8, 1900, UCC William O'Brien Papers, Box AKC).

Representation Committee. In such circumstances, a man who had earlier refused to become an English Liberal in the cause of Irish Home Rule could hardly accept the senior position in an organization designed to buttress an Irish party whose political preferences were decidedly Liberal. As for Dillon, the more he became a Parliamentarian, the less he became an agrarian. Moreover, he distrusted O'Brien's explicit program of putting the land question before Home Rule and gave reason to expect that his commitment to the tenants would not extend much beyond platform oratory, and doling out the last remaining shillings of the Evicted Tenants Fund. However, none of the three appears to have taken any action to head off Redmond's claim, which was based on the generally accepted cult of the leader—reason enough, perhaps, for their resigning themselves to the inevitable.

O'Brien was determined not even to accept the chairmanship of the convention, a position which certainly would have given him a tactical prominence at the event. He wrote to Dr. Patrick O'Donnell, Bishop of Raphoe, in an effort to get him to induce Archbishop Walsh of Dublin to take the chair. But Walsh had long ago decided to steer clear of dealings with the party. As he once wrote Archbishop Croke, "I never can overlook the action of Dillon and O'Brien in trying to oust Justin McCarthy from the Chairmanship . . . "[45] Redmond himself was obviously in no doubt as to the action he should take. His letter to Harrington quoted above shows he intended to capture O'Brien's organization and subordinate it to party Parliamentary interests. Nor did he hide from O'Brien his desire to take a strong hand: "I think it will be necessary to give some representation to the Parliamentary wing on the provisional and permanent governing body of the League."[46] Only time would tell whether the life O'Brien had given to the Nationalist movement would chart a new path in Irish Nationalism or merely perpetuate a policy which based the Irish demand, as Arthur Griffith feared, "on an admission of the validity of the so-called English conquest."

[45]O'Brien to Dr. O'Donnell (Bishop of Raphoe), May 10 and June 9, 1900, UCC William O'Brien Papers, Box AKB. For Archbishop Walsh's comment, see Walsh to Croke, May 12, 1892, Croke Papers, NLI microfilm p. 6013.
[46]Redmond to O'Brien, May 31, 1900, NLI William O'Brien Papers, NLI MS. 10496/2.

SIX

The Reunited Party

O'BRIEN, for the second time in his career, reached the pinnacle of national popularity when the Nationalist Convention met in Dublin on June 19 and 20, 1900. Thanks to his efforts in the past two years, the national seal of approval was given to the reunion of the party and the mantle of Parnell was handed to Redmond. Besides acknowledging the UIL as the national organization succeeding the Land League and the Irish National League (conveniently ignoring the Federation's long tenure of office), it also promulgated the Constitution and Rules of the UIL as drawn up by O'Brien. The basic demands—self-government, abolition of landlordism by compulsory sale, reinstatement of evicted tenants—had not changed since Parnell's time. There were several new features, however: ending the graziers' monopolies; establishment of a Catholic university (first mooted by Healy's Association); promotion of measures for the housing of the working classes; and last (and probably least), the preservation of the Gaelic language.[1] And as a reminder of O'Brien's personal struggle with Balfour, one other new demand called for the repeal of the Treason Felony Act, which confounded political offenses with ordinary crime. There were also structural changes, which by comparison with the rules of the old League greatly favored the constituencies. Parnell's central executive, which had garnered 75 percent of all branch collections, had dominated the county conventions. The new National Directory, however, only got 25 percent of the funds, the remainder supporting the activities at branch and divisional levels, where greater

---

[1]See pamphlet in UCC William O'Brien Papers, Box AKC, item 36; F. S. L. Lyons, *The Irish Parliamentary Party, 1890–1910* (London, 1951), 219–220. In 1902, in acknowledgment of the growing strength of the labor movement, the constitution was amended to include as one of the objects of both the League and the party, the urging on public bodies to observe the rules as to hours and wages adopted by trade unions and to contract only with employers who did likewise.

autonomy also resided. Although membership of the national organization was to be open to all Irish Nationalists, members could not be
chosen as Parliamentary candidates unless they adhered to the old "sit,
vote, and act" pledge of the Irish party.[2] O'Brien could well feel proud
of his achievement as the reunited party prepared to fight its first election on the program of the United Irish League.

Among the problems facing Redmond in the summer of 1900 were
those of Healy and the party's finances. The latter were, of course, a
perennial problem and would always have to be dealt with on a con-
tingency basis. Healy was a problem mainly because of O'Brien's absolute insistence on expelling him from the party—a demand O'Brien
had made of Dillon in 1895. This time, however, O'Brien made the expulsion a condition of his own membership in the party.[3] Whatever
considerations had acted on Redmond before the October election, they
counted as nothing after the electoral eclipse of the Healyites in which
only Healy, J. L. Carew, and one or two others were returned. O'Brien
had the pleasure of proposing the ejectment of Healy and Carew at the
December convention. The only notable opposition came from
Harrington, who accused O'Brien of once more creating two Irish parties in the House of Commons. This was, of course, overly pessimistic,
as was apparent from Healy's own amusing reflection on his downfall.
When O'Brien declared in the House that the UIL had deposited a
united Irish party there, Healy countered, "As a matter of fact it has
deposited two parties, of which I am one."

O'Brien, returned at the general election for his old Cork City constituency, was once more in the inner circle of party managers. One of
the questions on which he and Redmond were unlikely to agree was
how and by whom the funds of the organization were to be distributed.
As the Parliamentary leader, Redmond wanted a war chest to conduct
the affairs of the party at Westminster and fight elections in Ireland.

[2]The party pledge in its then existing form was first formulated in 1884 and continued
with only minor changes in wording as long as the Irish party survived. It ran: "I . . . pledge
myself that in the event of my election to parliament, I will sit, act, and vote with the Irish
parliamentary party; and if at a meeting of the party, convened upon due notice, specially to
consider the question, it be determined by resolution, supported by a majority of the Irish
party, that I have not fulfilled the above pledges I hereby undertake to resign my seat."
There is an 1891 proof copy of the pledge in J. F. X. O'Brien Papers, NLI MSS.
13418–477/folder 13. A copy for the year 1908 is in Redmond Papers, NLI MS. 15188/2. See
also C. C. O'Brien, *Parnell and His Party, 1880–90* (Oxford, 1957), 143.

[3]O'Brien to Redmond, November 9, 1900, NLI William O'Brien Papers, NLI MS.
10496/12. Redmond was reluctant to the end to desert Healy and was overborne only by
O'Brien's strength at the convention (see Redmond to Blake, November 21, 1900, Blake
Papers, NLI microfilm, p. 4683).

This was the reverse of O'Brien's views, for he still had little regard for the idea of conducting the national struggle in the House of Commons. As long as there was still work to be done at home (and the UIL had a mountain of that to do if its goals were to be attained), the natural arena for Irish politicians was the Irish countryside. The payment of members of Parliament was a particular burden, which would become more pressing as time went on, for the reorganization effected by O'Brien would return the more impecunious, though more "racy-of-the-soil" members. Redmond had to bolster his appeals to O'Brien for an American fund-raising tour by citing the inability of some members even to come to Dublin for meetings "unless their expenses are paid, and we have no Funds available for such a purpose."[4] Little help could, however, be expected from O'Brien, whose own organization had borne most of the election expenses. O'Brien, if anything, wanted to lessen the party's control of funds by attempting to force on Redmond the idea of a direct UIL divisional executive veto on the trustees' allowances to members, in order to keep them in line.[5]

O'Brien had come to regard the united Irish representation as a kind of Irish Parliament which could best serve the interests of the people by absenting itself from Westminster for the session. Though his conception bears a superficial resemblance to the policy of withdrawal and noncooperation later known as Sinn Fein, it was not as unconstitutional as it sounded. O'Brien fully recognized the de facto right of the British Parliament to legislate for Ireland until Home Rule was achieved. What he wanted was the settlement of the land question, which required the cooperation of all Irish M.P.'s in rousing the people to continue the struggle. In addition, a fighting policy would attract funds from America and elsewhere. But Westminster would still have to be relied on for the redress of Irish grievances. Thus, there was only a difference in degree between O'Brien, on the one hand, and Redmond and Dillon on the other. While the former's policy could be described as Parliamentarianism plus action, the latter's was Parliamentarianism plus expenses. Yet, with a Conservative government, half a million un-purchased holdings, and new forces surfacing in Ireland, the difference was vital, and O'Brien was almost driven to despair in his efforts to resolve it. So little did some individuals understand the work O'Brien was trying to do that no less important and respected a member than

[4]Redmond to O'Brien, June 28, 1900, NLI William O'Brien Papers, NLI MS. 10496/2.
[5]Redmond to O'Brien, November 9 and 10, 1900, *ibid.* (folders 12 and 3).

T. Harrington could write to Redmond that he was holding back from supporting the UIL because it weakened Redmond's powers as party chairman, because it was probably an anti-Healy front, and because a large body of Nationalist opinion was against it.[6]

When the Parliamentary session opened in February 1901, O'Brien attended only for the debate on the address. He treated the House to something of his old vitriolic style in denouncing the expected application of renewed coercion against the antigrazing agitation and in warning that such methods would force the Irish members to abandon the field to the secret societies.[7] This was the signal for O'Brien's withdrawal from Parliament and return to Ireland to test the Administration. Unfortunately, he could no longer call on Davitt for help, for the latter was absent in America for most of 1901, having succumbed at last to an intense longing for a complete rest "after the horrible nightmare of the past decade."[8] Worse still, O'Brien himself was ill-equipped for the expected confrontation, being unable to maintain a high pitch of nervous excitement for very long without complete physical collapse. He sought to resign the seat he had won in the recent election but was dissuaded by the knowledge that the vacancy might create an ugly contest in Cork, where he had ousted Healy's brother despite clerical opposition. With O'Brien in declining health and Redmond bent on continuing with Parliamentary matters until the end of the session, the movement had to be carried on in Ireland by the *Irish People* and by the local branches of the League.

The agitation which did occur was hardly such as to send shivers of fear through the corridors of Dublin Castle. Police reports for the first half of 1901 all testify to the peaceful state of the country, with reports of a lack of UIL progress, dormancy of League branches, and decline of their funds.[9] Despite this, however, the Nationalists felt the sting of the old methods in the outlawing of League meetings, the packing of juries, and the heavy hand of the district inspectors of the RIC. Yet, it is difficult to find much more behind the Administration's forceful action against the League than the traditionally extreme sensitivity of the Irish Executive to the tamest signs of popular unrest. The landlords, too, were a factor, of course, as evidenced by the Prime Minister's minute to the King:

[6]Harrington to Redmond, November 30, 1900, Redmond Papers, NLI MS. 15194.
[7]*Parliamentary Debates* 89 (22 February 1901):920.
[8]Davitt to Redmond, January 26, 1901, Redmond Papers, NLI MS. 15179.
[9]SPO, CBS Inspector General Reports, Carton no. 2 (Reports for 1901).

The condition of the West of Ireland, especially the counties of Sligo and Galway, was the subject of some discussion. In some districts the power of the United League [sic] acting by means of boycotting has been organized by Mr. Smith [sic] O'Brien and Mr. McHugh into a formidable tyranny and the landlords are clamouring to have these districts proclaimed, in order that the Crimes Act may be applied.[10]

Part of the reason for the lull in activity was the almost total nervous prostration of O'Brien during most of 1901. Redmond, though he was determined to keep the League at arm's length in order to avoid becoming embroiled in the agrarian agitation against his will, nevertheless appreciated the propaganda effect such activity would have had in American circles. Well might he admit in a letter to the secretary of the newly-founded UIL of America, therefore, that O'Brien's "absence from the House of Commons, serious as it is, is not nearly so serious as his absence from the platforms of the UIL in Ireland."[11] Indeed, that old indicator of unrest, agrarian outrages, had fallen to the level of those quiet days before the Land League. The constabulary's own records showed a mere thirty-five cases of boycotting for 1901. There were no causes célèbres such as had stirred the country in the 1880s, and the Administration, fully cognizant that the so-called agitation was confined to isolated districts, resisted throughout 1901 the clamor of Irish landlords for the proclamation of whole counties.

Controlled Agitation

As soon as the Parliamentary session ended in August 1901, the UIL provisional directory issued a resolution calling for active agitation in Ireland during the recess. A few days later, Redmond, responding to O'Brien's call for a winter program for the people, publicly endorsed the directory's demand, and for the first time in almost four years O'Brien was about to obtain the official assistance of Irish M.P.'s. Needless to say, Redmond's action was not unrelated to the favorable impression Irish agitation would create in America, where a fund-raising campaign was contemplated (it was usual for such a mission to include a "victim of coercion").

O'Brien clarified what he meant by a winter program in a vigorous speech at Bangor Erris on September 15, in which he called for a "great National strike against ranching and grabbing," though one not to be

[10]Salisbury to the King, July 13, 1901, PRO, Cabinet Minutes, CAB(1901) 41/26 no. 17.
[11]Redmond to John O'Callaghan, April 26, 1901, Redmond Papers, NLI MS. 15213/3.

soiled by violence.[12] Most assuredly, he did not mean by this another Plan of Campaign, as subsequent events showed. What he wanted was boycotting and the filling of Irish jails. What he got was the support of barely a score of Irish M.P.'s and the imprisonment of thirteen of them over the next few months. Redmond and Dillon also joined in the up-roar, the former warning that the agitation should be kept "well within the laws both of God and man," and the latter mindful that only lawful and moral means be employed.[13] Their efforts apparently did not please O'Brien, for Dillon had to complain to him of criticism he (Dillon) was being subjected to in the *Irish People*. O'Brien's reply was not apologetic: "I cannot help thinking that, with a little more than the trouble you are taking at present, you could even still do wonders for the settlement of this mighty question in the West, which alone can give the momentum for the settlement of the bigger question." Whether it was the result of his admonition or not, Dillon for the next two months made a series of powerful fighting speeches against the government, against the landlords, and against his *bête noire* Horace Plunkett, whose brainchild, the new Agriculture Department, he considered a deliberate attempt to undermine the Nationalist cause in Ireland.[14]

The agitation O'Brien called for appears to have quickened by December 1901. The Inspector General (RIC) in his "General State of the Country" reports to the undersecretary outlined the "criminal methods" of the UIL in boycotting and in that largely ineffective tactic, intimidation:

Distinct increase . . . of open intimidation by assembled groups at residences of grabbers etc. . . . the real power of the League has been but little affected by [extra police] . . . the League as an intimidatory power is, in my judgment, at the present moment generally stronger than it has ever been.

Whatever it was that so affrighted the guardians of law and order, it certainly seems that Inspector General Chamberlain lacked to an ex-traordinary degree that renowned British capacity for understatement in reporting that in some Irish counties "a state of affairs exists . . .

---

[12] *Irish People*, September 21, 1901.

[13] *Ibid.*, September 28, 1901.

[14] Dillon to O'Brien, October 9, 1901; O'Brien to Dillon, October 10, 1901, NLI William O'Brien Papers, NLI MS. 8555 (folders 9 and 8); *Irish People*, November 16, 1901. The graz-ing problem was, indeed, far from being solved. The first record (May 1902) of grazing acreage unlet because of agrarian agitation showed that only 12,181 acres out of a total graz-ing acreage of upwards of 500,000 acres were affected (SPO Intelligence Notes 1906–1914, Report for 1910/11).

which, I imagine, is unparalleled in any civilized country at the present time."[15]

However, O'Brien had set a trap for himself by counseling that caution be thrown to the winds in the winter of 1901/02. The trouble began on the DeFreyne estate late in 1901, where the tenants, no doubt spurred on by agitators like John O'Donnell and Conor O'Kelly, stopped paying their rents. By January 1902 the half-yearly rents received by the landlord had dropped from over £2,600 to less than £200.[16] O'Brien, who was abroad at the time to restore his health, received news from his editor, McCarthy, that the tenants on the DeFreyne and Murphy estates were conducting their battle on the lines laid down by O'Brien. His reply was violent, blasting the unfortunate McCarthy for misunderstanding his position on the land agitation in the West:

I never for one moment contemplated a no-rent movement. I knew only too well it would only land us in ruinous responsibility for a few bankrupt estates. The only suggestion I made as to the West was the Commission of Inquiry with the boycotting of grabbers and graziers and what I suggested as to the rest of the country was to rouse the landlords to the necessity for compulsion by *boycotting* every landlord who refused abatements exactly the same way as grabbers are boycotted—not for a moment by entering upon a hopeless no-rent campaign.[17]

Once bitten, O'Brien was shy of raising another mare's nest *à la* New Tipperary, but he could not publicly desert the tenants by giving his true feelings, "words cannot tell you what a blow it is to me." Apparently, there were limits to O'Brien's championing of the tenants, but considering the manner in which he and Dillon had been left to bear the burdens of the Plan of Campaign, it was not unreasonable for O'Brien to draw in his horns on this occasion. O'Brien, in fact, thought that the no-rent idea had been suggested to the tenants by a speech of Dillon. Furthermore, the landlord himself in his legal action accused Dillon of starting the trouble. However, although Dillon's words could easily be

[15]Reports of League activity for 1900–1902 are summarized in SPO, CBS, Inspector General Reports (carton no. 2). The "General State of the Country" reports referred to are for January and February 1902.

[16]Details of the DeFreyne case in which the landlord brought suit against twenty-nine prominent members of the party (including O'Brien) and the *Freeman's Journal* are in Redmond Papers, NLI MS. 15241/6 (copy of affidavits).

[17]T. McCarthy to O'Brien, February 2, 1902 (incorrectly dated 1900); O'Brien to McCarthy, February 16, 1902, UCC William O'Brien Papers, Box AM.

construed to their liking by the tenants, he gave no support to the tenants' independent action.[18]

As can be seen, O'Brien had no objections to boycotting or, as he liked to put it, combination on trade-union principles. When he returned from his four-month absence abroad in April 1902, he threw himself into this work once more, hoping that a general struggle against the landlords would detract from the notoriety of the DeFreyne case and give the landlords something else to think about. This time he had Davitt back again as his comrade-in-arms, but help from the M.P.'s had noticeably slackened. Part of the problem was the continuous drain on the funds of both the League and the party. Even Davitt felt constrained to invoke Redmond's and Dillon's aid in putting a stop to the demands of local branches for legal costs in connection with trials of coercion victims.[19] This financial pressure was doubtless in Redmond's mind as he reflected on the consequences of his encouraging the vigorous agitation undertaken in the previous winter.

The year 1901 had been a particularly bad one for the financial fortunes of the party. The Irish subscriptions, representing about 80 percent of party receipts, were barely enough to keep the party apparatus going, and the news from America was most discouraging. Bourke Cockran, an influential Irish-American supporter, wrote to Redmond on the difficulty of getting contributions in the face of propaganda against Parliamentary agitation organized by the Clan na Gael: "the movement seems to provoke no popular support."[20] Devlin's mission in the spring of 1902 put some life into American subscribers, but by then the Irish subscriptions had fallen off, and the financial situation seemed as hopeless as ever. Alfred Webb, one of the party treasurers, included the church, the Gaelic League, the tenant farmers, and labor among those who were allowing the party to starve. "The falling-off in Irish subscriptions," he told Redmond, "is extremely embarrassing. There has been so far this year little over half from Ireland what there was last year."[21]

Situations like this always highlighted the cruel dilemma posed by the party's dependence on public generosity. Whenever the treasurers

---

[18]F. S. L. Lyons, *John Dillon* (London, 1968), 225.

[19]Davitt to Redmond, May 9, 1902, Redmond Papers, NLI MS. 15179.

[20]Cockran to Redmond, January 7, 1902, *ibid.*, MS. 15236/3. The gross receipts from America during 1901 totaled only £133 (*ibid.*, MS. 15231/3, subscription list dated July 10, 1903).

[21]Webb to Redmond, June 9, 1902, *ibid.*, MS. 15231/2.

reported that finances were flourishing, subscriptions inevitably fell off. Admissions of near-penury, on the other hand, betrayed a weakness which could result in public apathy. Under these circumstances, continued adherence to O'Brien's program when public support was insufficient to maintain the party's solvency prompted second thoughts in Redmond's mind. That he began to veer back toward a more timid policy as early as February or March 1902 can be fairly deduced from a constabulary communication, whose information turned out to be remarkably accurate.[22]

A speech O'Brien made at Limerick July 5 triggered an ultimatum from Redmond. Both men were present at this meeting to further the fighting policy of the League. While Redmond's thoughts were couched in the usual vague terms of a general call for agitation, O'Brien gave specific advice: "Shun, picket, and boycott any landlord or grabber who won't sell," and thus fill the jails. And while he was careful to point out that he was not advising a no-rent policy, he suggested that perhaps a "no-rates" policy might be in order. The tenants had not received such explicit advice from a party platform since the Plan of Campaign. Only Davitt ever approached O'Brien in the fiery and impassioned intensity of his speeches, and, of course, the *Irish People* fanned the fires each week. In the next month O'Brien almost passed the torch to other hands when he warned that "for many of the younger generation who are growing up in Ireland today it is no longer a question between English Rule and Home Rule but it is a question between Home Rule and an Irish Republic." His catch phrase was "Throw toleration to the winds; the time is come for intolerance."[23] Redmond thought otherwise.

O'Brien was awakened to the reality of his own isolation by a letter from T. P. O'Connor telling him that most of his colleagues (they were not named) were out of sympathy with his call for "a violent and rapid movement." The reasons given were the expected poor response from

[22]W. V. Harrel (Assistant Commissioner, DMP) to Chief Commissioner, March 5, 1902, SPO, CBS Files 1902/26449/S. The letter refers to serious differences of opinion among the party leaders: "John Redmond does not approve of the methods adopted to push the League and thinks that the organisation and in particular its funds as well as the country was not prepared to undertake such work as combination of tenants with possible evictions . . . " Harrel's information also indicated that Dillon would not be likely to oppose Redmond's view of the situation, which was to push the national question at the expense of the agrarian problem.

[23]*Irish People,* July 12 and August 16, 1902.

the tenants, the disadvantages of any imprisonment of the leaders, and the danger of clerical opposition:

The country which has passed through ten long years of dissension must be allowed to recover with some slowness from all the paralysis and discouragement of that awful time. In other words, to fall back upon a phrase of Parnell's, the true policy is to keep the pot simmering but not to let it boil over.

O'Connor also weighted his argument with that old gambit the anti-Irish feeling that extreme agitation might incite in England at a time when wavering Liberals were being restored to their faith in Home Rule. In fact, he threw in every argument he could make, including the state of O'Brien's health and did not even hesitate to presume that "in their heart of hearts, even the Tory Majority are foreseeing the early termination of our struggle for some form of self government"! O'Connor also indicated that his comments reflected the "inner souls of those without whose cooperation you cannot go on," an apparent reference to Redmond and Dillon.[24] O'Brien himself later included Davitt in this group. But, while one might hesitate to ascribe any timidity to Davitt, the fact remains that he sought to influence Redmond to conserve funds and was so far in accord with party policy that he accompanied Redmond and Dillon to the United States in October.

O'Brien's brief reply, especially since the moderating counsel was expressed by one whose service to the cause had not been marked by undue discomfort, was remarkably restrained. It almost seemed as if he really believed that public support for his policy was lacking: "of course I should not dream of pressing my views upon unwilling colleagues . . . I hope you will see no objection to my communicating your letter to Redmond, as if he shares those views, it will not be difficult to hit upon some method of watering down my influence on the movement." A few days later he did write to Redmond wondering if he were of the same opinion as "T. P. and Dillon" that nothing serious ought to be attempted, adding that "it would be madness for me to incur so much odium and anxiety if my principal colleagues thought it trouble thrown away, if not positively mischievous." The carefully worded reply from Redmond left no room for maneuver. He repeated O'Connor's arguments (except for the egregious expectation of a Tory turnabout on

---

[24]O'Connor to O'Brien, August 12, 1902, UCC William O'Brien Papers, Box AM; Davitt to Redmond, May 9, 1902, Redmond Papers, NLI MS. 15179; W. O'Brien, *An Olive Branch in Ireland* (London, 1910), 138.

Home Rule) indicating both his agreement with them and the fact that all these views had been expressed at a meeting in London with O'Connor, Dillon, Blake, and himself present. He assured O'Brien he was all for vigorous agitation (whatever that meant), but he parted with him on the Limerick speech:

Where I differ from you is as to means . . . I do not agree with the wisdom of preaching boycotting wholesale . . . I am not impatient at the progress we have made . . . [I am] in favour of every reasonable fight that may arise . . . but I am not in favour of openly preaching universal boycotting.[25]

O'Brien's capitulation was tinged with bitterness as he promised Redmond to stay in the background and work to bring home to George Wyndham, the Chief Secretary for Ireland, the necessities of the congested districts:

It is only too plain to me that a great many of the Party desire to save themselves from the trouble of any practical fight and are only too ready to receive the suggestion that moderation and vagueness are the best policy . . .

Nothing will be easier than to save the League from any risk of suppression and in any case only suppression in a limited area was to be feared and I am better convinced than ever that such suppression would bear infinitely better fruit than allowing ourselves to be influenced by the electoral fortunes of English Parties.[26]

The final word in these discreditable proceedings was Dillon's, who wrote to Redmond: "I returned O'Brien's letter which I read with great relief. The proclamation of Dublin and the impending attack on the *Irish People* had a good effect on him. *This is not the first time that the Government has extricated us from serious difficulties by timely action.*"[27] Behind all this cross talk, however, lay the inescapable fact that neither the provincial directory nor the local branches of the League had sufficient motive power to impel an agitation, irrespective of what the leaders thought. Though he never lost faith in the tenant farmers, O'Brien's calculations, now as in the past, foundered not only on the political preference of his colleagues but on the adamantine materialism and conservative instincts of the Irish peasant. The land question was never again to

[25]O'Brien to O'Connor, August 14, 1902 (typed copy), Redmond Papers, NLI MS. 15212/9; O'Brien to Redmond, August 20, 1902, *ibid.*; Redmond to O'Brien, August 22, 1902, NLI William O'Brien Papers, NLI MS. 10496/6.

[26]O'Brien to Redmond (copy), August 25, 1902, NLI William O'Brien Papers, NLI MS. 10496/12.

[27]Dillon to Redmond, September 12, 1902, Redmond Papers, NLI MS. 15182/3. The italics are mine.

assume such a large role in Irish agitation, but only because it was already on the way to its final solution in the autumn of 1902, unsuspected by even the most sanguine of agrarians.

Conciliation Emergent

The four years of almost ceaseless activity O'Brien had put into his League work had not provided the benefits for the tenants for which he had hoped. True, his movement could be credited with the great work of giving the Parliamentary party a new lease on life. But the Conservatives had ruled uninterruptedly in England since 1895 and looked as if they would complete a decade of rule without effecting anything substantial in the way of land purchase for the land-starved tenants. However, one factor was working in O'Brien's favor, for recent tradition had shown that though Home Rule was out of the question under Tory governments, progressive land legislation was part and parcel of their policy of killing Home Rule with kindness.

Hitherto, the funds made available for land purchase either through Land Acts or the Congested Districts Board had been too small to make more than a slight dent in the hegemony of the landlords. But there were several reasons why further attention would be given to the problems of land distribution after 1900. First of all, George Wyndham, Chief Secretary since 1900, was not the "silken cad" depicted in the diatribes of the *Irish People*. His resistance to coercion was only overcome by the pressure of Lord Cadogan, the Viceroy, and a majority of the Cabinet. Wyndham's genuine affection for Ireland was probably not unrelated to the fact that he had family ties with the romantic patriot Lord Edward Fitzgerald. He first developed sympathy for the half-starved population of the west of Ireland when he had accompanied Arthur Balfour on his tour of Connaught and Donegal in October 1890. "The place is a beautiful, stagnant desolation," he later wrote to his fellow poet W. E. Henley, "the problem is can you make the men fish; can you make the women work at lace, hand-made curtains and tapestry? . . . If you can't they must go. But there they are, dreaming and singing and drinking, making 'potsheen' and hitting each other on the head with the stones that abound."[28]

The existence of O'Brien's United Irish League and the conversion of the Ulster Protestant tenant leader T. W. Russell to compulsory land

[28]Wyndham to Henley, February 10, 1901, Henley Papers, PML MS. MA1617/R–V.

"WHEN LEAGUE MEETS LEAGUE."

Conciliatory advances by the landlords result in the Land Conference of December 1902. From *Punch or the London Charivari*, September 24, 1902.

purchase were also of undoubted influence in convincing Wyndham that there was more than just "a piece of Roman work" to be done in Ireland. There was also the stagnation in land purchase under the earlier acts, which was mainly due to the excessive legal costs to the landlord and to the rapid decline in the value of land stock. Furthermore, the workings of the Fair-rent provisions of the 1881 Act were progressively grinding to a halt, with thousands of cases backlogged in the courts since the second-term review of rents in 1896. Another impetus to reconsideration of the land question was the cost of maintaining a huge police force to quell agrarian unrest. Finally, one of the great advantages of landlord status had been swept away by the Local Government Act of 1898, which abolished the old landlord-dominated grand juries, producing Nationalist-controlled county government in the Catholic areas of the country.

O'Brien had already shown that he was not immune to Tory advances in anything that could redound to the good of the tenants. He himself had worked closely with the Congested Districts Board on several occasions, and his League had showed it could put agitation aside when, as in the case of the estate of Lord Sligo, the board stepped in to arrange sales. In fact, O'Brien's receptiveness to Conservative intervention on the land question had annoyed one prominent member of the party, who made his complaints known to O'Brien: "You may have some special reason," wrote Andrew Kettle, "for tempting or touching Wyndham, but I fear I am getting out of line with your programme . . . if [the League] falls back on Parliamentarianism there will be no [Land] Bill or a bad one . . . Redmond wants no fight nor do I know any one who does but yourself."[29]

Just about the time O'Brien was whipping up enthusiasm for his winter program of boycotting and agitation late in 1901, Wyndham wrote to Balfour, then leader of the House and soon to be Prime Minister, that the time had come to construct a Land Bill. He backed up his suggestion by citing T. W. Russell's and O'Brien's common purpose in promoting agitation. Balfour's reply gave him the necessary go-ahead to prepare the groundwork for the Bill of 1902.[30] But, as Kettle

    [29]Kettle to O'Brien, August 29, 1901, UCC William O'Brien Papers, Box AL.
    [30]Wyndham to Balfour, October 18 and November 17, 1901, Balfour Papers, BM Add. MS. 49803. For Wyndham's favorable views on land purchase, see *ibid.*, Memorandum on Land Legislation for Ireland, no date (1900); and PRO, Cabinet Minutes, CAB(1901) 37/59 no. 15, Memorandum on Irish Land Question and Need for Legislation dated November 9, 1901.

feared, it turned out to be a "bad" bill. The measure introduced in the spring was criticized by O'Brien for its timid approach to the task of abolishing landlordism because it sought to provide only about one one-hundredth of the estimated amount of money needed. In any event, urged on by O'Brien, the party rejected those terms, and the measure was withdrawn.

During the summer of 1902 another initiative, this time nonpolitical and also non-Nationalist, was taken. At the request of the editors of the *Irish Independent* and the *Irish Times,* L. Talbot-Crosbie, a Kerry landlord, wrote a letter to the *Freeman's Journal* calling for a conference of moderate men "representative of the several parties" to work out a common agreement on the land question.[31] Conciliatory advances were not entirely novel at this time. On the Nationalist side, Redmond on two recent occasions had indicated he was in favor of conciliation, even if the landlords had to get better terms than they deserved from their past history.[32] In view of O'Brien's subsequent action, it is difficult to believe that the *Irish People's* branding of the Talbot-Crosbie scheme as "a stale and rotten red-herring across the path of the National movement" represented his own views. Redmond, however, refused to be dissuaded and in a speech at Taghmon on August 31 called for a joint settlement "which will not drive to ruin and destruction any class of landlords in Ireland." Obviously, there was enough conciliation in the air to generate the one scheme that would bring both parties together eventually. This came on September 3 in the form of a letter to the press written by another landlord, Captain John Shawe-Taylor. The letter ran along the lines of Talbot-Crosbie's earlier effort, but differed from it in suggesting several names from both sides as landlord and tenant representatives, which was the lame excuse cited by the *Irish People* for its jumping on the conciliation bandwagon in its September 13 issue. The tenant representatives named were O'Brien, Redmond, Harrington, and Russell.

What saved the Shawe-Taylor letter from the fate of Talbot-Crosbie's suggestion was its endorsement by the Chief Secretary, who grasped the chance to salvage his Land Bill for reintroduction on terms agreed to in advance by both interested parties. "You can scarcely conceive the 'hubbub' there is here over the prospects of a settlement," he

[31] *Freeman's Journal,* June 14, 1902. It is possible that Healy had a hand in this. Not only was he friendly with Wyndham and the only Irish M.P. to support the Land Bill, but he was also an intimate of W. M. Murphy, the owner of the *Independent.*
[32] *Irish People,* April 28, 1900; January 26, 1901.

informed Balfour, ". . . my task is sensibly lightened. They are so busy with purchase that, for the moment, Home Rule and the 'Land War' have dropped into the background."[33] O'Brien's and Redmond's first impressions apparently were a mixture of expectancy and disbelief. "I presume you attach no importance to Shawe-Taylor's proposal," O'Brien wrote. Redmond's reply was equally laconic, "Of course, S-T's suggestion only made me laugh."[34] Nevertheless, the timing of the letter may have afforded O'Brien some private satisfaction, considering the pressure lately exerted on him by the party leaders to defuse the agrarian agitation.

Shawe-Taylor himself was soon in correspondence with both men on the difficulties he was having in forcing the landlords to take up the conference idea, with Smith-Barry (now Lord Barrymore)—as so often before—being the main stumbling block. Those difficulties were temporarily solved, however, by the endorsement of the scheme by the Chief Secretary. Shawe-Taylor claimed in a letter to O'Brien that it was his own urging of Wyndham to use his official influence on Barrymore that prompted the endorsement.[35] By September 19 both O'Brien and Redmond had also agreed to throw in their support. O'Brien, who a few weeks before had been willing to flout English opinion, now explained to Redmond his desire to take advantage of it in order to make it difficult for the landowners to reject the conference:

It seems quite clear that S-T's proposal is awkward business for the landlords and will create a very bad impression against them in England if they should be the obstructors. That being so, I don't see why we should hesitate to write to Shawe-Taylor intimating that we have no objection if the representatives of the Landowners' Convention attend.

Redmond replied the same day requesting that O'Brien show his (Redmond's) answer to Shawe-Taylor to Dillon "and if he approves please post it for me."[36] In any event, the letter was posted and, in view of Dillon's provisional endorsement of the Land Conference idea at a public meeting on October 3, it would appear also that he had seen Redmond's reply.

[33]Wyndham to Balfour, September 19, 1902, Balfour Papers, BM Add. MS. 49804.

[34]O'Brien to Redmond, September 3, 1902, Redmond Papers, NLI MS. 15212/9; Redmond to O'Brien, September 6, 1902, UCC William O'Brien Papers, Box AM. For the text of the Shawe-Taylor letter, see W. O'Brien, *Olive Branch*, 140.

[35]Shawe-Taylor to O'Brien, September 12, 1902, UCC William O'Brien Papers, Box AM.

[36]O'Brien to Redmond, September 19, 1902, Redmond Papers, NLI MS. 15212/9; Redmond to O'Brien, September 19, 1902, NLI William O'Brien Papers, NLI MS. 10496/6; *Irish People,* September 27 and October 11, 1902.

With the release of O'Brien's and Redmond's letters to the press
(O'Brien gave the approval for this to Shawe-Taylor), there was no
turning back. O'Brien also offered a public endorsement in strong
terms at a meeting at Claremorris on September 25. Dillon, who was
also to have spoken at the meeting, was significantly absent, but
O'Brien's words must have made him wince when he read them, for
they were probably the first step in a process of estrangement which
finally saw them bitter enemies. O'Brien branded as an idiotic untruth
the notion that Nationalists wanted to keep the land question unsettled
for political reasons: "I, for one, have never wavered in the belief that
the better off and the better educated our people are, the stouter Irish
Nationalists they will be." Nevertheless, in the interests of unity, Dillon
spoke at a Nationalist meeting in Dublin some days later and, while
holding up little hope for repentance by the landlords, associated
himself "most heartily with the attitude taken up by Mr. Redmond and
Mr. O'Brien."[37] The new watchword was conciliation, despite the fact
that several M.P.'s and more than a score of Leaguers were either in
prison or awaiting sentencing under the Crimes Act.

The Land Conference

In selecting O'Brien and Redmond, Shawe-Taylor had chosen his men
well. As we have seen, Redmond had been putting out conciliatory
feelers for over two years. O'Brien, the greatest agrarian in the
Nationalist movement, was unlikely to obstruct any plan for land
purchase which seemed likely to achieve his cherished dream of
abolishing landlordism. His past services to the Nationalist movement
were all bound up with the cause of the tenants. For him the primary
National question was not Home Rule but the settlement of the land
question. Dillon had written to Blake three years earlier of O'Brien's
absorption in this problem:

He [O'Brien] then went on to make some general observations on the
parliamentary situation: that any one who asked the Liberal leaders to make
Home Rule the first plank in their platform would be an idiot; that they ought
to be set free of this dead weight; . . . and that whatever Party came in next
time the most they could do would be to carry a good land bill.[38]

O'Brien was not unaware that many Irish Nationalists, especially

[37]*Irish People,* October 4, 1902 (O'Brien's speech); *Irish Times,* October 4, 1902 (Dillon's
speech).
[38]Dillon to Blake, October 2, 1899, Blake Papers, NLI microfilm p. 4682.

Dillon, would be opposed to this arrangement of the priorities. Actually, his conception of the national goal was in many ways identical to that expressed by Parnell in 1884 when he said that the settlement of the land question on a secure basis would leave "no class interest in Ireland of sufficient strength capable of offering an obstacle to the triumphant march of our people towards national self-government."[39]

As for the landlords, their convention voted 77 to 14 on October 10 against having a conference. Ignoring this setback, however, several of the landlords set themselves up as a provisional committee of a proposed Land Conference and began to canvass all landlords possessing over 500 acres (4,000 out of an estimated 13,000 Irish landlords) for their opinions. Of the 1,706 replying, over 65 percent approved of the idea, and this was enough for Shawe-Taylor, Talbot-Crosbie, the Earl of Dunraven, and a score of others to start the negotiations which would provide four adversaries for the waiting Nationalist representatives. [40]

While those negotiations were proceeding, Redmond and Dillon had departed on their fund-raising tour of the United States, which left O'Brien the effective leader of the Irish party until Redmond's return in mid-November, six weeks later. It so happened that in addition to keeping the flag of conciliation flying in Ireland, O'Brien now also became responsible for the action of the party in the English Education Bill then winding its way through the Commons. The significance of this measure for the Irish members was that they were under pressure from the Catholic hierarchy, both English and Irish, to support a Conservative Bill which promised to put the upkeep of voluntary schools on public funds—a boon for the financially-pressed parochial schools of Irish Catholics in English cities. The party had voted for the second reading in May and gave consistent support to the bill throughout the early committee stages in June and July. It cannot have been pleasant for the party whips to fill Conservative division lobbies with unnecessary Irish votes (government majorities were usually overwhelming) and so risk alienating their erstwhile Liberal allies, especially when the Irish pro-Boer attitude in the recent war had distressed many Liberal Imperialists and had, as many thought, turned the Earl of

[39] United Ireland, April 19, 1884; R. B. O'Brien, The Life of Charles Stewart Parnell 1:291–292.

[40] See NLI MS. 10907 for activities of the Land Conference committee prior to convening of the conference in December 1902. There was a ground swell of "respectable" support for the conference idea soon after the appearance of the Shawe-Taylor letter. The Archbishop of Dublin, the Irish Hierarchy, 358 county councillors (only three dissenters), and almost 80 percent of the county lieutenants and deputy lieutenants all signified their approval.

Roseberry against Home Rule. After the summer recess, however, the attitude of the Irish Parliamentary party changed to a policy of "diplomatic inaction." O'Brien's own attitude all along had been one of neutrality; he had not been on hand for the vote on the second reading and had similarly avoided the divisions in October although he had been present and voting on other Parliamentary issues. He was not one who took kindly to clerical dictation, but he never openly expressed himself on this issue as had the real anticlerical of the Nationalist forces, Michael Davitt. Nor was he considered by opponents, such as the *Irish Independent,* as malign an influence on the success of the bill as T. P. O'Connor. In fact, he won praise from that newspaper for promoting the policy of neutrality on all English bills while Redmond was absent in the United States, thus scotching the alleged efforts of Davitt to get the party to vote against the bill. What the bishops wanted, however, was positive support, so O'Brien's stock with them hardly improved when on October 20, at the height of the debate, he took the opportunity of the government's refusal to discuss the operation of the Crimes Act to withdraw the party from Westminster. Only mavericks like Healy and Jasper Tully remained to demonstrate their loyalty to the "supreme and sacred claims of religion." The hierarchy, naturally, was furious and was not consoled by explanations that more important work needed to be done in Ireland on behalf of Irish tenants than swelling government majorities in Westminster. Of course, the bill was never in any danger, and in December, after Redmond had returned, a full surrender was made to the bishops when the Irish members, including O'Brien and O'Connor, were whipped back to the lobbies to protect the bill in its final stages. As Lloyd George's slogan had it, "Rome had been put on the rates."

All these proceedings, while not central to O'Brien's part in Irish politics, nevertheless left their mark as they nurtured imputations of anticlericalism. O'Brien had already incurred clerical suspicion during the general election of 1900, when many he had helped elect to Parliament—"O'Brien's new men"—had gotten there without the support of the clergy, who had supported Healyite candidates. In fact, it was believed that the independence of the party from the clergy had taken noticeable strides after that election and that an anticlerical spirit had at that time begun to invade both the leaders and the rank and file of Irish Nationalism. In any event, O'Brien had emerged with the taint of anticlericalism, and it is significant that in later years, when he was leader of his own opposition faction, his policies had no clerical support, always an important element in Irish politics.

The deliberations of the Land Committee meanwhile had produced four delegates to meet the tenants' representatives. These turned out to be the Earl of Dunraven, the Earl of Mayo, Colonel William Hutcheson-Poë, and Colonel Nugent Everard, who possessed 2,500 acres in County Meath which had been held in direct succession for seven hundred years. It was entirely fitting that a scion of the original invader should be among those called to reverse the consequences of the Conquest. Among them, Dunraven soon emerged as a capable leader with a genuine sympathy for a settlement and an interest in Irish affairs transcending mere land questions.[41] Dunraven and Redmond, as leaders of their respective delegations, now met at the end of November to draw up a scheme that would be fair to landlord and tenant alike. There was every confidence that victory and exciting new possibilities would result from such cooperation. Redmond, after meeting with Dunraven, reported to O'Brien that Wyndham and Sir Antony MacDonnell (the new Undersecretary) were, as he put it, "breast high for a big deal" and that Dunraven himself clearly had further ideas as to some kind of Home Rule afterwards.[42]

At this stage, O'Brien was the only prominent party member who could be expected to give Redmond full support in the forthcoming negotiations. Therefore, in order to ensure the support of his own colleagues, Redmond sent a letter to each Irish M.P. for his approval of the four names originally suggested as tenant representatives by Shawe-Taylor. Many might have expected that Dillon, or even such legislative wizards as Healy and Sexton, should have been selected, but the first was still canvassing in America, and the others were either *persona non grata* (Healy) or out of touch with the party (Sexton). In any event, Redmond weighted his request with the opinion "that the holding of a

[41]Dunraven was the owner of over 16,000 acres in Limerick, Kerry, and Clare. In 1886 he had been selected by Lord Grey to move the rejection of the Home Rule Bill if it reached the House of Lords. His attitude to Home Rule had softened over the years, however, and he certainly was not the bigoted Unionist portrayed in the Nationalist press up to this time.

[42]Redmond to O'Brien, December 1, 1902, NLI William O'Brien Papers, NLI MS. 10496/6. An amusing bit of conspiracy resulted from these negotiations. Dunraven had complained to Redmond that he was being greatly embarrassed by UIL members' interference with the hunting pleasures of the gentry in County Limerick, and Redmond wrote to O'Brien that Dunraven "begs of us for a month or so, to induce our local branches to do nothing of this nature" (*ibid.*). The matter was arranged immediately (see P.J. O'Shaughnessy, M.P. to Redmond, December 4, 1902, Redmond Papers, NLI MS. 15241/11).

meeting of the Party for the selection of names might be inconvenient and it appears to me really unnecessary."[43] Except for a few Dillonite supporters there was general agreement on the original selection.

O'Brien outlined his views on the terms to be discussed at the proposed Land Conference in a long letter to Redmond. He advised against any elaborate agenda or publicity, especially since it could not be expected that any headway would be made on the question of compulsory sale to the tenants. It would be victory enough if agreement on general principles were obtained (obviously, any Land Bill would have to come from the government, not the conference). The overriding problem was what amount the tenants should pay in purchase annuities and what income the landlords should receive in payment. Dunraven's and O'Brien's views coincided, and the latter provided the details of an agreement which (a) gave a substantial reduction in second-term rents (reduced rents fixed from 1896) as the basis of the annuity, (b) yielded an income equivalent to the second-term rent to the landlord, and (c) requested the government to supply the funds necessary to bridge any gap between what the tenant could afford to pay and what the landlord would expect. The formula was simple enough and was expected to handle about 430,000 of the 480,000 occupiers, with those 50,000 or so who had lands in excess of 250 acres each, requiring special treatment.[44] The gap-bridging mechanism was to be a government bonus payable to the landlords, a very enticing incentive for divesting themselves of their decaying patrimonies. So confident was O'Brien that a golden age of social peace was dawning that he figured the annual cost of the bonus to the Treasury could be recouped by suspending RIC recruiting.

Thus, finally, the eight delegates met in Dublin on December 20, 1902, in a conference publicly hailed by Redmond as "the most significant episode in the public life of Ireland for the last century." The conference report adumbrating a vast purchase scheme along the lines framed by O'Brien was published on January 4, 1903. Specifically, it made eighteen recommendations which included the abolition of dual ownership in favor of tenant proprietary, the establishment of an equitable price for the landlords (second-term rents or their fair

[43]For a copy of Redmond's circular letter, see Redmond to J. F. X. O'Brien, December 2, 1902, J. F. X. O'Brien Papers, NLI MSS. 13418–477/folder 2.

[44]O'Brien to Redmond, December 4, 1902, Redmond Papers, NLI MS. 15212/9. For Dunraven's views, see Redmond to O'Brien, November 22, 1902, NLI William O'Brien Papers, NLI MS. 10496/6.

equivalent), inducements to the landlords both to sell (by receipt of a Treasury bonus) and to remain in Ireland, exceptional treatment for the population of the congested districts (though *not* compulsory sale), as well as settlement (undefined) of the evicted tenants problem.[45]

The report was received favorably by people holding most shades of public opinion. The Irish party passed a unanimous resolution supporting the terms of the agreement and deploring criticism. Thirty-nine members, not including Dillon or Devlin, were present at that meeting, and it is fair to assume that they were carefully stage-managed by O'Brien. But little direction should have been required to induce acceptance of the recommendations of men who had sacrificed themselves for over two decades in the cause of the tenants especially now that the hopes of hundreds of thousands of those same tenants stood a chance of being realized. The assembled Catholic bishops, with one exception, praised the report, the lone abstainer being Archbishop Walsh of Dublin, who from this point on began to use the press to belittle the conference terms and to undermine the authority of the tenants' representatives. The news from Ulster also appeared hopeful, with both the *Belfast Newsletter* and the *Northern Whig* acknowledging the very favorable terms ceded to the landlords. The latter journal went so far as to urge the election of only those local government candidates who expressed support of the forthcoming Land Bill.[46]

O'Brien gave his expected public blessing to the report, which owed so much to his work and enthusiasm, in a public meeting at Claremorris on January 6. Conceding that the landlords' terms (second-term rents) were "splendid," he reminded his listeners that he himself had preached those figures four years earlier and that he had devised the bonus scheme also, as early as 1896.[47] Little had O'Brien realized in those earlier years that not only was he to reunite the Irish party but also to set in motion events of decisive importance in reversing the consequences of centuries of alien domination and in undoing the confiscations of Philip and Mary, Elizabeth, the Stuarts, and William III. Nor could his landlord opponents ever have dreamed that the archrepresentative of Nationalist "criminality" would sit in harmony with their representatives to distribute the largesse of Irish land sales on terms which by any standard were more than the landlords could feel

[45]For the full text of the Land Conference Report, see W. O'Brien, *Olive Branch*, 475–479.
[46]For the various comments on the report, see *Belfast Newsletter*, January 5 and 7, 1903; *Northern Whig*, January 5, 8, 16, 1903; *Evening Telegraph*, February 28, 1903.
[47]*Irish People*, January 10, 1903.

they were entitled to. There is no reason to doubt O'Brien's sincerity in viewing the settlement of the land question as the first step in the attainment of Home Rule. The problem was that few others had the same outlook, and for this he was to suffer. Though he could point to the great strides that erstwhile Unionist landlords like Dunraven and Tory politicians like Wyndham were making in coming to terms with Nationalist Ireland, he made the mistake of imputing to this tiny sector of progressive conservatism the elements of an eager vanguard of Protestant missionaries for Irish self-government. The fatal results of such millennial hopes were to be brought home to O'Brien within the next decade.

SEVEN

Triumph and Defeat

T HE ATTENTION of Ireland was now riveted on the developments surrounding the Land Conference Report—how it would be acted upon by the government and how received by the politicians and the people. The task of preparing a favorable climate of opinion for what was to be one of the most revolutionary pieces of legislation in Irish history—the Land Act of 1903—devolved naturally on O'Brien and Redmond. In the few months preceding the Land Conference these two had preached "unity" and "conciliation." Now their advice was to be tested before a formal party conclave. Both O'Brien and Redmond were aware of Dillon's native dislike of meddlesome Unionists, and they had also observed that Davitt had been active in condemning the "conciliation chatter" by citing the failure of this type of approach when it had been tried by Mitchel, Lalor, and even Parnell. The difficulties were to center around two areas of contention: the effect of any such wide-ranging reform on Home Rule, and the cost to the tenants for the purchase of their holdings. Many Nationalists, O'Brien among them, believed that the destruction of landlordism could only hasten Home Rule inasmuch as the need to protect the Ascendancy class against spoliation by an Irish legislature would thereby be removed. There were some also, and Dillon and Davitt were among these, who felt that the Nationalist senti-ment was not as indestructible as O'Brien was wont to maintain. For them, peasant proprietary would strengthen the allure not of Home Rule but rather, in Alfred Webb's phrase, "horse racing, cycling and other amusements." This was also the view of the government and many of the Unionist supporters of the Land Bill. Ulster Unionists were somewhat more realistic: for them vigilance would always be the watchword. As for the second problem, the success of any land-purchase scheme would inevitably hinge, as far as men like Davitt and

Dillon were concerned, on the cost to the tenants as measured by the number of "years purchase" of judicial rents. For some years past, vendors had sold at prices equivalent to seventeen to eighteen years' worth of accumulated rent payments or, in the jargon of land-reformers, "seventeen to eighteen years' purchase." Any notion that tenants would have to pay more would, it was claimed, be a dangerous threat to settlement of the land question. Although it was clear to the diehards in the Irish party that the Land Conference terms were particularly generous to the landlords (the Landowners' Convention admitted as much), a revolt, if it should come, would at least await the Land Bill.

Davitt was the first to ruffle the uneasy calm, and O'Brien was soon hoping that he could be persuaded to go on another Australian tour! O'Brien wrote apprehensively to Redmond: "I suppose it was only surprising that Davitt did not come out sooner. Very likely the best course is to make no reply. The only awkwardness is that it will give the call to every crank in the country to hark in . . . I do think you ought to take some opportunity of speaking out. Up to the present as usual the whole torrent of abuse is turned against me."[1] Davitt's attitude was no surprise to Redmond, but he was more worried about what action Dillon, just back from America, would take. O'Brien, who had had a long conversation with Dillon, assured Redmond that "he [Dillon] has his reservations about the Conference but is most reasonable and I would say has not the least notion of uniting with Davitt."[2] In other words, Dillon, according to O'Brien, would not hold himself responsible for anything in connection with the settlement nor yet would he be responsible for creating disunity in the party.

Redmond, however, was not comforted, and for the next few weeks his letters to O'Brien reflect his alarm and despondency. One adverse blast from Dillon, of course, was enough to drown the plaudits of a hundred League branches. The worries preying on his mind were many. First, he was dismayed that the country was accusing him and O'Brien of giving sporting rights to the landlords (those rights were actually left to mutual discussion between landlord and tenant). Then there was talk that the tenants would have to pay thirty-three years purchase; that

---

[1] O'Brien to Redmond, January 12, 1903, Redmond Papers, NLI MS. 15212/10. Redmond refused to appear on the same platform with Davitt at this time: "It would be extremely distasteful to me to go with Davitt to Ballinrobe . . . There are reasons which would make it very unfortunate for him and me to come into conflict on the same platform" (Redmond to O'Brien, January 29, 1903, NLI William O'Brien Papers, NLI MS. 10496/7).

[2] O'Brien to Redmond, no date (probably January 20, 1903), Redmond Papers, NLI MS. 15212/10.

resolutions hostile to the Conference Report would be proposed at the National Directory meeting; that Dillon's clerical supporters were intriguing to oust him from the chair of the April convention of the League; that the refusal to present Addresses of welcome to the King on his visit to Ireland would do harm. O'Brien was literally bombarded with questions: "Have you any information about the *Freeman?* What do they mean? Have you been able to feel the pulse of the country at all?"[3]

On February 16 the National Directory and the Parliamentary party gave their approval to the Land Conference terms. Fortunately, the loyalty of Dillon and Davitt held true. Davitt's position was perfectly honest—to encourage public discussion of the terms. His straightforwardness is illustrated by his reluctant refusal to speak on a League platform in criticism of the conference, fearing that his presence would make it seem as if he were trying to work up popular feeling against Redmond and O'Brien. As he explained to an official of the Galway executive of the UIL: "it has not been, nor will it be, any plan or purpose of mine to encourage in any way, a weakening of the popular support which Mr. Redmond and the Parliamentary party require from the country in the important work which lies before them in the present session."[4] The *Freeman's Journal,* on the other hand, was under no obligations of loyalty or friendship and the thunder of that Nationalist daily, managed by the hostile Sexton, was more than a match for the lesser voice of O'Brien's faltering weekly, the *Irish People.*

Meanwhile, the stage was being set for the introduction of the Land Bill. The negotiations with Irish leaders were being conducted by the Undersecretary.[5] On February 6, O'Brien and Redmond therefore met Sir Antony MacDonnell for informal talks; Dillon and Davitt, though invited, had declined to attend. It appeared that the matter of the Treasury bonus was causing some trouble, so the anxious O'Brien sought to stiffen Redmond before he met with Wyndham: "make it clear that twenty-five years' purchase for the tenants is not even dis-

[3]Redmond to O'Brien, January 22, February 10 and April 3, 1903, NLI William O'Brien Papers, NLI MS. 10496/folders 7 and 8.

[4]Davitt to T. Higgins, February 28, 1903, NLI MS. 2159.

[5]MacDonnell was no ordinary Undersecretary. He had already had a distinguished career in the upper reaches of the Indian Administration and was both a Roman Catholic and the brother of a member of the Irish party. He accepted his appointment only on condition that he could influence the action and policy of the Irish Administration toward settling the land question and reforming that Irish Administration along the lines of the progressive legislation instituted by Balfour [J. W. Mackail and G. Wyndham, *Life and Letters of George Wyndham* (London, 1925) 1:80–81].

cussable and that our last word is 20 percent off second-term rents for a period that will make it equivalent to the seventeen or eighteen years' purchase of first-term rents [i.e., the market price]."[6]

The bill to achieve social reconciliation in Ireland was finally introduced by Wyndham on March 25, 1903. It accepted in general the suggestions of the Land Conference but seriously weakened them in several features. Not 17 or 18 years but 18½ to 24½ years' purchase was to be the range on first-term rents (fixed for fifteen-year term under the 1881 Act) and up to 27⅔ years on second-term (reduced) rents. Worse still, rather than let free bargaining operate between landlord and tenant, a zonal system for different areas of the country was set up which allowed reductions of as little as 10 percent on second-term rents as a basis for the tenant's annuity, the latter being fixed at a low 3.25 percent.[7] These were the main faults now seized upon by the diehards Sexton, Davitt, and Dillon. The influence of Sexton at this stage was more harmful than that of the others: there was no letup in the criticisms of the *Freeman's Journal*.[8] But the criticism was not all on the Nationalist side. Even T. W. Russell, one of the Land Conference delegates, had serious reservations, and he wrote O'Brien of the impossibility of final settlement because of the lack of a compulsory-purchase clause. Neither did he think more than 21 to 23 years' purchase of second-term rents should be paid.[9] The landlords, on the other hand, were determined to resist any loss of income resulting from an increase in the maximum reduction within the zones desired by the tenants' representatives. They were fully aware that the success of the act would hinge on the tenant's annuity. Previous experience had demonstrated that the tenant would always elect to purchase if his combined payment for interest and sinking fund was at least 20 percent less than the rent for his holding. He would not be deterred by the number of years he mortgaged his property. And such reduced outgoings is what the bill envisaged: a rental of £100 sold at, say, twenty-three years' purchase or £2,300 would yield an annuity of 3¼ x 23 or £75, less

[6] O'Brien to Redmond, February 12, 1903, Redmond Papers, NLI MS. 15212/10.

[7] For details of the bill, see J. E. Pomfret, *The Struggle for Land in Ireland, 1800–1923* (Princeton, 1930), 294–296. A detailed criticism of its various features is made in M. Davitt, *The Fall of Feudalism in Ireland* (New York, 1904), 708–711.

[8] One particular tactic of the *Freeman's Journal* must have sorely embarrassed O'Brien and Redmond. The paper had printed its criticisms in pamphlet form, and some member of the UIL Standing Committee ordered 1,500 copies for distribution to all the League branches, "a very mischievous expenditure"! (John O'Donnell to Redmond, July 10, 1903, Redmond Papers, NLI MS. 15218/2).

[9] Russell to O'Brien, April 8, 1903, UCC William O'Brien Papers, Box AN.

than the previous rental. Thus the landlords' bargaining power was strong and, essentially, they retained the upper hand in the face of Nationalist warnings on the inadequacy of the zonal reductions.

When the Landowners' Convention met in April, it acclaimed the bill as "by far the largest and most liberal measure ever offered to landlords and tenants by any Government in any country." O'Brien himself was rather shocked at the introduction of the zones, and Davitt wrote to Dillon that O'Brien had muttered something to him about rejecting the bill.[10] This, if Davitt heard aright, could not have meant more than a momentary overreaction on O'Brien's part. Nevertheless, it was clear amid all the adulation and ululation that a major turning point had arrived in the history of the Irish land question. An Irish party whose one hope of survival lay in wheedling ameliorative legislation from the British Parliament could not but accept such a revolutionary measure. On April 16, the Nationalists also held a Convention in Dublin to pronounce on it. With Dillon abroad for his health, the only real threat could come from Davitt, and, as at the UIL Directory meeting two months earlier, he declined to question the authority of Redmond. In any event, the preparations for the meeting were expertly handled by O'Brien. In the preceding weeks the party had disseminated only notices favorable to the Land Conference report. And O'Brien effectively bulldozed the Convention itself by introducing a series of resolutions which, in contravention of the usual practice, had not been distributed in advance to the delegates. In any event, the virtually unanimous support of 3,000 Nationalists, applauding the bill, was given to O'Brien's resolutions, as they, in O'Brien's effulgent and misleading description, "pledged the troth of the Irish nation . . . to the vital principles of the policy of national reconciliation."[11] What they had in fact done was to consign to Redmond and O'Brien full discretion in guiding the bill through the House of Commons. At this stage there was little open dissent at what had been accomplished. Numerous county and rural district councils endorsed by resolution the actions of the party. Important party members such as J. F. X. O'Brien and David Sheehy stood firmly on the side of O'Brien, and the *Cork Examiner's* endorsement was a counterweight, if a provincial one, to the thunder of the *Freeman's Journal*. Even Joseph Devlin, soon to be an indefatigable enemy of both O'Brien and the Land Act of 1903, wrote encouragingly to Redmond from America:

[10]F. S. L. Lyons, *John Dillon* (London, 1968), 230.
[11]W. O'Brien, *An Olive Branch in Ireland* (London, 1910), 229.

Everyone here is well satisfied with the result of the Convention. Of course the croakers have raised the cry that if the Land question is settled the people will lose their national spirit, but the men who are worth anything in America heartily rejoice at the promise of the passage of the Bill.[12]

O'Brien took a prominent part in the Commons debate on the bill, noting that it was weakest in those instances where it departed from the Land Conference spirit. In particular, the Treasury bonus offered by the government (£12 million) was inadequate and would result in an additional two years purchase to the tenants. Also, the bill failed to provide for the decadal reductions in annuity payments recommended by the Land Conference. Inevitably, amendments were called for, and it was the task of O'Brien and Redmond to negotiate them with Wyndham. The go-between this time was that noted diarist and relative of the Chief Secretary Wilfrid Scawen Blunt. Redmond urged several essential points for consideration, mainly having to do with the abolition of the maximum rate of reduction within the zones and the provision of compulsory powers for the redistribution of the Connaught grasslands. As the debate wore on, the tone hardened. Redmond conveyed O'Brien's exasperation to Blunt:

If the present attitude of obstinate insistence on the zone limits is persisted in, nothing can prevent a series of angry debates which will make it impossible to proceed with the Bill. . . . The opposition to the Bill is intense and is rapidly growing uncontrollable. Some of us have had to strain our influence to prevent its showing itself in a much more dangerous form than anything that has occurred yet.[13]

The situation was saved, however, by the action of Dunraven and his friends, who were instrumental in getting an amendment accepted that took most of the sting out of the zonal impediment by allowing judicial tenants, i.e., those who had had their rents fixed under the Land Act of 1881 (about two-thirds of all occupiers), to conclude mutual agreements with their landlords for reductions outside the zone limits. This cooperation was a practical illustration of the conciliation preached by Redmond and O'Brien.[14] If Redmond had been swayed at

[12]Devlin to Redmond, April 24, 1903, Redmond Papers, NL. MS. 15181/1. For the various resolutions and letters endorsing O'Brien's stand on the bill, see correspondence for February through October in UCC William O'Brien Papers, Box AN.

[13]Redmond to Blunt, June 17, 1903 (copy of O'Brien's draft initialed by Redmond), *ibid.*, MS. 15171/1.

[14]Redmond had also worked with Dunraven to help defeat an amendment inimical to the interests of the poorer landlords, urging however that that particular battle be waged in the House of Lords: "it is not a matter that the Irish Party would care to fight in the House of Commons" (Redmond to Dunraven, August 5, 1903, *ibid.*, NLI MS. 15187/1). However

this stage by the inordinate suspicions of Dillon, however, things might well have turned out otherwise. The congested districts fared less well, because it was impossible to get a Conservative Cabinet to insert a word as lethal to property as *compulsory* in the bill. But O'Brien was not prepared to jeopardize the bill on that account, even for tenants he had been fighting for since 1898. For, as he said, "whatever may be its short-comings, the bill as it stands is a great bill, and is capable of producing better and wider results than any Act ever passed by the English Parliament for Ireland." It cannot be denied that this was, in fact, the case. Alas, no such credence could be placed in his claim that it would be "the fault of English statesmen, and not the Irish people" if the spirit of conciliation did not lead to settlement of the larger question—Home Rule.[15] The time for conciliation on the national question, which had begun with some hope in 1870, had long passed. Not the least effective individual in dividing the "two Irelands," through his long association with *United Ireland* and his relentless harrassment of the landlords, was William O'Brien himself.

The Parting of Friends

The passing of the Land Act in August 1903 was the outlet the "irreconcilables" needed to mount a full-scale attack. Hitherto, the danger of jeopardizing the bill had kept Davitt and Dillon from translating their sullen distaste into open defiance. At critical moments, such as the directory meeting of February 16, both men had decided not to attend rather than voice public opposition to the Land Conference terms. Then in April Dillon, again shirked being placed in "a very awkward position," by managing to be in Egypt "on doctor's orders" when the National Convention met to endorse the Land Bill.[16] Davitt attended but only dared a "friendly" amendment, which he withdrew when challenged by Redmond and O'Brien.

Now, as in 1881, the tenants would make their own decisions while their Parliamentary representatives would take up an exercise they had developed into a fine art—venting their spleen on one another. On the surface, the conflict was between the support of the Land Act by Red-

---

much O'Brien and Redmond desired the abolition of landlordism, they had no intention whatsoever of depriving the country of the "stabilizing influence" of landlords in their own demesnes.

[15] *Parliamentary Debates* 124 (29 June 1903):848; 125 (21 July 1903): 1351–52.

[16] Dillon to Redmond, March 11, 1903, Redmond Papers, NLI MS. 15182/4.

mond and O'Brien on the one hand and the opposition to the Act by
Davitt, Dillon, and Sexton on the other. It was also a conflict of per-
sonalities—the exuberant, impatient, fanatical O'Brien *versus* the
austere, hesitant, intransigent Dillon. Men who had fought England
hard when they sought to end dual ownership of land, now fought even
more bitterly against each other after that point had been virtually conceded. There was no question here of abasement of the national honor
or diminution of the national claim. O'Brien cited his own case in his
characteristically optimistic fashion:

We had won the property in the entire soil of Ireland for our people by a
mortgage for 68½ years to pay from 20 percent to 40 percent less than their existing rents, they having been hitherto mortgaged, not for 68½ years but for all
time to pay from 20 percent to 40 percent more, not as freeholders, but as
tenants whose obligations had to be settled by a lawsuit, renewable every 15
years![17]

O'Brien's statement, though true in theory, breaks down when set
against the actual results. Within a few years the financing under the
Land Act began to break down, and it was discovered that almost twice
as much money as the £100,000,000 estimated by Wyndham would be
needed to accomplish the original goal. Nevertheless, by 1909 seven
million acres (about 230,000 holdings) had been purchased under the
Act, leaving nine million more to be dealt with.[18] Besides, if the tenants
had to pay their annuities (which were less than their old rents) for
seven or eight years longer than was bargained for, this was of less moment to O'Brien than the fact that they were now the full owners of
their holdings. Considering the past history of landlord-tenant relations
and the long struggle he had personally waged on behalf of the tenants,
one can forgive O'Brien's seeing the Land Act of 1903 as the talisman to
banish the racial and sectarian enmities that had embittered Anglo-
Irish relations. Had he been less of a dreamer and more of a politician,
however, he would have realized the futility of his hopes at that stage of
Irish history.

Beneath all the haggling about prices and annuities, conducted
mainly by Sexton in the pages of the *Freeman's Journal*, lay the much
deeper question of O'Brien's entire policy of conciliation—the desire to
reach out the hand of forgiveness and, as Dillon caustically mocked, to

[17]W. O'Brien, *Olive Branch*, 257.
[18]A. J. Kettle, *Material for Victory* (Dublin, 1958), 129; Earl of Dunraven, *Past Times and Pastimes* (London, 1922) 2:23.

"advance more or less under their [the landlords'] inspiration along the smooth and easy and short road to that goal of Irish freedom for which we have so long and so arduously struggled."[19] As we have seen, both O'Brien and Redmond had openly promoted a conciliation policy before the Land Conference. Then, however, conciliation had meant merely a discussion between authorized landlord and tenant representatives to work out a settlement of the land question, and even Dillon gave his approval to that meeting when it transpired. But when O'Brien tried to make conciliation part of a larger policy, he came up against a blank wall as far as the Nationalists were concerned. Dillon, in addition, was obsessed by the notion that the settlement of the land question endangered the larger national question. Between these conflicting attitudes Redmond adopted a defensive role. Though basically conciliatory in nature like O'Brien, he was too much of a politician not to see the implications of his colleague's policy. No Nationalist leader could afford to be compromised by the affections of Unionists. Gradually, therefore, Redmond began to ease himself clear of the importunate O'Brien, who was pestering him with demands to assert his leadership against the open "mutiny" of Sexton.

Enraged at the daily charges of the *Freeman's Journal* that the landlords were combining to demand as much as twenty-seven years' purchase, O'Brien presented Redmond with a resolution for the September 8 Directory meeting which sought to pressure the Nationalist press into supporting the policy of conciliation. Redmond balked at this, fearing a rupture with Sexton and Dillon and the end of unity in the party.[20] Nevertheless, the Directory still appeared to be on O'Brien's side, approving a policy designed to test the Act by methods originally set up by Parnell, with O'Brien's aid, in 1881. Dillon was not invited to this meeting, but it appears nevertheless to have been weighted in O'Brien's favor in advance as John O'Donnell, the League Secretary, on his own responsibility sent out a secret circular to the most reliable members of the Directory stressing the need for attendance at what "will be the most important [meeting] held since the starting of the organization."[21] His tactic failed, however, owing not only to continued attacks from the Nationalist opponents but also to a growing intransigence of the landlords in holding out for higher prices.

[19] *Freeman's Journal*, October 21, 1903.
[20] Redmond to O'Brien, September 7, 1903, Redmond Papers, NLI MS. 15212/11; W. O'Brien, *Olive Branch*, 264.
[21] John O'Donnell to Redmond, August 20, 1903, Redmond Papers, NLI MS. 15218/2.

It must have been embarrassing for O'Brien to report to Redmond within two months after the Act was passed that "the landlords are evidently acting in combination and making extravagant demands."[22] Even the Chief Secretary himself became alarmed and wrote Balfour that the time was propitious for taking up the university question: "It is important to give the Irish something to think about and to argue about, if only to divert their undivided attention from the prices under the Land Act."[23]

O'Brien was undeterred by these setbacks, and he next adopted a new tactic in an effort to counter the torrent of propaganda from the *Freeman's Journal*—a symposium on the Land Act in the pages of the *Irish People*. Several notable figures were to be invited to air their views. He outlined the project to his new ally, Dunraven:

I intend to devote myself for the next few months to the directorship of the *Irish People* newspaper, with a view to preparing the country, and especially the young people for the new conditions of Irish life. Among other features, I intend to open a special department for the free expression of opinions by all sorts of influential thinkers whether in agreement with our views or not.[24]

O'Brien hoped Dunraven would be the first in the fray and that opinions would follow from Horace Plunkett, the Archbishop of Tuam, George Moore, and "all sorts of influential people." Although he was assured of support by lightweights like Justin McCarthy (then retired), Douglas Hyde, and Lord Mayo, the big guns, such as Lord Monteagle, Horace Plunkett, and Bishop Patrick O'Donnell of Raphoe (Croke's successor as the paramount clerical Nationalist) absolutely refused.[25] This scheme soon came to nought, but at least it elicited from Dunraven a statement on Home Rule which must have given O'Brien food for thought, especially since Dunraven and his friends had just entered Irish politics with their Reform Association: "An independent Parliament—dualism under the link of the Crown—seemed and seems to me impracticable. Irish representation in the Imperial Parliament will be insisted upon and if the negation of that principle be an essential of Home Rule I am opposed to Home Rule." Instead of lecturing his noble friend on the indestructibility of the Nationalist sentiment,

[22]O'Brien to Redmond, October 6, 1903, *ibid.*, MS. 15212/11.
[23]Wyndham to Balfour, September 17, 1903, Balfour Papers, BM Add. MS. 49804.
[24]O'Brien to Dunraven, no date (end of September 1903), NLI William O'Brien Papers, NLI MS. 8554/2.
[25]See UCC William O'Brien Papers, Box AN (letters from various correspondents dated September and October 1903).

O'Brien strangely (or perhaps tactically) replied, "I am no more than you, at the present moment, in a position to give, in an actual scheme, a definition of Home Rule . . . all that is necessary is to try to discover as many points of contact as possible."[26] It seemed indeed that O'Brien had done for himself what he had urged the party to do for the Liberals four years earlier—he had set himself free from the "dead weight" of Home Rule.

Throughout October O'Brien appealed in vain to Redmond to take action against the "malignant dishonesty" of the *Freeman's Journal* and Dillon's attacks on the policy of conciliation. In a letter October 29, he branded the party chaotic and contemptible and hinted darkly at his resignation. Redmond's reply to this tirade was hardly calculated to mollify him, for it indicated clearly that Dillon and unity were preferable to O'Brien and disunity:

I don't agree with you as to the Party. With the exception of a mere handful I consider the men quite sound, but what I fear is that if the present difference as to the best price were to degenerate into an open and undisguised split with Dillon on the other side, the Party would instantly be rent asunder . . . Davitt does not count for much, allowance is made for him by the country. Dillon is going away on 1 December for 6 months. The *Freeman* is making no impression. The tenants are taking our advice and not theirs.[27]

O'Brien's response was to resign from the Directory on November 4 and to relinquish his seat in Parliament, much to Redmond's surprise and the dismay of all his own friends. In addition, he ceased publication of the *Irish People* for two years.

The progressive decline in the relations of O'Brien with his oldest comrades in the Nationalist movement forms one of the saddest episodes in the history of the Irish party. Nowhere is this decline more evident than in the manner in which Davitt's friendship with O'Brien was shattered beyond repair. The old Land Leaguer had recaptured some of his agrarian zeal when he became president of O'Brien's League in its formative period. Unlike Dillon, Davitt felt Land Reform and Home Rule could go hand in hand, but he could not swallow land purchase on terms excessively generous to the landlords or utopian attempts to enroll them in the fight for Home Rule. He coupled Redmond with O'Brien on these issues and in a letter to Dillon accused

[26]Dunraven to O'Brien, October 26, 1903; O'Brien to Dunraven (copy), October 27, 1903, NLI William O'Brien Papers, NLI MS. 8554/2.

[27]Redmond to O'Brien, October 31, 1903, *ibid.*, MS. 10496/9.

both of them of destroying the Nationalist character and purpose of the constitutional movement. Though the two former campaigners never spoke to each other again, Davitt's generous regard for all those who had ever worked for Ireland's good never allowed him to descend in public to the splenetic verbiage of the excitable O'Brien. In one speech to his constituents Davitt actually defended O'Brien against his detractors: "I don't know any man alive today who has done better work for the rest of Ireland [i.e., areas unaffected by the 1903 Act] than Mr. O'Brien. I differ with the present views and the present policy of Mr. O'Brien, but I could not permit any man to deprive him of the credit due to him for his past services. I believe he has been deceived by Mr. Wyndham and Lord Dunraven."[28]

The rift with Dillon, though it did not occur until 1903, had deeper roots. The friendship between the two campaigners must have weakened, in Dillon's case, during those lean years of the 1890s when O'Brien cut himself loose from the Irish party, leaving Dillon to fight alone with paltry funds and declining membership. Nor could the relationship have improved after O'Brien's dismissal of Dillon's chances in the contest for leadership of the reunited party in 1900. The final blow was O'Brien's bulldozing of the April 1903 Convention to consider the Land Bill, when he had the good fortune to have Redmond on his side. Dillon got his revenge when Redmond refused O'Brien's demands to take action against Dillon, Davitt, and the *Freeman's Journal* for their attacks on the Land Act and their rejection of the spirit of national conciliation detected by O'Brien. One can only sympathize with Redmond's choice—in terms of party unity the actual support of Dillon, Davitt, and Sexton was infinitely more attractive than the alleged support of the mass of tenants O'Brien claimed to represent. It is difficult, also, not to sympathize with Dillon's outburst of mixed emotions and generous feelings in a sad letter to Edward Blake a few months after the final parting:

Sometimes I do think his [O'Brien's] mind must be unhinged. I find it so difficult to recognise the William O'Brien I knew for twenty-five years in the writer of these monstrous diatribes or to find any trace of any old friend in this wilderness of baseless dreams . . . To think of such a personality, so amazing and so unfailing a source of political energy and influence, all gone to rack and ruin.[29]

[28]Lyons, *John Dillon*, 238; *Irish Times*, July 4, 1905. Davitt died in May 1906 and even in death showed a compassion that his colleagues would have done well to imitate in life: "To all my friends I leave kind thoughts, to my enemies the fullest possible forgiveness . . . " (from his will).
[29]Dillon to Blake, April 3, 1904, Blake Papers, NLI microfilm p. 4683.

Conciliation Defeated

O'Brien's resignation threw the Irish party into a state of turmoil not experienced since the Parnell crisis in December 1890. Redmond, genuinely surprised and alarmed, implored O'Brien on November 5 to recall his notice to the press, but to no avail. Dillon was concerned about the damage O'Brien could do if he were to rally his friends to bring up the question of his retirement and the reasons for it at the November meeting of the party and the UIL Directory. When Redmond invited Dillon to attend that crucial meeting, the latter agreed only on condition that there would be no discussion regarding O'Brien other than a resolution asking him to reconsider his resignation. Redmond agreed to this strategy.[30] O'Brien's case, however, was not helped by his own violent counterattack in letters to the press, demonstrating, as Davitt once remarked, that capacity "to keep silence and efface himself in 30 columns and 50,000 words." Redmond sought to remain on good terms with him, deploring his retirement and purporting to align himself with O'Brien's policy: "as for the policy of conciliation as I understand it, I stand by it. I intend to deprecate controversy and to appeal for continued unity."[31]

To give Redmond his due, he adhered to this conciliatory stand as far as support of the Land Act was concerned. Even as late as May 1904 Dillon became alarmed at the extent to which Redmond was tending to conciliation. He told Blake he was full of uneasiness at Redmond's lack of any real "policy of combat."[32] However, when invited to the UIL Directory meeting on November 24, O'Brien refused to bury the hatchet, much to Dillon's alarm. The latter was convinced O'Brien was once more out to wreck the Irish party. "There is no intention of retiring from politics," he wrote to Redmond of O'Brien, " . . . and unquestionably his power for mischief on those lines is enormous."[33]

O'Brien was not being entirely honest in the way he was holding up his former colleagues to public odium. Nothing was heard from him in public of complaints he made privately to Dunraven on the intransigence of the landlords: "The trouble has arisen also, to a shocking ex-

[30]Redmond to Dillon (copy), November 4, 1903, Redmond Papers, NLI MS. 15182/5. For Dillon's attitude, see Lyons, *John Dillon*, 242.

[31]Redmond to O'Brien, November 14, 1903, NLI William O'Brien Papers, NLI MS. 10496/9.

[32]Dillon to Blake, May 14, 1904, Blake Papers, NLI microfilm p. 4683. For examples of the Redmond attitude which troubled Dillon, see Redmond's public speech at Limerick on November 15 and his private letter to Blake on November 27 (*ibid.*, p. 4684).

[33]Dillon to Redmond, November 26, 1903, Redmond Papers, NLI MS. 15182/5.

tent, from the unreasonable demand of the landlords . . . I confess I am no longer sanguine."[34] The extent of that demand was eventually revealed in figures released by the Treasury in 1908, which disclosed that the average price within the zones was 22 years' purchase for first-term and non-judicial rents, and 24½ years' purchase for second-term rents. These amounts were well in excess of those which even the tenants' representatives thought should have been paid. O'Brien had become so fanatical about the alleged miracle wrought by Wyndham that he seemed to lose all sense of proportion in attempting to dragoon Redmond and the party into adopting a policy of conciliation which, however laudable in other circumstances, inspired little popular support in 1903.

Nevertheless, O'Brien's resignation was a very serious matter for the party, and it had repercussions both at home and abroad. They were immediately felt within the League itself. Laurence Ginnell of the central office reported the dismal facts of decline to Redmond—22 lapsed divisional executive bodies by December 18 and 489 lapsed branches by the spring of 1904; the League was wholly dead in West Mayo and almost extinct in Dublin. This situation did not improve and caused much anxiety within the party during the next two years concerning the funds of both the party and the League. The strength of the League in the country continued to decline. Tim Harrington, a member of the National Directory and O'Brien's colleague at the Land Conference, observed that "the party so far as I can see has very little influence anywhere. It certainly has none here in Dublin." The same gloomy report was received from Haviland-Burke, one of O'Brien's original UIL organizers: "Over large districts, the organisation is barely more than nominal even where it exists and the subscriptions speak for themselves . . . other organisations are being actively pushed in all districts and largely utilised for the purpose of drawing away thousands, particularly the younger men, from any support whatever of the parliamentary movement." When an attempt was made to restart the UIL in one of the Dublin wards, the meeting was broken up by members of antiparty Nationalist groups who advocated abstention from Parliament.[35]

The decline in the prestige of the party was not, of course, due solely

[34]O'Brien to Dunraven, November 12, 1903, NLI William O'Brien Papers, NLI MS. 8554/2.

[35]Data on the decline of Nationalist strength are contained in several letters of Laurence Ginnell to Redmond during January and February, 1904 in Redmond Papers, NLI MS.

to O'Brien's resignation. Actually, the Nationalist movement had never really recovered from the effects of the Parnell Split fifteen years before, and even O'Brien's League never restored it to its former primacy. But at a time when the party was fast losing its hold on the country's youth, it could ill afford opposition from dangerous mavericks like O'Brien. Moreover, he had not publicly compromised himself with Unionist elements other than to preach conciliation on the Land Act, a stance that several prominent Nationalists, such as T. D. Sullivan, had thought perfectly correct. For this reason, and because of lack of direction in the Irish party itself, O'Brien continued to remain a thorn in the side of Dillon and his friends until a reconstituted alliance with the Liberals from 1909 onward enabled the party to recover some of its impetus.

The effects were also felt in the American organization, the resignation being viewed there as giving a fillip to the Clan na Gael's criticism of the Parliamentary party. Davitt, who returned from a visit to the United States in the spring of 1904, wrote to Redmond: "The organisation [UIL] in the U.S. is virtually dead. It is useless to dwell upon the cause of this. Finerty [League president] blames O'Brien for it . . . Some of the 'Clan' leaders came to me in New York and they were jubilant over the situation."[36] Henceforth, the Clan made great use of O'Brien's diatribes against the party, and John Devoy customarily devoted the first page of his *Gaelic American* to them, not as an endorsement of O'Brien's policies but rather as a stick to beat the party.

O'Brien's defiance of the party also encouraged Unionists like Lord Dunraven, Shawe-Taylor, and Talbot-Crosbie, who, since the Land Conference in 1902, had, like O'Brien, been contemplating further development of the conciliation policy. O'Brien had had contact with Dunraven early in 1904 and continued to impress on him the importance of extending the Land Conference spirit and fighting the anti-Land Act policy of the *Freeman's Journal*. Dunraven was agreeable and hoped that something might be done later in the year but, he wrote,

---

15191/2. See also, A. Webb to Redmond, May 12, 1904, *ibid.*, MS. 15231/4; Dillon to Redmond, August 19, 1905, *ibid.*, MS. 15182/7; Harrington to O'Brien, January 21, 1905, UCC William O'Brien Papers, Box AO; Haviland-Burke to O'Brien, January 23, 1905, *ibid.* Official records of UIL activity in Dublin are in SPO, DMP–CBS: UIL meetings 1900–1905.

[36]Davitt to Redmond, May 5, 1904, Redmond Papers, NLI MS. 15179. For further details of the League's position in America and its decline in funds, see John O'Callaghan to Redmond, December 7, 1903, and January 5, 1904, *ibid.*, MS. 15213/5.

"there are difficulties; the construction of any kind of platform; the danger of a taint of landlordism sticking to your skirts."[37] The platform was to be provided sooner than expected, however, when Sir Antony MacDonnell, anxious to satisfy his secret urge to do something for Ireland, joined Dunraven's group at the latter's invitation and began to draft a scheme. Preliminary details were conveyed to O'Brien by Shawe-Taylor on August 1: "During the autumn the proposition is to reform this Committee into an Irish Reform League. Its platform has not yet been settled, but will probably be (i) a settlement of the University Question, (ii) a possible further extension of the principle of self-government to Ireland." Redmond also appears to have been advised of these plans, though in his case the reference to self-government was omitted, a natural caution considering the fact that the Irish party properly regarded itself as the only standard bearer of self-government.[38] Meanwhile, O'Brien himself corresponded with Talbot-Crosbie urging the necessity for "a bold pronouncement on self-government." On August 31, the Irish Reform Association released a preliminary report calling for the devolution of larger powers of local government to Ireland. This was followed on September 26 by the publication of a detailed scheme envisioning administrative control over Irish finance by a partly-elected council with authority to promote bills for purely Irish purposes. O'Brien's views on the vague devolutionary proposals outlined in the August report convey little excitement at the giant step contemplated by his landlord friends:

The self-government portion of the Manifesto is, considering all the difficulties, quite satisfactory as the preliminary declaration of a body of Unionist gentlemen. If we once come to particulars in a friendly spirit, in conference with representatives of English Parties, there would not be much difficulty in arriving at an agreement on main points.[39]

O'Brien was chiefly interested at this time, however, not in devolution but in how the Land Act could be improved. He would have preferred the Association to concentrate first on recovering the good will of the tenants—"who are fearfully and I think naturally sore at the high rate of purchase"—by working for the reinstatement of the evicted and the restoration of decadal reductions in the repayment of loans as

[37]Dunraven to O'Brien, July 26, 1904, NLI William O'Brien Papers, NLI MS. 8554/3.
[38]Shawe-Taylor to O'Brien, August 1, 1904. UCC William O'Brien Papers, Box AN; Shawe-Taylor to Redmond, no date, Redmond Papers, NLI MS. 15226.
[39]Talbot-Crosbie to O'Brien, August 13, 1904; O'Brien to Talbot-Crosbie (copy), September 1, 1904, UCC William O'Brien Papers, Box AN.

provided by the Land Act of 1896. O'Brien's fertile mind was toying with the idea of setting up yet another organization concerned specifically with improving the Land Act, yet having in it the seeds of his future All-for-Ireland program. He wrote optimistically to Dunraven that he soon hoped to sweep Munster with the conference spirit and expected reciprocal support from Dunraven's Association.[40]

All these projects came to an abrupt end in November with the storm raised by the publication of the Dunraven scheme, and the involvement in it of Sir Antony MacDonnell, the Undersecretary, coupled with Chief Secretary George Wyndham's public disavowal of Home Rule in a devolutionary or any other guise. It was a sudden and disastrous blow to the hopes of O'Brien and Dunraven for conciliation. It was also a personal tragedy for Wyndham, who was forced from office and into disgrace by the retaliatory onslaught of Ulster Unionism, furious that an attack on the Union should emanate from within the Irish Administration of the Tory party.[41]

The entire affair had developed in confusion and was in reality something of a flash-in-the-pan as far as conciliation was concerned. Wyndham mislaid and never read the letter MacDonnell had sent him in September advising him of his role in the formulation of the devolution scheme. Hence the consternation at the Chief Secretary's dashing of the hopes of the conciliationists when the storm broke. Even Lord Castletown, an influential Southern Unionist, whose support O'Brien felt necessary to any policy of conciliation, held aloof from the affair, recognizing full well that devolution was "too advanced for the Unionists and not sufficiently so for the Nationalists."[42] The basic weakness of the Reform Association's position was noted by one of its own members in a letter written to the Undersecretary, even before the devolution scheme appeared in the press:

The portion of our Manifesto which has created most adverse comment is that anent "devolution" . . . I agree with Lord Dunraven in feeling that until we can

[40]O'Brien to Dunraven, September 2 and 6, 1904, NLI William O'Brien Papers, NLI MS. 8554/5.

[41]For the program of the Irish Reform Association, see the Earl of Dunraven, *The Outlook in Ireland* (London, 1911), 273–280. For the development of the devolution crisis, see F. S. L. Lyons, "The Irish Unionist Party and the Devolution Crisis of 1904–5," *Irish Historical Studies* 6 (March 1948):1–22. There is an interesting letter by MacDonnell on his motives for launching the devolution scheme in MacDonnell to Mrs. Alice Stopford Green, September 1, 1904, A. S. Green Papers, NLI MS. 15089/4.

[42]Lord Castletown to O'Brien, September 15, 1904, UCC William O'Brien Papers, Box AN.

count upon a far larger and more representative body of support than we at present possess, there is great danger to the movement failing from the ridicule which is being directed against the weakness of our personnel.[43]

If Dunraven, the head of the Reform Association, felt thus about the lack of support, one is forced to conclude that the scheme had been pushed forward by the forceful MacDonnell. In any event, if one had conspired to discredit the policy of conciliation and destroy further Conservative concessions to Home Rule sentiment, one could hardly have done better than to use the bungling methods of the Reform Association. Unfortunately for O'Brien, he failed to learn the obvious political lesson from the affair.

Devolutionary Designs

O'Brien was now without a party and shorn, temporarily, of a policy. He had been returned unopposed for Cork City in 1904 but refused to take the Irish party pledge when sworn in as a new member in May 1905. His only following was in County Cork, and as the *Irish Times* jocularly put it, "his Parliamentary following could still be accommodated, with a little squeezing, upon one 'outside' car." Even his most avid supporter in the party, John O'Donnell, saw ruin for his own prospects in Galway if he opposed the party, and both he and other O'Brien followers such as E. Crean, M.P.; J. Gilhooly, M.P.; and D. D. Sheehan, M.P., were advised by O'Brien to hold to their opinions in silence.[44] Despite the deficiencies of the Land Act, he could take some pride in its workings since its passage in 1903. The social effects of the Act were immediate. The year 1903 alone saw a 33 percent drop in reports of intimidation, a 70 percent decline in boycotting cases, 60 percent fewer people needing police protection, and a 50 percent decrease in the number and acreage of grazing farms unlet or unstocked because of agitation.[45] This state of affairs did not deteriorate until the start of the cattle-driving campaign in 1907/08, but even then agrarian violence of the type that provoked a coercive response from the government did not reappear. As far as the transfer of the land itself was concerned, the

[43]Hutcheson-Pöe to MacDonnell, September 16, 1904, MacDonnell Papers, The Bodleian Library, MS. C351.

[44]O'Donnell to O'Brien, January 27, 1905; O'Brien to Crean, February 4, 1905, UCC William O'Brien Papers, Box AO.

[45]SPO Intelligence Reports 1906–1914, Carton no. 2 (Report for 1910–11). See also, Appendix A.

rush of tenants to purchase was halted only by the parsimony of the Treasury in advancing loans. Nevertheless, in the period 1903 to 1909 over 200,000 peasants became owners of their holdings under the Act. Nor was the Home Rule cause set backward by such social improvement. In fact, the ironic thing is that O'Brien's opponents in the Irish party who prated most about the inviolability of the Nationalist claim were within the next decade driven by Unionist militancy and cajoled by Liberal entreaties to weaken the integrity of that claim until the party's fatal concession regarding Ulster in 1914.

Though no longer a party member, O'Brien retained enough of the party spirit not to contest the right of Dillon and Redmond to represent Irish opinion. Dillon, on the other hand, did not cease to regard O'Brien as a threat, for experience had made him aware of O'Brien's facility for starting projects and building them up from nothing quite rapidly. As the general election loomed closer, therefore, Dillon's letters to Redmond take on a note of urgency—stressing the need to combat O'Brien's takeover of the agricultural laborers movement (the Land and Labour Association), to start a party-controlled weekly paper in opposition to the revived *Irish People,* and to head off any complications at the forthcoming National Convention.[46] Dillon also realized that the party's troubles would be immeasurably increased by the return of the Liberals to power because of the pressure from Ireland to demand Home Rule pledges as a condition of the party's supporting the government. In fact, the threat from O'Brien turned out to be much less of a problem than that posed by the overwhelming Liberal victory in January 1906.

One thing was clear about the 1906 election—it was not fought on the issue of Home Rule. The election speeches of prominent Liberals dismissed Home Rule as something for future Parliaments to grapple with. Lord Elgin, for example, agreed to join the Cabinet only after receiving assurances that Home Rule did not form part of the government's immediate program. Asquith at Sheffield, echoing Sir Edward Grey's comments, asserted that it would be "political dishonesty" for Home Rule to be introduced by a government elected on the issue of free trade. Augustine Birrell, the darling of the Nationalists for the next ten years, insisted in a speech at Bristol that Home Rule could not come by any action in the next Parliament. Strangest of all

[46]Dillon to Redmond, August 19, 23, 30, and September 25, 1905, Redmond Papers, NLI MS. 15182/7.

was the speech of T. P. O'Connor at Liverpool on January 5, a speech
not reported (for obvious reasons), in the Nationalist press:

Mr. O'Connor said the attempt of the Tory party to place Home Rule as the
issue before the country instead of protection was contemptible and dishonest
. . . He believed that in the next five years, with good sense on the part of the
Government and of the Irish people, more would be done for Ireland than had
ever been done.[47]

Such pronouncements gave added power to the carping of O'Brien,
now one of the foremost critics of the Irish party. The party was once
again face to face with the reality of political dependence on the
Liberals. Worse still, O'Brien's represented only one critical voice
among several ominous noises from more fervid (because anti-
Parliamentarian) Nationalists of the older school of patriotism, who
wanted no truck with the step-by-step Home Rule to which the party
had resigned itself. The party would have been even more dismayed
had it known of the private opinions on Home Rule of James Bryce, the
man who had become the Liberal Chief Secretary:

The forces of nature seem to me to be working for Home Rule, and it will come
about under one English party just as much as under another *if*—an important
if—the Irish continue to press as strongly for it. That is perhaps not so certain.
When they have the land, much of the steam will be out of the boiler . . . That
Home Rule will come in our time seems unlikely.[48]

O'Brien, on the other hand, would not have been at all dismayed at
the advice Bryce took on Irish legislation as soon as he assumed office.
In February 1906, Sir Antony MacDonnell, retained as Undersecretary, resurrected the old Dunraven (i.e., his own) scheme, which was to
become Bryce's stillborn measure of step-by-step Home Rule. Though
it was essentially an extension of local government as envisaged in the
old Reform Association program, MacDonnell claimed that Redmond
was not unfriendly to it (provided it offered a council at least two-thirds
elected) when he (MacDonnell) discussed it with him.[49] Actually,
O'Brien and Redmond had each adopted a moderate position on
Home Rule, and O'Brien, especially, would have given his support to
any scheme emanating from either Conservatives or Liberals, however

[47]P. Rowland, *The Last Liberal Governments: 1905–10* (London, 1968), 19; *The Times,* London, January 5 and 6, 1906.
[48]Bryce to Dicey (copy), February 3, 1905, Bryce Letters, NLI MS. 11011. Bryce apparently was the only member of the Cabinet who argued for the retention of the Coercion
Act—a sore point with Nationalists—as an essential safeguard against lawlessness
(Rowland, *The Last,* 134).
[49]MacDonnell to Bryce, February 11, 1906, Bryce Letters, NLI MS. 11012/2.

little it approached the vaunted goals of the Irish claim. Redmond was more restricted in his actions, of course, because of his responsibility as leader of the Nationalists and because of the fact that he was answerable to National Conventions which, as time was to show, could not always be "managed."

O'Brien, as an outsider, could not work directly with the Liberals. His extra party contacts continued to be the Irish Unionists, especially Dunraven and also Lord Rossmore[50] and the Southern Unionist Lord Castletown. His belief was that individuals like these could use their influence to persuade members of the government or other influential persons to hold a conference to resolve outstanding issues of Irish legislation. In fact, his contacts were useful enough to enable him to see Bryce's draft proposal six months before it was officially shown to Redmond! This was the proposal for legislation which MacDonnell had tentatively discussed not only with Redmond but also with Dunraven. O'Brien's notes of a conversation with his unknown informant (presumably Dunraven) in April 1906 indicate that the discussion centered on what was eventually to be shown to Redmond in October as a draft of the devolutionary measure to be introduced in the 1907 session. O'Brien disliked the name *Irish Council* for the proposed administrative body, preferring the more grandiose *National Council of Ireland*. He also advised that all Irish M.P.'s and representative peers of Ireland be ex officio members of the Council in addition to the Council members elected for each of the existing Parliamentary constituencies. Irish representation in the Imperial Parliament should be continued, perhaps nominated by the Council. While he thought that the absence of legislative power in the Council would be a "terrible damper" on Ireland, he reflected that the annual receipt of £1,000,000 as a bonus from the Imperial Exchequer would make up for it. O'Brien was obviously hoping the Council would be a large body of more than two hundred members which would take over part of the Irish Administration—this would look more like a Parliament than any smaller part-elected and part-nominated body. And he reckoned that the inclusion of the Irish M.P.'s was essential to secure the approval of the Nationalist party.[51]

[50]Rossmore was an Orangeman, who in 1883 headed a noisy demonstration at Clones, County Monaghan, against a Nationalist registration meeting. He was suspended from his justiceship of the peace because of his veiled threats of violence against this Nationalist "invasion" of the electoral rolls. Not the least of his detractors in the 1880s was O'Brien's *United Ireland*.

[51]Notes of conversation dated April 6 (1906), item AO-281, UCC William O'Brien Papers, Box AO. In his memoirs, O'Brien admitted this collaboration (*Olive Branch,* 416).

The scheme Redmond was shown bore none of the marks of O'Brien's recommendations. The council was to consist of fifty-five members, two-thirds indirectly elected and one-third nominated.[52] Even the title *Irish Council* had been replaced by the insulting *Lord Lieutenant's Council*. The proposal was roundly condemned by the Nationalist leaders and rejected as impossible in a private memorandum to Bryce signed by Redmond, Dillon, and T. P. O'Connor. Devlin, writing to Redmond from abroad, said that "if it were not for the criminal conduct of O'Brien in offering such encouragement to MacDonnell and Co. in the name of 'rebel' Cork they would never have the indecency to formulate such a scheme."[53] The party was given temporary relief from the further embarrassment of discussing the scheme when Bryce abruptly gave up his post in December to become Ambassador at Washington. As Bryce had earlier feared, "They [the party] care more for a showy bird (very much) in the bush than a plump little bird in the hand."[54]

Among the party's many troubles during 1906 was O'Brien's increasing activity in the ranks of the Land and Labour Association. This Munster organization of agricultural laborers and small tenants had been started years earlier by D. D. Sheehan of Cork, one of the staunchest supporters of O'Brien's ideas in the Irish party. O'Brien, however, was more inclined to use the Association as a springboard for his conciliationist program. Dillon wrote to Redmond after one large meeting of the Association urging him to squelch that body by getting a few of the reliable Munster M.P.'s to start a new Land and Labour group and claim it as the legitimate continuation of the original Association! This would effectively confine Sheehan's (or, as Dillon called it, O'Brien's) group to part of Cork and Kerry, otherwise "the whole of Munster will be gradually poisoned, and no seat will be safe in case of vacancy."[55]

O'Brien's object, however, appeared to be to rejoin the party. Several letters from Limerick, Cork, and Kerry branches of the Association suggested to Redmond the possibility of a friendly conference. One

[52]Lyons, *John Dillon*, 289.

[53]Devlin to Redmond, January 2, 1907, Redmond Papers, NLI MS. 15182/2. For Redmond's comments on the draft measure and a detailed criticism by Blake, see M. A. Banks, *Edward Blake, Irish Nationalist 1892–1907* (Toronto, 1957), 312–316.

[54]Bryce to Campbell-Bannerman, October 10, 1906, Campbell-Bannerman Papers, BM Add. MS. 41211.

[55]Dillon to Redmond, March 25, 1906, Redmond Papers, NLI MS. 15182/10. Redmond declined Dillon's suggestion, being loth to proliferate the Nationalist associations further. However, a rival association was set up eventually.

proposed that Redmond, Dillon, Davitt, Sexton, Healy, and Harrington meet O'Brien and one of his friends to promote unity. The usual party response was that no conference could take place unless O'Brien first took the party pledge. In any event, the chances of reunion were hardly increased by O'Brien's inability to refrain from wildly attacking the party in the resurrected *Irish People*. Dillon and Redmond generally tended to ignore O'Brien's public statements, on the grounds that the less the differences between them were aired, the more united the party appeared, especially to supporters in America and elsewhere. Dillon tried to close off discussion about O'Brien by advising Redmond that "any toleration of his proposals of Conference would of course be absolutely fatal to the Party. The only possible way to make peace with him is to show that we can get on without him."[56]

O'Brien would not let himself be ignored, and before long Dillon was plagued once more by his "extremely dangerous" moves on the evicted tenants question. The inability of the party to persuade successive English governments to do anything for those unfortunate people in the past twenty-five years constituted one of its most notable failures. Nor could it take pride in the manner in which the question had been shelved in recent years, to be resurrected every time a National Convention required the pious recitation of the old demand for reinstatement. It has also been noted how shamelessly those same tenants had been deserted by the other Irish farmers. Now, during the summer, O'Brien had begun to promote the idea of reassembling the old Land Conference to bring the matter before Bryce's Administration. He had Dunraven working to influence Lord Mayo, Nugent Everard, and Hutcheson-Poë, while he himself wrote to Russell and Harrington, expecting the latter to tempt Redmond into cooperating. Only Redmond and Mayo declined to attend the conference, which was held by six of the eight original Land Conference delegates in Dublin in October 1906. Dillon prepared Bryce for the overtures he was certain to receive, warning him somewhat gratuitously that the conference was really an attempt to wreck the party and that he should ignore any communication and work only through Redmond as chairman of the Irish party. Dillon's suspicions of O'Brien were so great that he regarded a request from one of the party members to start a special fund for the evicted tenants as a plot to syphon off contributions from the Parliamentary fund.[57]

[56]Dillon to Redmond, August 2, 1906, *ibid.*, MS. 15182/12.

[57]Dillon to Bryce, October 17, 1906, Bryce Letters, NLI MS. 11014/2; Dillon to Redmond, September 29, 1906, Redmond Papers, NLI MS. 15182/12.

Dunraven's legislative suggestions duly reached Bryce, tempting him with the advice that O'Brien, not Redmond or Dillon, was the man to follow—a choice between conciliation and the extreme demand of independence.[58] Though Bryce did ignore the conference, the following year brought an end to the tenants' travail with the passage of the Evicted Tenants Act in August 1907. The party naturally took the credit, though in fact it had done less than O'Brien to keep the issue before the public and it had been prepared to sacrifice the tenants rather than let an iota of credit accrue to the member for Cork City.

The Irish Council Bill

The prospect of O'Brien's return to the party had been part of the sideshow of Irish politics since the election in January 1906. At that time both O'Brien and the party desired to avoid electoral contests against each other in Cork, and George Crosbie, proprietor of the *Cork Examiner,* had been most active as mediator between Redmond and O'Brien. Though nothing came of those efforts to reunite, a deal had been patched up regarding the Cork seats. The party's resentment against O'Brien carried over to his supporters Sheehan and O'Donnell, who were both dismissed from the party later in the year on flimsy excuses. Upon D. D. Sheehan's expulsion, O'Brien threatened action against the party in connection with the distribution of funds to Irish members of Parliament (Sheehan and O'Donnell were refused the usual quarterly stipends once their names had been removed from the list of Nationalist members). This evoked a distasteful reaction from John O'Callaghan, UIL Secretary in America. His letter to Redmond rivals the intemperate mud-slinging of the party quarrels in the 1890s:

It was an old tradition down around my own place near Mallow, that there was a connection, near or remote, between O'Brien's family on the mother's side and Pierce Nagle, the "Informer" [a renegade Fenian of 1867]. Perhaps a hint or two in that direction, with a quiet suggestion that before he demands an accounting of the American and Australian funds he should give an accounting of the Jewish funds himself, might do something to steady his nerves at this time.[59]

<hr>

[58]Dunraven to Bryce, October 27, 1906, Bryce Letters, NLI MS. 11014/2. Needless to say, the three landlord representatives dissented from the compulsory expropriation advocated by their companions.

[59]John O'Callaghan to Redmond, January 15, 1907, Redmond Papers, NLI MS. 15213/10.

O'Callaghan's plan was to have others send letters to the Irish papers in the same malevolent strain. Though it is extremely unlikely that Redmond would have approved such action, the Nagle story did eventually get a public airing.

The motive behind this type of attack on O'Brien was the seemingly hopeless position of the Irish party both at home and abroad as the year 1907 opened. The return of the Liberals to power and their expressed attitude to Home Rule legislation made the Nationalists all too aware of how great a friend Gladstone had been to them. Against this background O'Brien's criticisms tended to have a disproportionate effect. Redmond seemed to be utterly incapable of giving any lead to the country and so far removed had he, Dillon, and the older members become from the popular movement that without Devlin the party apparatus must have collapsed altogether. Actually, Devlin's absence on his Australian mission during 1906 had been sorely felt in Ireland. T. P. O'Connor had been forced to desert the comforts of London society to retrieve the party's fortunes in America. "I am rather concerned," he wrote to Redmond, "to find from your letter that things are so critical. I did not realise that they had got to this point." No doubt, "Tay Pay" got his contributions from the well-to-do, judging by the somber reflections he conveyed to Blake while in America: "New York woke me very thoroughly to the distance that separates us from the great days of old. The movement there was almost dead and I do not flatter myself so far as to think that I have thoroughly revived it."[60]

The weakness, of course, was within the party itself and could not be attributed solely to factionists like O'Brien. Devlin discerned the cause in a letter to Redmond: "If the members of the Party kept more in touch with their constituents . . . we might laugh at every attempt to destroy the movement . . . But we cannot blind ourselves to the fact that not twenty per cent of the Party trouble themselves once the elections are over." Dillon himself would have added the *Freeman's Journal* to the list of woes for its lack of "loyal, active and intelligent support" of the party.[61] Even the party-controlled Young Ireland branch of the UIL added to these worries, with its repeated calls for an economic boycott of British goods.

[60]O'Connor to Redmond, September 17, 1906, *ibid.*, MS. 15215/1; O'Connor to Blake, October 28, 1906, Blake Papers, NLI Microfilm p. 4683.
[61]Devlin to Redmond, January 2, 1907, Redmond Papers, NLI MS. 15181/2; Dillon to Redmond, July 31, 1907, *ibid.*, MS. 15182/15.

But O'Brien's was not the only carping voice outside the party ranks. At least a dozen Nationalist movements of one kind or another were vying for recognition in 1907. The party, of course, could count on the United Irish League, the national organization which was now greatly weakened in numbers and finances. Supporting the party in Ulster was Devlin's sectarian counterpart to the Orange Order, the Board of Erin. That group was an ultra-Catholic organization whose crude bossism and roughhouse tactics alienated many of the more moderate elements in the party. Also known as the Ancient Order of Hibernians (AOH), it had little in common with the benevolent and philanthropic body of the same name in the United States. Arrayed against the official Nationalists were small groups of activists in Sinn Fein, the Daughters of Erin (the women's Sinn Fein group led by Maud Gonne), the Dungannon Clubs (the university-student Sinn Feiners), and, below the surface, the IRB. The activity of these extreme elements had also brought about the "melancholy change" loyalist observers like the *Irish Times* had espied in the assaults on British soldiers and the antienlistment drives that were being conducted in various parts of the country. These opponents of the Nationalists received popular support from the ostensibly nonpolitical Gaelic League and GAA membership. Webb, party treasurer and one of the oldest members of the party who over the years had almost lost hope for the old cause, warned Redmond in a doleful letter of the effects of the party's apparent abandonment of the fight for Irish nationality:

I am greatly impressed with the character of the support being given to the Gaelic League, Dr. Hyde, and the Sinn Fein movement, as compared to the character of the support we are receiving. The cream of the youth and spirit of the country are being gathered into these movements . . . Who are being left us in the country?[62]

The appointment of Augustine Birrell as Chief Secretary in January 1907 brought the party to grips once more with the Liberal down payment on Home Rule. Redmond, Dillon, and O'Connor were undoubtedly aware, after their experiences of the previous year, that any proposal would be devolutionary and, as such, in the spirit of the Dunraven scheme championed by O'Brien. After all, MacDonnell, the

---

[62]Webb to Redmond, June 26, 1906, *ibid.*, MS. 15231/5.

originator of that scheme, was still Undersecretary. It is easy to appreciate the ridicule which met the introduction of Birrell's Irish Council Bill in May. It proposed to set up an administrative body with control over seven of the most important Irish governmental departments (excluding the police and judiciary) but having no legislative power. Birrell was more concerned with the effect of such a measure on non-Nationalists and moderates than with the claims of the Irish party. For this reason he refused to yield to the party's demand that the entire Irish representation in Parliament be ex officio members of the 107-member Council, something O'Brien had also felt to be necessary when he had commented on Bryce's draft of the bill the year before. Birrell had scant regard for the sensibilities of his Irish friends and justified his stand to the Cabinet in terms that might have been uttered by O'Brien: "to inspire confidence, and to conciliate moderate opinion in Ireland, the Council must be recruited from the most business-like and substantial men the country affords . . . an infusion of new blood is essential if the scheme is to work."[63] Paltry in financing and marred by an absence of trust in the Irish M.P.'s, to whom Home Rule had been pledged for twenty years, the Dunraven scheme almost seemed advanced by comparison. It took that balladeering muse of Irish history, the Shan Van Vocht, to do justice to the egregious measure:

> Is it this you call Home Rule,
>   Says the Shan Van Vocht;
> Do you take me for a fool,
>   Says the Shan Van Vocht.
> To be sending round the hat
> Five and twenty years for that
>   Isn't good enough for Pat
>   Says the Shan Van Vocht.

O'Brien, however, was pleased at the bill's introduction. Though he was abroad at the time, his articles in *Nineteenth Century* in July and August 1907 reveal that he accepted the Prime Minister's judgment of the bill as a great measure. It did not trouble him that as a concession of self-government the bill was "stingy to the verge of beggarliness." He firmly believed that the establishment of any representative body in

[63]PRO, Cabinet Minutes, CAB(1907) 37/88 no. 54, memorandum dated April 27, 1907.

Ireland, no matter how limited, would necessarily lead to the full concession of Home Rule. Redmond obviously believed this also, but the day had long gone past when the members of the Irish party could safely promise the Irish people's acceptance of any formula the government deigned to offer. This was a point O'Brien chose to ignore and Redmond or Dillon could not dare ignore.

Half hoping for a favorable response, Dillon and Redmond were finally forced to bow to the howl of derision that rose up on all sides, from Cardinal Logue, Archbishop Walsh, Healy, the *Independent,* and almost every county council and UIL branch in the country. The Ulster Unionist Council and the *Irish Times,* mouthpiece of the Southern Unionists, naturally urged opposition to the measure, reasoning that no protection was afforded to the interests of the minority! Even the *Freeman's Journal* joined in the hostility. Indeed, the unpredictable Patrick Pearse, attracted by the favorable educational clauses, seemed the only voice publicly calling for endorsement of the bill. At any rate, O'Brien became the scapegoat for the party's disappointment as it alleged that it was his support of the Dunraven scheme that caused the plan of Home Rule "by installments" to be taken up by the Liberal party. Redmond himself proposed the rejection of the bill at the National Convention on May 21, and the bill was dropped soon after. Birrell's natural good spirits deserted him, and he was even prepared to resign. He attributed the failure of the bill to the opposition of the clergy to the creation of a new education department in Ireland, and to the justifiable disaffection of the Irish M.P.'s, who had been kept utterly in the dark about the terms of the bill by Redmond and Dillon. He also had some sober reflections on the Undersecretary's involvement and some afterthoughts which would have found favor with O'Brien:

Our poor dear Sir Antony still thinks that if the Bill had been *much less* it would have got through!! Our mistake has been to have touched *Devolution* at all. *Home Rule* we could not give. We should have contented ourselves with *Land* Reforms and the *University* Question and . . . we should have taken altogether our own line and left Sir Antony in the lurch.[64]

[64]Birrell to Campbell-Bannerman, May 24, 1907, Campbell-Bannerman Papers, BM Add. MS. 41239, Folio 250b. However, "poor dear Sir Antony" MacDonnell may not have been displeased at the result. Writing to Bryce some days earlier, he bemoaned the increasing lack of cooperation he was receiving from Birrell and stated he looked forward to the rejection of the bill by the Nationalists because it would enable him to extricate himself from "an unpleasant position" (MacDonnell to Bryce, May 15, 1907, Bryce Letters, NLI MS. 11015). MacDonnell actually resigned one year later, a bitter conclusion to the career of one of the foremost British civil servants of his time. "And so," he wrote to his friend Alice Stopford Green, "one more Irishman leaves the field broken in hopes and in health because his

The Return to the Party

Thus, in Ireland in the summer of 1907, the prestige of the party had sunk to a very low ebb. Even A. J. Kettle, an honorary treasurer of the party, gave a nod to O'Brien's policy by calling, in vain, for an All-Ireland movement to encompass all classes and creeds because the Nationalist organization was too narrow to attract wealthy capitalists and landlords. In July, Dublin saw one of its first great public propaganda meetings of Sinn Fein. That organization had only just been strengthened by the adherence of Nationalist M.P.'s James O'Mara, C. F. Dolan, and Sir Thomas Esmonde, chief party whip. The *Irish People*, under a new editor, John Herlihy, was behaving very amicably toward Sinn Fein at this time. Herlihy had suggested to his employer, still abroad, that the time was ripe for endorsing the abstention policy. O'Brien, however, was still too much of a constitutionalist to abandon Westminster, although he did acknowledge the threat of Sinn Fein in a *Nineteenth Century* article, warning the party not to be surprised if their actions had brought the policy of abstention "within the pale of discussable politics."[65] But, short of that policy, he would have no objection to cooperating with Sinn Fein, and attempts to undertake this on O'Brien's behalf were contemplated at the end of the summer. O'Brien, having returned to Ireland, hoped that Tim Harrington could be induced to approach Sinn Fein but a party man as loyal as Harrington could hardly oblige. The object as Harrington saw it was not to destroy the party but to save both it and the League from the onslaught of Sinn Fein. He gently chided O'Brien, "Much mischief has been done in my judgment to the cause of re-union by the attitude taken up by the *Irish People* on this Sinn Fein policy especially with reference to the recent meeting at the Mansion House."[66] O'Brien's tolerationist policy, however, received encouragement from Sir Thomas Esmonde, recently recruited to Sinn Fein from the party ranks:

---

brother Irishmen mistrusted him and denied him their support." (MacDonnell to Mrs. Green, May 10, 1908, A. S. Green Papers, NLI MS 15089/12).

[65]William O'Brien, "The Breakdown in Ireland," *Nineteenth Century* 62 (August 1907):323–344. See also, Herlihy to O'Brien, May 30, 1907; O'Brien to Herlihy (copy), July 22, 1907, UCC William O'Brien Papers, Box AP.

[66]Harrington to O'Brien, October 12, 1907, UCC William O'Brien Papers, Box AP. The Mansion House reference alludes to a Sinn Fein disruption of a Nationalist meeting in that historic Dublin center by forging eight hundred admission cards, for which tactic Sinn Fein was praised by the *Irish People*.

The [Nationalist] movement has gone to the dogs. If it is to be saved it can only be saved on your lines as I have repeatedly said. Don't think for a moment that you are not doing good. You are doing splendidly and if you can manage to obtain the support of the young element in the country which is now looking on and doing nothing the future, such as it is to be, is yours.[67]

The negotiations appear to have gotten as far as Captain Shawe-Taylor's actually making contact with someone in Sinn Fein, though Arthur Griffith's biographer makes no mention of any such episode. O'Brien's intention was to hold a united demonstration in Dublin in January 1908, before the opening of the Parliamentary session. Brimming over with misplaced optimism, O'Brien told his ally Dunraven of his plans:

I am glad to say Capt. Shawe-Taylor's mission has been completely successful. The Sinn Feiners jumped at the idea. They quite recognised that there must be no attempt to turn the demonstration into one in favour of their own peculiar doctrines. They are quite content with the one principle of National Unity on the broadest possible basis, with a view of settling Irish questions among Irishmen themselves and are willing to do as much or as little as we may think judicious to forward the success of the demonstration . . . The grand difficulty is under what auspices it should be called? It would never do to have it summoned by the Reform Association or by any existing organisation whatever . . . we will have to be most careful to avoid alarming public opinion by anything that might look like a movement for the destruction of the Party.[68]

It required an alarming degree of self-deception for O'Brien to assume that Sinn Fein would enter such a blind alley in an effort to prop up a group of powerless landlords or a set of discredited Parliamentarians. Though nothing came of the scheme, the pressures that had been building up against the party rescued O'Brien from the hopeless situation in which his nonparty Parliamentarianism had landed him.

On the face of it, the chances of O'Brien's becoming reconciled to his ex-colleagues in the Nationalist party seemed quite remote in 1907. The year had opened with his claim for £5,000 damages against the *Freeman's Journal* for allegations it made in the previous year that O'Brien's policy on the Wyndham Act had rendered "unnatural services to insatiable landlordism" and that, furthermore, he had conspired with Lord Dunraven's devolutionist friends to set up a moderate Center party in opposition to the Nationalists. The libel suit had been

[67]Esmonde to O'Brien, November 21, 1907, *ibid*.
[68]O'Brien to Dunraven, December 28, 1907, NLI William O'Brien Papers, MS. 8554/9.

heard in Limerick during March, and all the old dirty linen had been washed anew in the courtroom and the press. O'Brien used his opportunity to depict Redmond as one kept in "degrading bondage" by Dillon and O'Connor, to brand the rank and file as "degraded slaves" of the leadership, and to denounce the Irish party in general as a "political murder club" for its expulsion of Sheehan and O'Donnell for their support of conciliation. The jury found that certain published speeches by Dillon and Redmond were indeed libels, but the one farthing damages it awarded was considered contemptuous and somewhat tempered O'Brien's victory. What the jury did not know, however, was that O'Brien was not being truthful when he asserted during the trial that from the time of his resignation in November 1903 until his reelection for Cork in August 1904, he had no communication of any sort with Lord Dunraven. Such a lapse from the truth is rare in O'Brien's case, and perhaps we should allow that he lied only to protect Dunraven. It is clear from the correspondence already cited in connection with the Reform Association that O'Brien in fact communicated with Dunraven all through 1904. Dunraven's own words reveal the engaging "conspiracy":

As we have to play-act at conspirators and approach each other shrouded in long cloaks and slouch hats, I suggest that you come here [described by Dunraven as a "temporary and practically unknown asylum"] tomorrow.[69]

We know, of course, that O'Brien would not have long maintained his secrecy. Had the Reform Association not been scotched by the Ulster Unionist uproar, O'Brien's All-for-Ireland program would not have had to wait five years to get under way. Given these dealings, however, the one farthing damages in the libel suit seem rather more just than contemptuous.

The most disconcerting aspect of this episode from the party's point of view was that Tim Healy acted as counsel for O'Brien. Inveterate enemies during the 1890s, O'Brien and Healy had moved closer together after the former's withdrawal from the party in 1903. In 1905 Healy was retained by O'Brien to defend John O'Donnell in a legal action, and in the next year a close collaboration developed for the preparation of O'Brien's libel suit against the *Freeman*. Besides, one of O'Brien's staunchest supporters among well-known Irish nationalists

[69]Dunraven to O'Brien (pencilled date "June 1904"), *ibid.*, MS. 8554/4. O'Brien's evidence is given in O'Brien, *Olive Branch*, 366.

was T. D. Sullivan, Healy's father-in-law. Now the two found common cause in their hostility both to Dillon and to the unrelenting *Freeman*. But if such common purpose were to profit by the protection extended to Healy by Cardinal Logue, who was regarded by Dillon as an irreconcilable enemy of an efficient and independent Party, then the threat to the party of the brilliant organizer O'Brien could reach formidable proportions. Thus, however dangerous Healy's presence might be within the party, the danger to the party of keeping both him and O'Brien at bay might prove even worse. Besides, as indicated above, the Sinn Fein was becoming an ever more menacing and effective threat to the party, as well. Conditions were therefore ripe for further attempts to entice the dissidents back to the ranks on terms which would destroy neither the independence nor the authority of the party. Nevertheless, the party would have to swallow a certain amount of its pride in accepting so venomous a critic back into the fold, particularly when young party bloods like Tom Kettle were giving blow for blow in their fight against "Dunravenism, Devolution, and sham Home Rule."

The first official attempt to readmit O'Brien and Healy to the party had taken place at the UIL National Directory meeting in June 1907. There the unity amendment of Thomas O'Donnell, M.P., found only eight supporters. Thereafter, however, the pressure on Redmond to restore the party's falling stock in Dublin, the center of Sinn Fein activity, forced his hand. First he enlisted the aid of Tim Harrington, a senior party colleague and former three-time Lord Mayor of Dublin, to reorganize the moribund UIL central branch in that city. The moderate Harrington also happened to be favorably disposed to O'Brien's conciliation policy; he had attended the latter's "reassembled Land Conference" on the evicted tenants question in the previous year. Feeling the need to broaden the base of the party in any quest for the men of substance it had always sought to attract, Harrington gave Redmond some cogent reasons for realigning with his former colleague, stressing in particular the need to divest the party's image of the sectarian bigotry introduced by Devlin's Ancient Order of Hibernians:

Their [AOH] program so far as I can learn . . . is in direct opposition to our policy of uniting all creeds and classes of Irishmen and though at the present they are all right and giving us good services the day of division and dissension will come . . . I believe now as I always did in union and conciliation as essential for the success of the cause . . . I believe your own position would be easier and more pleasant with the strong old hands such as O'Brien and Healy and if possible Sexton around you than to be in a position to be checked by every recruit within a few months or years of his admission to Irish politics.[70]

Notices also began to appear in the press from August onward urging the party leaders to call a unity conference with O'Brien and Healy. These came from district councils, boards of guardians, and UIL branches throughout the country. Pressure also came from Edward Lahiff, a member of the National Executive of the UIL of America, stressing that his contacts revealed O'Brien to be "ardently anxious" for a meeting. Whatever the degree of O'Brien's ardor, his erratic nature kept him playing with impossible alternative combinations, for during the second half of 1907 not only was he negotiating with Sinn Fein as recounted above, but he was also urging Dunraven to get some of his landlord friends to help lay the groundwork for a joint propaganda campaign on the conciliation theme.[71] Despite his capacity for self-delusion, however, O'Brien must have realized the hopelessness of his isolated position. This rendered him amenable to the approaches of the several negotiators then probing the possibility of reunion— Harrington, Crosbie of the *Cork Examiner*, Lahiff, and Alderman Stephen O'Mara of Limerick.

O'Brien's terms were conveyed separately to Crosbie and O'Mara and by them in turn to Redmond. He had four main principles, none of which seemed in any way objectionable:

1. The attainment of the fullest measure of Home Rule should be the first object of the party;
2. that pending the settlement of that question the party should work to obtain a Land Amendment Bill and a University Bill next session;
3. that the assistance of others outside the Party should not be rejected if offered; and
4. that every member of the party should be pledge-bound and that the pledge should be defined.[72]

Immediately, Redmond wrote to Dillon pointing out that a refusal to consider reunion "would be extremely bad and many of our best friends would think us in the wrong . . . If a bitter fight goes on I foresee very serious results and for myself I am about sick of it."[73] On the following

---

[70]Harrington to Redmond, August 20, 1907, Redmond Papers, NLI MS. 15194.

[71]Lahiff to Redmond, October 10 and 12, 1907, *ibid.*, MS. 15201/4. W. O'Brien to Dunraven, no date (July 1907), and Dunraven to O'Brien, December 26, 1907, in NLI William O'Brien Papers, MS. 8554/9.

[72]Crosbie to Redmond, November 15, 1907, NLI Redmond Papers, MS. 15177/5; S. O'Mara to Redmond, November 15, 1907, *ibid.*

[73]Redmond to Dillon (copy), November 16, 1907, *ibid.*, MS. 15182/15.

day, November 17, Redmond, appearing at a public meeting in Ennis, indicated his willingness to meet O'Brien in informal consultation and invited him to return to the party. When this was followed one week later by O'Brien's release of his proposals at a meeting in Ballycullane, County Wexford, it only remained to set the date for the informal meeting. This was duly held at the Mansion House on December 13, where Redmond and Bishop O'Donnell were confronted by O'Brien and his clerically-outweighed supporter the Reverend J. Clancy of Kilkee.

The preliminary negotiations broke down almost immediately on two main points: Redmond's insistence on the binding force of the party pledge, and O'Brien's demand for a formal convention to be summoned ad hoc to confirm any declaration of principles. While O'Brien himself would not have objected to the strict interpretation of the pledge (i.e., to "sit, act, and vote" with the party both *in* and *out* of Westminster), Healy, whom O'Brien insisted be included in any reunion, had long held convictions on the looser interpretation, which allowed a member freedom to follow his own political opinions outside Parliament. Fortunately for O'Brien, Healy was much less concerned at this time with reunion than with the Irish University question (in fact, he had only with difficulty been induced to become involved with the party once more). Accordingly, O'Brien was finally able to persuade him to agree to the strict interpretation. As to calling a convention, Redmond and O'Brien must have reflected that their respective positions were exactly the opposite of those they had held in the reunion negotiations in 1900—O'Brien on that occasion being anxious to avoid a formal party gathering. Redmond, however, would not budge on the convention ploy, holding—quite rightly—that O'Brien, with far less authority than in 1900, was again attempting to dictate to the party.[74] There were some anxious moments during the next few weeks as both sides strove to compose their differences. Dillon warned Redmond of the danger of stretching out the negotiations, while O'Brien comported himself as the champion of unity at public meetings: "I consider that a *very* serious situation has now arisen. O'Brien with great astuteness has to a very considerable extent outmanouevered the Party."[75] Admittedly, O'Brien was never one to make agreement easy. He was wont to protest his own

[74]O'Brien to Redmond, December 19, 1907, *ibid.*, MS. 15212/12; Redmond to O'Brien (copy), December 22, 1907, *ibid.*
[75]Dillon to Redmond, December 21, 1907, *ibid.*, MS. 15182/15.

innocence on all occasions, even when his newspaper was lambasting all and sundry. Davitt had once remarked that he was "more autocratic than the average Tsar." In the event, however, it was O'Brien who capitulated. On January 17, 1908, in a chracteristic about-face, he wrote to Redmond stating that he and his colleagues (Healy, A. Roche, D. D. Sheehan, and John O'Donnell) would answer the summons to the next party meeting. Sir Thomas Esmonde recanted his recent adherence to Sinn Fein and also returned to the party. The final act in all these wearying proceedings was the suspension of that citadel of faction, the *Irish People*. Thus ended, for a while at least, a disastrous phase of O'Brien's career.

Any study of Redmond's actions from 1902 onward suggests that he and Dillon were strange bedfellows. His approach to the Land Conference, his refusal to condemn the Land Act, his hailing of Dunraven's devolution scheme, his attempts to pacify O'Brien, and his acceptance of gradualism on the question of Home Rule—all this places him firmly on the side of O'Brien's views. His success in retaining the leadership of the party lay in the virtual dictatorship exercised by himself, Dillon, and the lately-coopted Devlin. He was also fortunate in that neither of the latter two aspired to first place. No tensions existed within the party between O'Brien's resignation and Birrell's Irish Council Bill to merit a rapprochement between the like-minded Redmond and O'Brien.

O'Brien, of course, could have done incalculable harm to the party if he had been less of a Parliamentarian. His allies obviously should have been Arthur Griffith and Sinn Fein, as well as those Nationalist-minded elements who, though not revolutionary, had become disillusioned by the party's remoteness from the cultural awakening that seemed to have more of the national spirit in it than the interminable party resolutions on land purchase, evicted tenants, artisan dwellings, redistribution, and the congested districts. But O'Brien himself was also hopelessly out of tune with the New Ireland. He remained as much a nineteenth-century agrarian as Dillon and as much a Parliamentarian as Redmond. Actually, he was so bereft of a popular policy that for years he did little besides repeating ad nauseam the iniquities of the "wreckers" and "shamfighters" who had mangled the Land Act of 1903.

His insistence on the efficacy of representation at Westminster probably cost him the support of Sinn Fein in 1907, as it definitely did in 1910. The one policy to which he stuck through thick and thin was that of conciliation or, as he indelicately called it, "conference plus business." He had a fanatical and childish belief that roundtable conferences could solve any problem, and his promiscuous though well-intentioned canvassing of this panacea, especially from 1910 onward, must have created as much boredom as his breeches had caused merriment twenty years earlier. He was also incurably blind to the obvious distrust of his program among those Southern Unionists who alone could give substance to his unceasing claim that a new spirit of conciliation was abroad in the land. The influential *Irish Times* rarely lost the opportunity to bring the implications of his policy before its readers:

So far as the maintenance of the Union is concerned we, perhaps, ought to wish him away, for there is a far greater danger of the British people being wheedled into conceding something in the nature of Home Rule than of their being bullied into it. The methods of Mr. Dillon and Mr. Davitt would never have induced the British people to lend £100 million on the security of Irish land . . . [76]

[76]*Irish Times*, May 11, 1905 (editorial); see also, *ibid.,* October 22, 1906 (editorial).

EIGHT

The All-for-Ireland League

S INCE O'Brien's official break with the party in 1903 he had
worked against it in a private capacity only—dabbling with devolution, waging a one-man press war against the *Freeman's Journal*, encouraging the opponents of the party, and using every opportunity to
accuse his former colleagues of deserting the interests of the rural population. But he had not before 1910 elected to capitalize on his influence
and wealth by organizing any formal opposition to the party. In fact, he
had made some electoral compromises with the party in Cork at the
general election of 1906. Also, after the Irish Council Bill was mooted in
1907, O'Brien began preparing to swallow the bitter pill of rejoining the
party. This, as we have seen, was effected in January 1908. It soon
became evident, however, that his return to the Nationalist fold could
not endure. Conflict was bound to ensue in that very year because the
government had been pledged to introduce legislation designed to
amend Wyndham's Act of 1903. Since the fourteenth meeting of the
National Directory of the UIL in August 1904 and at semi-annual
meetings thereafter, the order of business had always included
resolutions pointing up the deficiencies of the Land Act and demanding
amending legislation. The last such meeting had occurred on January
15, 1908, two weeks before the appearance of O'Brien and his friends at
the party conclave in London. Therefore, no sooner had O'Brien taken
the party pledge than he began to embark on the conference trail to ensure that some opposition would be presented to any proposals of the
government to water down land purchase.

What had in fact happened to land purchase was that the tenants
had applied for more loans than the Treasury felt able to finance. In
1909 £56,000,000 in sales agreements were pending, compared to
£28,000,000 of actual sales concluded since 1903.[1] Obviously, the ten-

[1] J. E. Pomfret, *The Struggle for Land in Ireland, 1800–1923* (Princeton, 1930), 302. The
Treasury had decided that only about £5,000,000 per year would be provided for the purposes of the Land Act, hence the large number of sales pending by 1909.

185

ants had had little desire to follow the advice of Dillon or the *Freeman's Journal* not to partake in the alleged O'Brien-inspired capitulation to the landlords in all that time. The landlords, too, had realized the advantages of the Act—cash payment to the vendor instead of in fluctuating stock, a 12 percent bonus, and the zonal system. However, in the same six-year period the price of land stock had fallen as low as twenty points below par, the cost of the difference being borne by the Treasury. By some maleficent design, the framers of the Act had provided that charges for any excess stock issued to raise cash to pay the landlords would be thrown on the Irish ratepayers if the Guarantee Fund (an Imperial contribution to Irish revenue, from Irish sources) was insufficient to absorb the charges. By 1909 the latter fund was exhausted. The landlords had realized the dangers and had rushed to sell before the axe fell.

A report of a departmental committee of the Treasury appointed to inquire into Irish land purchase finance was released early in 1908 which highlighted the breakdown of the financial provisions of the 1903 Act. The annuity payments from the tenants were not providing any margin to defray charges incidental to the working of land purchase or to meet losses on the excess land stock issued to raise the cash payments for the landlords. Since the government was not prepared to bear the burden of loss consequent upon the stock being at a discount, and putting the cost on the Irish ratepayers would be intolerable, the obvious course, therefore, was to restrict land purchase pending the return of a more favorable financial climate. O'Brien, therefore, was once more back in the position of defending the Act, not only from Dillon but now also from the designs of the government. In March, he wrote to his landlord friends to get up support for yet another reassembling of the Land Conference. The noes outnumbered the yeas. Lord Mayo would only join in conference if Redmond would. Nugent Everard felt too out of touch with his landlord friends to be of much use. Horace Plunkett also begged off, remarking that any conference in which he appeared would only invite the bitter hostility of Dillon. Wyndham wrote in kindly but practical terms, aware that not the party but the fall of Consols (British Government stock) had killed land purchase as he and O'Brien had conceived it.[2] Of course, nothing could come of any conference without Redmond's cooperation, and this was not forthcoming. In fact,

[2]Wyndham to O'Brien, April 14, 1908, NLI William O'Brien Papers, NLI MS. 11439/3. Dunraven's report on the attitudes of his various landlord friends is in Dunraven to O'Brien,

the latter had seen to it that O'Brien's efforts at a party meeting in April 1908 to denounce the Treasury report and recommendations (a graduated bonus and a higher purchase annuity) were defeated by 42 votes to 15. From this point on the amendment of the Act only became a matter of time.

Before the end of the year O'Brien had decided that his political future could no longer encompass membership in the Nationalist party. Still, it was not going to be easy to proceed alone, as his conversations with Dunraven disclosed. He conveyed his apprehensions to his wife:

We are quite at one as to the future. All he [Dunraven] lacks is energy. I suggested it would now be perfectly possible to move the farmers if five men would subscribe £1,000 apiece to defray the expenses of organisation. *He did not know any such five men* . . . without organisation and funds, nothing can be done to give expression to our views and neither men nor money are available. It looks more and more as if I will simply have to efface myself for the next session and stay quietly at home and await events.[3]

But since O'Brien had the energy of ten men and the optimism of a hundred, lack of support would never deter him for long. For the moment, he decided to brave the National Convention which had been called for February 9, 1909, to consider the Land Bill just introduced by Birrell. O'Brien was under no illusion that his views would receive a favorable hearing. He fully expected "Molly Maguire" to preside.[4] Undoubtedly, Devlin had prepared his forces well in advance by importing his Belfast peak-and-muffler brigade to stifle any vocal support for O'Brien's views. O'Brien now found himself at the receiving end of a scheme of organized bulldozing of opinion which he, ironically, had demonstrated so successfully at the April 1903 party convention which had endorsed Wyndham's Land Bill.

The convention, dubbed the "Baton" Convention by O'Brien because of the rough-housing of his friends by Devlin's "ushers," was

---

April 17, 1908, NLI William O'Brien Papers, NLI MS. 8554/12. For Plunkett's view, see Plunkett to Gill, April 6, 1908, Gill Papers (Plunkett Letters 1902–1923).

[3]W. O'Brien to Sophie, no date (from internal evidence, December 11, 1908), UCC William O'Brien Papers, Box BH. The italics are mine.

[4]O'Brien to Dunraven, January 4, 1909, *ibid.*, Box AR. *Molly Maguire* is the pejorative name given by O'Brien to Devlin's AOH organization, the Board of Erin. By 1909 that group claimed a total membership of 65,000, having benefited from the removal in 1905 of a ban by the Irish hierarchy directed against its sectarian secret-society proclivities. Cardinal Logue, however, continued to regard the Board with much distaste [P. G. Cambray, *Irish Affairs and the Home Rule Question* (London, 1911), 119–120].

one of the stormiest meetings ever held by the Nationalist organization. When O'Brien tried to speak against Birrell's proposals to whittle down the land purchase arrangements of the Act of 1903, his voice was drowned by noisy interruptions. The same hostility was accorded the speeches of his supporters, Father James Clancy and Thomas O'Donnell, MP. O'Brien's motion to reject the Bill found only twelve supporters. This was not the only protest at that meeting. Francis Sheehy-Skeffington proposed amendments critical of the party because of its weakness on Home Rule, and Laurence Ginnell, hero of the cattle-driving campaign in Leinster, called on the party to abandon Westminster and organize the Irish people to put an end to landlordism. The Land Bill was soon passed into law, having incorporated the recommendations of the Treasury Committee. Henceforth, landlords would be paid not in cash, as under the terms of the 1903 act, but in guaranteed 3 percent land stock which the vendor would have to accept at its nominal value. Considering the fact that the market price of the stock was then about 80 percent of its face value and had not been above par for over 10 years, the inducement to sell would clearly be affected. Furthermore, the 12 percent bonus on the price of each sale was discarded in favor of a sliding-scale bonus of from 3 to 18 percent, the largest amount being given for the least number of years' purchase. Thus, to obtain his 12 percent bonus under the 1909 act, the landlord would have to sell at twenty years' purchase of second-term rents, about five years' purchase less than the prevailing average rate. And as for the tenant, his annuity was increased from 3.25 to 3.5 percent, perhaps the sharpest impediment to land purchase. The government, with the compliance of the Irish party, had achieved its purpose—not to abolish land purchase entirely but rather to slow it down. By 1908, the number of holdings (including those under one acre) transfered or pending transfer under all previous land purchase acts amounted to about 316,000. This left over 280,000 holdings still unsold. Obviously, O'Brien's dream of abolishing landlordism was unlikely to be realized under the Liberals.

These were the circumstances which impelled O'Brien to ignore all odds and announce the All-for-Ireland program he had been planning in opposition to the party in the following month. Among O'Brien's supporters in Cork at this time was a small group of Sinn Feiners, and among them was Edward Sheehan. O'Brien had drawn up his proposed constitution for the All-for-Ireland League before the Nationalist

Convention and had given it to Sheehan for his comments. The latter sent an enigmatic reply:

One or two shrewd heads in Sinn Fein here in Cork are of opinion that your statement of principles would be better if you dropped the self-government references altogether . . . Of course, there will be people for a long while to come who won't see the reason for allowing the ex-landlords a footing in the national movement. All the colossal ignorance of the country is against it and Dillon will be obsessed by it through pure "cussedness" till he goes to the grave.[5]

Feeling more encouraged than forewarned, O'Brien reopened negotiations with Dunraven at the end of February: yet another "psychological moment" had arrived to unite "all classes and creeds." In his letter he could not refrain from claiming that "every section of Nationalists" in Cork—Gaelic League, Sinn Fein, GAA, UIL, and Land and Labour Association—was only waiting for the call to jump on his bandwagon. Such a statement, if not a figment of O'Brien's vivid imagination, could only have sprung from faulty intelligence of a kind which once assured him that Patrick Pearse "certainly . . . is no Nationalist."[6] In any event, he could at least count on the sympathy of Cork farmers who had not yet purchased their holdings and who would now find it increasingly difficult to do so. Many others also would adhere to his movement out of regard for his own great popularity or because it offered an opportunity to formalize their opposition to the party without going to the extreme of supporting Sinn Fein—after all, O'Brien was as little (or as much) compromised on the concept of Irish Nationalism as Redmond or Dillon. But would a movement confined to one—though large—corner of Ireland pose a threat to the official party? Moreover, would it attract those wealthy and influential landlord and Protestant elements needed to give it the spirit of mutual toleration that O'Brien thought necessary for viable self-government?

Dunraven's reply was both ambiguous and discouraging. While admitting that the time was ripe for an organization for conciliation and landowners' defence, he felt that politics was the rub: "for a general moderate policy including moderate and progressive Home Rule I am very doubtful . . . I do not think I could raise even so small a sum as £3,000 or £4,000 [to start a paper] among devolutionists and the few

[5]E. Sheehan to O'Brien, February 2, 1909, UCC William O'Brien Papers, Box AR.

[6]T. McCarthy to O'Brien, no date (from internal evidence, 1902), UCC William O'Brien Papers, Box AL, item 128.

members of the Irish Reform Association." Dunraven, however, promised to provide £3,000 of his own money, a promise he more than redeemed in 1910 and thereafter. Another disappointment was the refusal of Antony MacDonnell, now elevated to the House of Lords, to appear at the proposed inaugural meeting of the All-for-Ireland League announced in the *Cork Examiner* on March 20. His excuse was that as a Liberal peer he could not be present on a platform organized to denounce a Liberal Land Bill.[7]

Without money and landlord support, even so indefatigable a fighter as O'Brien was forced to desist. His decision was no doubt aided by a complete breakdown in his health. During the past year his infirmities included phlebitis, neuritis, rheumatic gout, and an operation to remove a cyst. He resigned from Parliament for the third time and in April 1909 left for a nine-month recuperation on the Continent. Dunraven, always more realistic than O'Brien, both before and after events, reflected that "to be perfectly frank it was I think perhaps a mistake to start a new organisation under the circumstances."[8]

The Elections of 1910

While O'Brien was recuperating on the Continent during 1909, the situation continued to deteriorate for the Irish party. The great hopes anticipated from the amended Land Act only materialized in a mangled form, for the concession of some compulsory powers to the Congested Districts Board hardly balanced the effects of the increase in the tenant's annuity to 3.5 percent, the conversion of the landlord's fixed bonus to a sliding scale, or the payment of vendors in stock instead of in cash. Since the majority of the sales under the 1903 Act averaged 22 years for first-term and nonjudicial rents and 25 years for second-term rents,[9] the landlord's own incentive would decrease to 10 percent or no bonus at all, respectively, in such cases. The result was a virtual breakdown in land purchase when the landlords in large numbers refused to sell under those conditions. A comparison of the purchase agreements under both acts offers an instructive commentary on the achievement of the earlier act in helping to settle the Irish land question:

[7]O'Brien to Dunraven, February 22, 1909; Dunraven to O'Brien, February 24 and 27, 1909, NLI William O'Brien Papers, NLI MS. 8554/10; MacDonnell to O'Brien, March 1, 1909, UCC William O'Brien Papers, Box AR.

[8]Dunraven to O'Brien, March 31, 1909, NLI William O'Brien Papers, NLI MS. 8554/10.

[9]Irish Landowners' Convention Reports, report of special meeting, dated January 20, 1909, in NLI Pamphlet Collection, Series IR 330941/i8.

1903 Act Number of Purchase Applications	1909 Act Number of Purchase Applications[10]
*1904: 17,247	*1910: 3,473
*1905: 54,124	*1911: 4,314
*1906: 33,051	*1912: 5,668
*1907: 29,266	*1913: 3,991
*1908: 72,386	
*1909: 11,145	

*For year ending Oct. 31.

The decline in the prestige of the party was also reflected in the reduced contributions to the Parliamentary Fund. In the six years ending December 1906, the annual average subscription amounted to £12,000. For each of the years 1907 and 1908 less than £8,000 was subscribed. As we know, the party leadership had become desperate about their financial situation as early as 1906. Only Devlin's Australian tour and O'Connor's visit to the United States rescued the party from penury. The situation did not improve after that, however, for in 1909 another tour by "T. P." was needed to fight the election in January 1910. The major weakness was due to the falling off in the number of UIL branches. The National Convention held in January 1902 claimed 1,230 League branches. By 1909 this number had been cut in half, while the number of branches in O'Brien's stronghold of Cork had dropped from 109 in 1905 to 17 four years later.[11] Sinn Fein, on the other hand, was most active from 1906 onward and became a formidable opponent of the party in Dublin. On the credit side, the party held up the Town Tenants Act (1906) and the Housing of the Working Classes Act (1908), two specifically Nationalist-sponsored measures of social reform. In addition, the party claimed credit for other measures executed by the government of their Liberal allies—the Labourers Act (1906), the Evicted Tenants Act (1907), and the Irish Universities Act (1908). In any event, the failure on the Home Rule question considerably dimmed the luster of these achievements. Furthermore, the onset of the government's battle with the House of Lords over Lloyd

[10]*Ibid.*, Reports for 1909/10 to 1912/13. Even Dillon finally acknowledged to W. S. Blunt some worth in the 1903 Act: "He [Dillon] told me a number of interesting things about Ireland. Wyndham's Land Bill [*sic*] has had the effect of changing the whole character of the peasantry. Instead of being careless, idle and improvident, they have become like the French peasantry, industrious and economical, even penurious. Marriages are now contracted later, though the limitation of families had not yet begun owing to Catholic influences" [W. S. Blunt, *My Diaries* (London, 1932), 710, entry for March 31, 1910].

[11]F. S. L. Lyons, *The Irish Parliamentary Party, 1890–1910* (London, 1951), 215; Cambray, *Irish Affairs*, 116; Minute Book of UIL National Directory meetings, 1904–1918, NLI MS. 708.

George's 1909 budget, aimed at the rich, had repercussions in Ireland. The proposed taxes on the liquor trade invited the hostility of Irish publicans and distillers toward the party for its coquetting of the Liberals. With O'Brien's friends, Healy, Sheehan, and seven or eight others barking at its heels, it was plain to see that the party was in for a rough time on the budget.

During the latter half of 1909, attempts were made to bring O'Brien back into the maelstrom of Irish politics. In September the newspaper *Sinn Fein* announced somewhat prematurely O'Brien's intention to reenter politics. The paper reckoned that he would find himself largely in sympathy with the official policy of the Sinn Fein party.[12] His letter to Dunraven in November indicates that he did indeed intend to be in Cork for the election in order to defend the constituency against the Redmondites and retain the county as the nucleus of any future Nationalist movement, but as to reentering Parliament, he avowed that nothing would induce him to do so. More damage could be done to the party by not giving it a further opportunity to divert the country by attacking him.[13] He gave the same reply to his friend Alderman Forde of Cork, who had written to tell him he would be the choice of his old constituency at the general election. It was probably the speech of Asquith, the Prime Minister, at the Albert Hall in December, with its half-promise of Home Rule, that made O'Brien change his mind on contesting the election. In addition, he undertook his fourth newspaper venture as a means of publicizing his views. On January 1, 1910, four days before he himself returned to Cork, the first number of the *Cork Accent* appeared, its program being to save Ireland "from the Degrading Thraldom of an Incompetent clique, who have Ruined the Irish Cause, Betrayed the Irish Farmer, and have converted the Irish Party into the despised tail of British Liberalism." Whatever benefit the Italian sun had conferred on his health, it had little affected his spleen. O'Brien's hand is evident in every line of that first issue. It confessed to be anti-Dillon, anti-Radicals, anti-Budget, anti-*Freeman's Journal*, and anti-Molly Maguires. A noticeable effort was made to display friendliness to Sinn Fein, which stood to gain from any journalistic opposition to the pro-Redmond *Cork Examiner*.

There was a definite purpose in the favor shown to Sinn Fein. Even before his formal return to Irish politics, O'Brien had sent the

    [12]Quoted in *The Times*, London, September 21, 1909.
    [13]O'Brien to Dunraven, November 5, 1909, NLI William O'Brien Papers, NLI MS. 8554/10.

troubleshooting Shawe-Taylor on another mission to Dublin to sound out Sinn Fein on a possible alliance. O'Brien's contact was a Dublin solicitor and supporter, James Brady, who had been endeavoring to wean Sinn Fein away from its hostility to Westminster. The plan was to create a National Council in Ireland which would decide when the Irish representatives should attend Parliament and which would control their actions once there. O'Brien would provide funds to run Sinn Fein candidates in the Dublin divisions in return for Sinn Fein support of O'Brien's candidates in the south and west. It was hoped that Sinn Fein would join with Brady and his friends in putting forward candidates under these conditions. Shawe-Taylor, accompanied by Tim Healy, met Brady on December 8 and assured him that the money would be forthcoming to support this plan. Accordingly, Brady wrote the next day to G. Gavan Duffy (not the Duffy of '48 fame), a solicitor friend and Sinn Feiner, requesting him to stand for election along with Brady on this policy. On December 10 Duffy declined the offer. Meanwhile, a special meeting of the Sinn Fein Executive had been called for December 20 to discuss O'Brien's proposals as conveyed through Brady. A report of this meeting was given by W. Sears, a Sinn Feiner who was present, in a letter to Duffy, and it indicates how seriously these overtures were considered:

There was a large attendance, including B[ulmer] Hobson, Madame Markievicz, O'Flaherty, [P. T.] Daly and Ald. Kelly . . . The debate was very similar to the last one: arguments on both sides the same. Ald. Kelly, Cuffe, Clare, Milroy and others being in favour of cooperation in the founding of a National Council . . . Result: Regret cannot cooperate because the Constitution will not allow us. Mr. Griffith was in favour of cooperation if possible.[14]

This fateful attempt of O'Brien to break out of his encirclement in Cork came to nothing, although it almost created an open split in the Sinn Fein ranks. Griffith's inclination to cooperate was dictated by his chronic lack of funds. He had begun publishing *Sinn Fein* on a daily basis in August 1909 and was most anxious for it to continue (it failed at the end of January 1910). P. S. O'Hegarty, the journalist and Sinn Feiner who had exposed O'Brien's "conspiracy" in a special number of the *Irish Nation*, claimed in the January 15 issue that O'Brien had been prepared to supply the funds necessary to keep Griffith's paper alive. Though this exposure put a stop to further negotiations, it appears that

[14]Quoted in S. O'Luing, *Art O'Griofa* (Dublin, 1953), 202. This same source (pp. 199–205) carries an account of these negotiations with Sinn Fein, which lasted from December 1909 to March 1910. See also W. O'Brien, *The Irish Revolution* (London, 1923), 66–68.

Griffith was loth to discard the possiblity of cooperation. Milroy as late as March 1910 was considering the introduction of a resolution at the next meeting of the National Executive on the creation of a National Council along O'Brien's lines. He claimed Griffith's support for such a resolution, but, of course, O'Hegarty's deathblow scotched all these efforts.

O'Brien's success in the January election must have exceeded his own expectations: eleven Nationalists independent of the offical party returned, and seven of them followers of O'Brien. Healy's presence in the latter group boded ill for the party's dominance of Nationalist debate in the House of Commons. So the national organization was split once more, O'Brienites *versus* Redmondites. Notwithstanding O'Brien's personal success in Cork, the votes showed that a considerable Redmondite opposition existed in the city. In fact, O'Brien had to share the division with his former supporter, A. Roche, since gone over to the Irish party. Moreover, the combined vote of the two O'Brienites only exceeded that of the Redmondites by a few hundred votes and was less than a majority of the votes cast.[15] Worse still, it was felt that the Protestant vote had gone not to O'Brien but to the spoiler candidate and ex-Lord Mayor, Sir Edward Fitzgerald. The O'Brienite following in the rural areas consisted of small farmers and agricultural laborers (the bulwark of Sheehan's Land and Labour Association). However, he was woefully lacking in clerical support, the Bishop of Cork being a partisan of the Board of Erin. Nevertheless, O'Brien's return to the political arena was noted with some foreboding in UIL circles in America, where the hostility of Clan na Gael and the AOH was diverting much-needed funds from the Nationalist representative body there. "The evil about Healy and O'Brien," wrote M. J. Ryan of Philadelphia (president of the UIL of America), "is not the harm that they may do to you in Ireland or Great Britain, but their every objectionable utterance is heralded here as evidence of dissension, and with the obvious purpose of chilling American ardor." The same letter contained some disturbing evidence of the party's difficulties in redeeming the pledges of contributions given during T. P. O'Connor's fund-raising tour.[16]

[15]The votes were: W. O'Brien, 4,535; A. Roche (Redmondite) 4,438; M. Healy (O'Brienite) 4,229; W. Murphy (Redmondite) 3,776; and Sir Edward Fitzgerald (Independent) 2,061 (*Cork Accent,* January 20, 1910).

[16]Ryan to Redmond, February 27, 1910, Redmond Papers, NLI MS. 15236/24. Ryan himself threw in the sponge in the following year, citing "Redmond's avowals of loyalty to England as a kind of setting at naught all the hopes of my life's workings" (copy of Ryan's letter to John O'Callaghan dated May 10, 1911, in *ibid.*, MS. 15213/13).

O'Brien's success was little setback to the seventy-one members returned by the Irish party, for the Liberal minority government was once more dependent on Irish votes in circumstances vastly more advantageous to the Nationalists than those of 1886. The year 1909 had seen the culmination of the Liberals' battle with the House of Lords with the introduction of Lloyd George's budget and its rejection by the upper house. Before the election Redmond, cognizant of the tenuous base of his support in Ireland, had begun to harrass the Liberal leaders for firm action on the Lords' veto—only the announcement of a measure limiting the legislative veto of the House of Lords would ensure the Nationalists' compliance with the budget (they had voted against the second reading). But Redmond's bluffing tactics on the budget were not appreciated by the Cabinet. A. M. Murray, the Master of Elibank and the Liberal chief whip, took least kindly of all to Redmond's posturing. Pondering the political possibilities in the revival of the Nationalist split, Elibank was soon in communication with Healy, who was now of one mind with O'Brien against the People's Budget, which O'Brien claimed was "the most gross and flagitious breach of the Act of Union." Healy indicated that he and his friends were willing to come to terms with Redmond on the budget if the whiskey tax were dropped and the stamp duties withdrawn. However, the approach to Redmond would have to be made by the Master, and Healy suggested that the latter reopen negotiations with the party on the basis of information received that the O'Brienites were agreeable to compromise and that it would be impossible for the government to treat with a divided Irish party. Negotiations were, in fact, opened, and on March 18 Elibank saw Dillon to arrange a March 21 meeting with him and Redmond, "after which," O'Brien wrote to Healy, "he is to let me know. If (as seems likely) the Master and his friends stand true to their offers to you and me, whatever is the upshot, we are bound to come out on top."[17] O'Brien had not reckoned on Redmond's remaining true to his own stand, however, and the anticipated cooperation fell through. It was probably this intransigence of Redmond and Dillon that evoked the hostile feelings which Elibank committed to paper after the crisis had passed:

During all these Irish negotiations two men who impressed me very favourably were William O'Brien and Tim Healy. O'Brien was an honest fanatic—a kind

---

[17]Murray to Asquith, February 28, 1910, *ibid.*, folio 5; O'Brien to Healy, March 19, 1910, NLI William O'Brien Papers, NLI MS. 8556/3. For Redmond's part in this affair, see F. S. L. Lyons, *John Dillon* (London, 1968), 316.

of mad Mullah. And Healy played the game throughout. But dire necessity compelled me to keep my eye on the big battalions, although I confess I was sadly tempted at one time to finance 20 or 30 candidates in Ireland to assist Healy and O'Brien, and I would certainly have done so if the Redmondites had failed us on the Budget and the Veto.[18]

What lends credence to these intentions is a private investigation on Elibank's behalf conducted mainly in Munster during March of that year. The result was a very lengthy report on the political situation in Ireland based on travel, observation, interviews, and casual talks.[19]

The report derived from interviews with peers, priests, professionals, farmers, traders, publicans, and policemen. It concentrated on an analysis of O'Brien's and Redmond's relative positions in the wake of the election and was quite balanced. Cork was described as the Mecca of O'Brien's movement, although his followers had won seats in Kerry and Limerick and some support of his policies was also evident in Mayo: "No one but William O'Brien could have created such a movement. . . . Perhaps the most striking circumstance is that he can consort and confer with the Irish Tories without anyone daring to doubt his fidelity to the Cause of the Irish people." The sources of O'Brien's popularity were seen as the part he played in the "too successful" Wyndham Land Act and his condemnation of the budget. The clerical opposition to his movement was also noted. However, the struggle between O'Brien and Redmond, it was thought, would be decided largely by money, and in such circumstances it seemed to Elibank's informant out of the question that O'Brien would achieve a greater triumph than his initial success.

It was O'Brien and his supporters who finally voted with the Unionists against the budget while Redmond, secure in the knowledge of legislative action on the veto, helped to pass the bill which became law on April 29. The outcry of the Irish publicans now mattered little, and the party could safely condemn O'Brienite objections as the "hysterical shriekings of played-out politicians." The cogent question was asked by Devlin in a fine speech on the second reading on April 25: "Why do not some of these ex-democrats who exhibit all this passion for the distillers and the landlords think of their better and higher and nobler days when they fought for the people?"

[18]Personal memorandum of A. M. Murray quoted in A. C. Murray, *Master and Brother* (London, 1945), 48.

[19]Unsigned report dated March 31, 1910, and marked "Quite Confidential" in Murray of Elibank Papers, National Library of Scotland, MS. 8802 ff. 39–45. There is a copy of this report in Lloyd George Papers, Beaverbrook Library, C/20/2/1.

Conciliation Resurrected

O'Brien's electoral success revived his project of an All-for-Ireland League, and this time he discussed the idea with Healy, whose friendship with Cardinal Logue could perhaps be put to use. "I have just had a letter from the Cardinal," Healy replied, "who has no belief in the possibility of any rapprochement in Ulster, and expresses the opinion that the founding of a new organisation would not be approved by public opinion." The sage Dunraven also tried to deter O'Brien by claiming that a start at that time would be premature, and Castletown, though promising to attend the inaugural meeting provided he would not be asked to speak, felt that "we are a little *previous* in hoping for people to join us."[20] But it was typical of O'Brien to rush in where angels—or even a cardinal—feared to tread. With an aplomb that boggles the mind, he dismissed all counsel, preferring instead the wayward opinions of Lord Shaftesbury (ex-Lord Mayor of Belfast) that a growing number of Protestants in the North were in sympathy with his policy. He closed off all argument in a letter to Healy with the apocalyptic observation "The establishment of the All-for-Ireland League is not a matter of choice, but of life and death."[21]

Although O'Brien in his paper had indicated clearly what he was against, he left the positive aspects of his program vague. The inaugural resolution of the new League on March 31, 1910, hardly differed from official Nationalist policy on Irish government—the call for self-government in purely Irish affairs, the completion of land purchase, relief from overtaxation. The overall spirit of the appeal, however, was conciliatory—to guarantee the Protestant minority inviolable security for all their rights and liberties. This was the policy of conciliation which O'Brien asserted had been laid down by Parnell himself in the manifesto issued in the aftermath of the infamous Phoenix Park murders. Moreover, the political cooperation of Protestants and Catholics in the cause of Ireland had been the foundation stone of Butt's original Home Rule Association. O'Brien now felt that a social and political union of these forces could be sealed by some, presumably millennial, Imperial Settlement "which will place on the side of the Imperial connection those boundless Liberal-Conservative forces in

[20]Healy to O'Brien, March 18, 1910; Dunraven to O'Brien, March 26, 1910, NLI William O'Brien Papers, MS. 8554/12; Castletown to O'Brien, March 23, 1910, Davitt Letters, NLI MS. 913.

[21]O'Brien to Healy, March 19, 1910, NLI William O'Brien Papers, NLI MS. 8556/3.

Ireland whose essence it is to reconcile property with poverty, religion with liberty."[22]

The fact was, however, that O'Brien had no clearly defined program on Home Rule and had paid little attention to it in the preceding decade while he was obsessed with the land question. The national question was to be relegated to the future, however distant, until the working-out of a conciliatory policy had removed all the barriers to a Home Rule shared by Protestants and Catholics alike. Pressure of events, of course, brought O'Brien down to earth and rendered progressively irrelevant his incessant harangues against the Land Act of 1909. Asquith's statement in the House early in April on the proposed legislation to curb the power of the House of Lords revolutionized the situation as far as Ireland was concerned. Now, Home Rule would be the main topic for Irish politicians to haggle over. O'Brien was shattered and could only convey his anguish to his wife:

[Asquith's pronouncement] is for me a position of the most cruel difficulties. Under no circumstances could a man occupy a more unenviable position. Anything of a depressing nature I say will go wholly against the grain in Ireland, where Asquith's pronouncement is sure to create a sensation. On the other hand it would be effacement to remain silent—so that it is one of the most cruel dilemmas of my life.[23]

With the real battle for Home Rule begun, O'Brien was left hopelessly on the defensive in Ireland. His League, confined to Cork now that his overtures to Sinn Fein had been rejected, was a tender growth indeed. A study of its meetings reported in the *Cork Accent* listed a mere handful of small villages, mostly located in the northern part of the county and certainly numbering no more than twenty, as having representation. By May 14 the paper was only able to report the existence of twenty-four branches. Indeed, considering O'Brien's close collaboration with D. D. Sheehan, one is tempted to conclude that even those few outposts were equally adapted to membership in the older Land and Labour Association—at least, the same place names appear in the listings of both organizations. At any rate, the new League would certainly be no match for the UIL. Whatever power it did possess was in the municipal politics of Cork City, where a vote for O'Brien's nominees represented more a parochial reaction against the Dublin bosses of the local party organization (O'Brien, after all, was "one of their own") than an endorsement of the policy of conciliation. Op-

[22]W. O'Brien, *An Olive Branch in Ireland* (London, 1890), 472–473.
[23]W. O'Brien to Sophie, no date, Macdonagh Papers, NLI MS. 11440/3.

ponents attributed his municipal successes to his largess, which was supposed, over the years, to have inspired the "tuppence for a pint, sir" cry with which corner-boys greeted visiting dignitaries. The League platform had little programmatic quality, whether in relation to Home Rule or to some alternative acceptable to moderate Unionists. It also lacked the support of the clergy and never overcame the hostility of Bishop O'Callaghan of Cork, who regarded All-for-Ireland as an unnecessary divisive factor in the constitutional movement. And most damaging of all, at least for the prospects of conciliation, was the noticeable absence of support from local Protestant elements, which the financial contributions of a Hutcheson-Poë or the speeches of a Dunraven could not balance.

The Irish party on the other hand had virtually the full support of the Nationalist press, the ear of the government, and the advantage of a sudden decline in the fortunes of Sinn Fein. The latter reversal was attributable not only to the apparent success of the Parliamentary strategy but also, though less so, to the aforementioned revelations in P. S. O'Hegarty's *Irish Nation* regarding the collusion of Sinn Fein elements in O'Brien's attempts to compromise the anti-Parliamentarian Sinn Fein position. Nor was O'Brien's position helped by the potent ridicule his movement endured from the shoneen-baiting D. P. Moran in the *Irish Leader*. Not the least effective deflating tactic was the coupling of O'Brien with his landlord ally as "Lord Dunraven and William Never Done Ravin'." Moran's barbs against what he termed the All-for-William League were potentially more damaging than all the tirades of Devlin and Dillon combined. Denouncing him for persisting in faction while the very nation was decaying, the *Leader* damned O'Brien's policy of conciliating Protestants as humbug and pointed out in more lurid terms what Dillon had been saying all along. The inaugural meeting of the League was greeted by Moran as follows:

The half-slave breaks out in the order in which the names of the speakers occur. Conciliation is too much for some constituents so they flop before lords and a colonel . . . All sincere converts are welcome on the Irish nationalist platform . . . [but] when men who are not converts are welcomed . . . the fact indicates subserviency and weakness and not conciliation. The first name on the list is that of Lord Dunraven. When did he become a Home Ruler? We understood he was only a Devolutionist. The second name [Castletown] is that of the grand secretary of a pernicious secret society, the Freemasons in Dublin . . . The third name on the list is that of Col. Hutcheson-Poë; when did he become a Home Ruler?[24]

[24]*Leader*, April 2, 1910.

This type of sectarian realism found no place in O'Brien's thinking, however, which is, after all, to his credit, inasmuch as a place would obviously have to be found for the Protestant minority (it was too big to ignore) if Home Rule were to encompass thirty-two counties. O'Brien's error was to extrapolate from the minimal support afforded by a few devolutionists the conviction that a veritable host of Protestants was waiting in the wings to declare themselves at the propitious moment. The only real non-Nationalist convert to his movement who was willing to carry the All-for-Ireland banner into Parliament was Moreton Frewen, formerly a landlord in Cork, a Tariff Reformer, and a convert to federalism. But even Frewen was less interested in Home Rule than in using his position as member for Cork northeast to buttress property against the Celtic demos.[25] Actually, none of O'Brien's landlord friends was strong on Home Rule, and it soon became difficult to discern whether O'Brien was leading them or they him, in the approach to be adopted to self-government.

During 1910 O'Brien's cause was sustained by wide public discussion in Great Britain on the merits of a federal solution to the Home Rule problem. To some, federalism meant a union whereby Ireland would have a Parliament in Dublin which would rank with the Dominion Parliaments of Canada or South Africa. Others, like Earl Grey, Governor General of Canada, preached federalism as a basis for Home-Rule-All-Round. Still others, Dunraven and T. A. Brassey for instance, wanted an Irish Parliament run along lines which would make Ireland not a Canada but an Ontario or a Quebec. Brassey wrote to O'Brien in April 1910 promising generous contributions to his campaign funds if only he would state his approval of this latter solution.[26] Although O'Brien would not risk a public statement on those terms, it is clear from his correspondence with Frewen that he had gravely weakened his concept of Irish nationality. Could it possibly survive the small claims he made for it in that letter?

I am quite with you that the Federal solution would be an excellent one, but even that form of Home Rule would, I am afraid, be too strong meat as yet for the Protestant minority. The letter you sent me gives a fair glimpse of their timidity and inertia . . . Whenever our movement has reached a certain point of strength, the true way out of the situation will probably be in Conference . . .

[25]Frewen's active role as a propagandist on behalf of Imperial unity is discussed in A. J. Ward, "Frewen's Anglo-American Campaign for Federalism 1910–1921," *Irish Historical Studies* 15 (March, 1967):256–275.
[26]Brassey to O'Brien, April 6, 1910, Davitt Letters, NLI MS. 913.

For the moment, it is sufficient for us to insist upon the general principle of Domestic self-government, leaving its form to be defined hereafter.[27]

O'Brien's task was truly formidable, and the wonder is that he bore, virtually alone, the crippling burden of financing a movement and a newspaper on behalf of a minority that refused to be conciliated. The *Irish Times*, the Unionist organ, welcomed the symptoms of conciliation in O'Brien's League, but warned its readers that the O'Brienites differed from the Redmondites only in method, for they both put Home Rule ("an impracticable policy") in the forefront of their programs.[28] The *Irish Times* boycotted O'Brien's views as effectively as did the *Freeman's Journal*. His tenacity must have been due in part to the implacable hatred he had come to feel for Dillon and Devlin. In August, Frewen received a despairing letter from O'Brien indicating that all he wanted Unionists like Barrymore to do was to dispose their class "to a sympathetic consideration of any *proposals for increased Local Government* in Ireland."[29] But even this moderate request fell on deaf ears. Attempts to carry the fight into the camp of the enemy were also a failure. A meeting at Crossmolina, County Mayo, almost had fatal results when revolver shots were fired and O'Brien's audience routed by toughs and priests. O'Brien reacted in lesser coin with verbal abuse in the *Cork Free Press* (successor to the *Cork Accent*). His bitter flailing of the party evoked the distaste of his former admirer Lord MacDonnell: "I view with abhorrence O'Brien's campaign," he wrote Alice Stopford Green. "I don't as you know follow Redmond, but I believe Redmond would accept any scheme. I have not sought to weaken Redmond's forces. That is what O'Brien is doing."[30]

In December 1910 the voters prepared for their second election in twelve months. O'Brien retained his strength in Cork but lost Kerry and Limerick. None of the fourteen candidates he fielded outside Cork was returned. One of the casualties was Healy, who was ousted from his old seat in North Louth. Frewen gallantly offered Healy his own seat, but with equal chivalry Healy declined. The election had been a

[27]O'Brien to Frewen, May 25, 1910, Frewen Papers, LC Box 30.

[28]*Irish Times*, April 1, 1910.

[29]O'Brien to Frewen, August 19, 1910, Frewen Papers, LC Box 31. The italics are mine.

[30]MacDonnell to Mrs. Green, November 29, 1910, A. S. Green Papers, NLI MS. 15089/13. The Redmondite–O'Brienite battles sometimes required the police to take a hand. In May 1910 a serious riot occurred between the factions in Newmarket, County Cork, and when the police fired on the rioters one man was killed (SPO, CBS–IG Reports, 1908–1920, Carton no. 15, Report for May 1910). Wild fracases between the opposing factions became a recurring nightmare of Cork City politics between 1910 and 1914.

debilitating financial drain on O'Brien's resources. One of Frewen's attractions was the hope he had held out for large American funds, and one of his stratagems was an attempt to convince Asquith that he had been instrumental in getting an assurance of £25,000 from American sources so that O'Brien could fight the December election, the purpose being "to strengthen [Asquith's] hands in dealing with Redmond." Despite these grandiose claims, no more than £3,950 ever found its way to O'Brien at that time.[31] Other blind-alley projects of Frewen's were a £40,000 testimonial for O'Brien to be donated by ex-landlords and tenant proprietors and, *horribile dictu*, a banquet for O'Brien in the Kildare Street Club, the Southern Unionist stronghold in Dublin.

O'Brien's position was too weak to lose a Healy, and before long he was petitioning Dunraven to get Frewen to retire in favor of Healy. It would not be possible to disturb any of the other All-for-Ireland M.P.'s, for a seat to them meant the difference between relative poverty and riches—they had been regarded privately by Frewen, somewhat unjustly, as "duffers and unilluminates." Actually, it was to prove not too difficult to dislodge Frewen, for the latter was becoming increasingly disillusioned by O'Brien's reluctance to oppose the Parliament Bill which had been introduced in February 1911—another of O'Brien's "cruel dilemmas." O'Brien apparently would have preferred an accommodation between Asquith and Redmond on both the House of Lords and Home Rule rather than the "idiotic veto intrigue" and, presumably, uncompromising Home Rule.[32] But Redmond held the votes and, thus, the initiative on the matter, and it was extremely naïve to hope that Redmond would or could prop up a body whose capitulation was the prerequisite for Home Rule. Publicly, of course, it was not possible for O'Brien to oppose the Parliament Bill and survive politically as an Irish Nationalist. Frewen's promise of American funds was contingent on O'Brien's taking an active stand against the attack on property represented by that bill. He would not, however, take that fatal step, as Dunraven reported to Frewen (if nothing else, this decision indicated that O'Brien was not entirely immune to political realities):

---

[31]See Dunraven to Frewen, December 22, 1921, and January 6, 1922; Frewen to Dunraven, December 28, 1921, Frewen Papers, LC Box 56; Frewen to Asquith, November 11, 1910, *ibid.*, Box 32. Frewen applied the same questionable tactics with Redmond, assuring him of more money than he could use if only he would come over to O'Brien's movement (Frewen to Redmond, November 17, 1910, Redmond Papers, NLI MS. 15188/9).

[32]O'Brien to Frewen, May 10, 1910, Cockran Papers, NYPL Box 17; O'Brien to Captain Stewart-Bam, February 6, 1911, Davitt Letters, NLI MS. 913.

I practically told him all that you say concerning possible American assistance
. . . [O'Brien] repeats over and over again the formula we know so well that opposition to the Parliament Bill or to John Redmond's policy would sweep him
off the face of the earth. He cannot see beyond the immediate conflict in local
county councils and so on *relying solely on his personal influence in discarding principle*
. . . I beg you to be very tender and conciliatory in dealing with him . . . He
might fly off the handle at any moment and quit; and that would be to us and
our whole [federal] movement a disaster . . . It is impractical and inconvenient
to the last degree that he will not act on his real convictions.[33]

This letter reveals as much about Dunraven as O'Brien. The former
was now using O'Brien for his own federal ends, whereas O'Brien was
apparently willing to accept something less than even a federal solution,
provided the Protestant minority was thereby conciliated. Nor were
Imperial arrangements Dunraven's only concern, as is evident from his
letter to Lord Grey, Governor General of Canada, attempting to recoup
the financial losses which were being entirely borne by O'Brien and
himself: "If socialism is to be successfully fought and a satisfactory
measure of Home Rule attained it can only be through William
O'Brien's new movement."[34] Such were the allies and opportunities left
to the former peasant champion—a dinner at the Kildare Street Club
or a part in the fight against the redistribution of wealth.

Agonizing Reappraisals

The passage of the Parliament Act in August 1911 was something of a
watershed in O'Brien's relations with the Unionists. Stiffened by Healy,
he had refused to vote against the bill, despite the admitted hostility of
Frewen and Dunraven to any weakening of the House of Lords. This
was the signal for Frewen to give up his Parliamentary seat, ostensibly
to make way for Healy's unopposed reelection, but his real feelings were
otherwise. Naturally, those few Southern Unionists who were sympathetic to O'Brien's policy though they held his movement at arm's
length, drew the obvious conclusions from this apparent failure of conciliation. Frewen conveyed their feelings to his Irish-American friend
Bourke Cockran: "Barrymore said to me yesterday at dinner 'Because
you are to resign therefore we in Cork no longer interest ourselves in
O'Brien and his Party and that being so we shall take no trouble to
register our people and without our support O'Brien has no future'."[35]

[33]Dunraven to Frewen, July 3, 1911, Frewen Papers, LC Box 35.
[34]Dunraven to Lord Grey, December 27, 1910 (copy), *ibid.*, Box 33.
[35]Frewen to Bourke Cockran, May 31, 1911, Cockran Papers, NYPL Box 17. Frewen

In reality, however, conciliation had hardly existed outside O'Brien's mind, and Barrymore could do no ill to O'Brien's policy that public disinterest had not already done. Healy was painfully explicit about the situation:

Redmondism holds the field and commands both press and pulpit . . . we have merely abstractions and high phrases to offer an entrenched garrison to induce surrender . . . it is in my judgment useless to talk compromise or conference. It would inevitably be rejected by the Government because the specific bears your crest and brand, while the Orangemen would dis-heed it as involving a trap or a surrender.[36]

The appearance on League platforms of a handful of Cork landlords and as many Southern Unionists did not count for much in the political balance. The powerful Irish Unionist Alliance completely ignored O'Brien's abstractions and carried on a relentless propaganda against Home Rule in any form. And the Earl of Mayo, one of the Land Conference landlords, had made his position clear in the Lords' debate on the Parliament bill when he asserted "that we do not want any sort of Home Rule at all in Ireland, nor do we want any form of devolution either." Nor did the return of O'Brien's supporters to Parliament necessarily betoken an endorsement of the conciliation policy. Those individuals were Nationalists of the old school—men like Gilhooly, who had fought coercion in the 1880s, or D. D. Sheehan, who had championed the cause of the agricultural laborers since the early 1890s. That the movement was kept alive at all was almost solely due to O'Brien's own determination and his wife's financial resources. In March 1911, Healy wrote to his brother that O'Brien had told him he had sold £13,000 of his wife's investments to finance the League. By May, the *Cork Free Press* was losing L500 per month and that loss was increasing. The only sizable contributions from outside sources that O'Brien ever got besides Frewen's £3,950 were two sums of £5,000 each to contest the election. One came from Thomas F. Ryan, one of Frewen's American antisocialist friends, the other from Lord Carnarvon (son of the former Lord Lieutenant) via J. L. Garvin. By December even

---

sometimes carried his preference for Unionism over Home Rule to extremes (he signed the Ulster covenant in 1912); see Frewen to Walter Long, August 24, 1911, Frewen Papers, LC Box 34: "I, were that possible, would see Ireland wiped off the map, unless . . . we can institute . . . a relation . . . which will strengthen us."

[36]Healy to O'Brien, September 1, 1911, NLI William O'Brien Papers, NLI MS. 8556/5.

Dunraven seemed prepared to throw him over: "William O'Brien is beat and the movement a failure," he wrote to Frewen. "Now is the time to prepare for the real struggle." Among his requirements was £40,000 and a more moderate, less personal *Cork Free Press* devoted largely to antisocialism.[37]

For O'Brien this was a sad condition in which to face the climactic battle then developing over Home Rule. At the end of 1911 the government began to ponder the bill it was pledged to introduce in the following spring. O'Brien's views were requested by Asquith, but he, like most, had very little to offer. For him, practical politics dictated a reasonable compromise to meet Liberal and Unionist opinion in England and to conciliate the Protestants in Ireland—in other words, a conference to hammer out "a courageous but moderate measure of experimental Home Rule."[38] This call to take the Home Rule debate outside the maelstrom of party politics presumed a state of affairs which bore no resemblance to the ominous grouping of forces which was now taking place in Ireland and England. Speaking for the Irish Unionists, Sir John Lonsdale declared they would be satisfied with nothing less than citizenship in the United Kingdom and the protection of the Imperial Parliament, and he rejected Redmond's minority guarantees as "paper safeguards." The Nonconformist Unionist Association, committed since 1888 to maintaining the Union, was spurred to action by the powerful support of Balfour, Lord Lansdowne, Edward Carson, leader of the Ulster Unionists, and others. Even that old conciliator George Wyndham urged his Parliamentary colleague Leopold Amery to "declare for Ulster and never abandon her."[39] And in the Nationalist ranks a polarization of forces was under way which pitted the Nationalist mass movement against James Connolly's Socialists and the revolutionary IRB.

The Home Rule Bill introduced by Asquith on April 11, 1912, did little to realize the hopes of Irish patriots, living or dead. James Connolly termed it a "gas-and-water bill" designed to reduce the authority of the Irish Parliament to that of a municipal council. The Nationalist

[37]For various observations on the financial condition of O'Brien's League, see T. M. Healy, *Letters and Leaders of My Day* (New York, 1929), 2:503; Dunraven to Frewen, May 9, and December 25, 1911, Frewen Papers, LC Boxes 34/35; Sophie O'Brien to M. Macdonagh, January 22, 1936, Macdonagh Papers, NLI MS. 11443/2.

[38]O'Brien to Asquith, November 4, 1911, Asquith Papers, The Bodleian Library, MS. Asquith 36, folio 7.

[39]*The Times,* London, October 23, 1911; J. W. Mackail and G. Wyndham, *Life and Letters of George Wyndham* (London, 1925) 2:708.

Convention, staged by Devlin, accepted it with enthusiasm. Patrick Pearse, the IRB leader, retorted that by accepting the bill Redmond had "sold Ireland's birthright for a mess of pottage." The All-for-Ireland League also held a convention in Cork, which grudgingly accepted the bill. O'Brien saw the scheme envisaged in the bill as "federal devolution" and was willing to accept it as a compromise, though realizing it was not "the dream of Irish nationhood." The fine points of legislative detail did not trouble him as they did Redmond and Dillon:

Any bill that goes in the direction of securing that good will and cooperation [of the Protestant minority] would be to my mind of infinitely more permanent value to Ireland than any mere politician's point as to whether this or that particular power was given to or withheld from the Irish Parliament.[40]

The differences between this bill and Gladstone's measure of 1893 were mere matters of detail. As a sop to Nationalist sentiment, the legislative body was, for the first time since 1782, designated an Irish Parliament, though it was to be subordinate to the Imperial Parliament. The limitations were as great, if not greater, than before, and representation at Westminster was almost halved. Dublin Castle was, indeed, swept away, but that hated symbol of English ascendancy the Lord Lieutenant was retained in all his panoply.

Having had time for reflection, O'Brien spoke on the second reading and gave considerable attention to Ulster. He believed that the bill did not go far enough in this regard and therefore urged a minority representation in the proposed Parliament out of all proportion to Protestant numbers and geographical distribution.[41] As an indication of the unreasonable lengths to which O'Brien would go to avoid ruffling Unionist feathers, he even deplored Hutcheson-Poë's attempt to organize a Dublin meeting to condemn Ulster's rejection of Home Rule. Without equal denunciation of his bête noire, the Board of Erin, it would, he said, be an insult to Ulster.[42]

But Protestants, North or South, were in no mood to be put off with paper safeguards. The Earl of Midleton, a leader of the Southern Unionists and one of those Cork landlords to whom the All-for-Ireland appeal was particularly directed, pledged his support against any measure of Home Rule. This is evident in his letter to St. Loe Strachey of the *Spectator,* the archpropagandist of Ulster's cause:

[40] *Parliamentary Debates* 36 (11 April 1912): 1468–73.
[41] *Ibid.* 37 (30 April 1912): 1919–31.
[42] O'Brien to Dunraven, October 1, 1912, NLI William O'Brien Papers, NLI MS. 8554/11.

We got nearly 3,000 people together in Cork representing Munster and the result of our meeting was an immediate demand for others . . . I am not one of those who talk of active resistance on the part of Ulster, but if anything of the kind takes place I am quite sure that there will be an immense mass of passive resistance in the south of Ireland.[43]

In all his years of exhortation, O'Brien could never assemble three dozen of Midleton's people to give support to his policy.

Orange reaction to the Home Rule Bill was swift and menacing. The Ulster Covenant to resist the setting-up of a Home Rule Parliament was followed in January 1913 by the formal establishment of the paramilitary Ulster Volunteers. Nationalist reaction was on two fronts: the Sinn Fein–IRB-sponsored Irish Volunteer movement and the revolutionary socialist Citizen Army, which, under James Connolly's inspiration, looked to national independence as the prerequisite to a new social order. The Parliamentary Nationalists, with their AOH and UIL supporters, were mere spectators of this development. They were progressively losing much of their credibility in Dublin through their aloofness to the bitter social struggle of the workers during the strikes and lockout of 1913—a predictable stand for a party leadership whose bourgeois consciousness had had scant regard in the past for the miserable plight of the working class. Redmond himself was positively alarmed at these complications of the political situation at a time when he needed all possible authority to keep Asquith from indulging in his favorite ploy of compromise.

O'Brien's reaction, not surprisingly, was to settle matters by conference and consent. He and Dunraven had been incessant in their appeals for a government-sponsored solution to the Orange-Nationalist impasse. As Dunraven realized, they were helpless to do anything else:

The trouble is that, at present, we are of no use to anybody. Useless to Unionists because we are Home Rulers though anti-Socialists. Useless to the government because we are anti-Socialist though Home Rulers. Useless to Free Importers and Fair Traders because we take neither side.[44]

But these appeals for a conference found little support except among a handful of men of no political significance. One curious response came from Captain J. R. White, son of the hero of Ladysmith, who

[43]Midleton to Strachey, May 4, 1912, St. Loe Strachey Papers, Beaverbrook Library, S/21/9. Dunraven detested Ulster's intransigent stand and gave an opposite view of the Southern Unionist attitude to Bonar Law (Dunraven to Law, September 8, 1912, Bonar Law Papers, Beaverbrook Library, 27/2/10).

[44]Dunraven to O'Brien, February 1, 1913, NLI William O'Brien Papers, NLI MS. 8554/14.

wanted to found a movement of Ulster Protestant Home Rulers which would link up with the All-for-Ireland League. White's talents, however, were more appreciated by James Larkin, the union leader, to whom he gave the benefit of his military knowledge during the Dublin strike.[45]

The conference method attained more acceptance when taken up by stronger hands than O'Brien's and Dunraven's. The purpose was to head off any confrontation between the government and Ulster diehards, but the desired result was something O'Brien never could accept—the exclusion of Ulster from a self-governing Ireland. F. E. Smith, a Unionist M.P., wrote to Lloyd George suggesting a conference be called by the King and then left for Belfast to review the 50,000 Ulster Volunteers. Balfour, who had endured years of social strife in Ireland in the 1880s, was one of the few, if any, who considered the social implications of the gathering crisis over Ulster. "I look with much misgivings," he wrote to Bonar Law, "upon the general loosening of the ordinary ties of social obligation. The behavior of Suffragettes and Syndicalists are symptoms of this malady, and the Government, in its criminal folly, is apparently prepared to add to these a rebellion in Ulster." He went on in prophetic strain to consider all the attendant evils—expeditions of Orangemen from elsewhere, imitation by Nationalist rebels, resignation of officers in army and navy.[46] In that same month of September Lord Loreburn, a former Liberal Lord Chancellor, published in The (London) Times his famous appeal for an unfettered conference between the leaders to avert the rioting and disorder that were sure to occur if the bill were either accepted or rejected in its existing form. Ruling out the bill as a basis for discussion was, of course, unacceptable to the Nationalists, who, at this stage, would have only the bill, the whole bill, and nothing but the bill. O'Brien welcomed Loreburn's appeal and blasted Redmond's rejection of it as "the asininity of a blundering windbag or . . . the deliberate betrayal of a scheming hypocrite"—words that were hardly intended to calm the stormy sea of Irish politics. Though Asquith dismissed Loreburn's plan as impractical, it generated much discussion and was, in fact, to be the excuse needed in the following year by a government which flinched from the challenge of Edward Carson's Volunteers.

[45]White to O'Brien, September 4, 1913, UCC William O'Brien Papers, Box AS.
[46]F. E. Smith to Lloyd George, September 26, 1913, Lloyd George Papers, Beaverbrook Library, C/3/7/1; Balfour to Bonar Law, September 23, 1913, Bonar Law Papers, Beaverbrook Library, 30/2/18.

SECOND THOUGHTS.

In the autumn of 1913 the possibility of the Government's excluding either four or six Ulster counties from the operation of Home Rule in order to appease the Unionists caused considerable apprehension among the Nationalist leaders.

The fear of the Nationalists, a legitimate fear ever since Winston Churchill's ominous references to exclusion of "three or four Ulster counties" as far back as August 1912,[47] was that a conference could only end amicably in an arrangement which would make special provisions for Ulster, thus diminishing the full claim. The UIL National Directory meeting in February 1913 resolved that the rejection of any scheme of mutilation of the country represented the unchanging sentiment of the Irish people. Devlin spoke at Dundalk in October, vowing as an Ulster Nationalist that he would rather have his head cut off than be cut away from the rest of his fellow countrymen. The Orangemen and their influential Tory supporters had less regard for their blood brothers in the South. By October 1913, Carson and the other leading men in Ulster were obviously prepared to ditch the Southern Unionists, sentiments in which Bonar Law fully agreed. A few weeks later Law

[47]Churchill to Redmond, August 31, 1912, Redmond Papers, NLI MS. 15175/9.

wrote to Walter Long that Asquith had at last made up his mind: "He [Asquith] told me definitely that he would propose to the Cabinet the exclusion of part of Ulster, either the four or the six counties, probably the six; that if they agreed he would then see the Nationalists; and my impression is that he had definitely made up his mind that an agreement on these lines is the only alternative to a general election."[48]

The exclusion of Ulster was anathema to O'Brien. As we have seen, to please the Protestant minority, he was prepared to accept even so tame a concession as the mere extension of local government. In fact, as he was later to state, O'Brien preferred no Home Rule to Home Rule for only three provinces. He differed from Redmond in that the latter wanted to force Ulster's acquiescence by having the government call Carson's bluff, whereas O'Brien thought she could be won over to accepting an Irish parliament only by inducement. He was willing to make large concessions to accomplish this—a veto to the Ulster party on objectionable Dublin legislation, double representation for Ulster constituencies and power to appoint county inspectors (RIC) and perhaps county court judges.[49] By March 1914, however, Asquith and Lloyd George had finally beaten down the opposition of Redmond, Dillon, and Devlin to the temporary exclusion of Ulster. All that fierce Nationalist rhetoric about "the interests of Ireland" fizzled to nought before the unwavering resolve of Ulster. O'Brien warned that if Ireland were once divided, she would remain divided. In fact, Bonar Law had decided this for himself even before the amending bill providing for six-year exclusion of Ulster was introduced in the House of Lords.[50] In a last desperate effort O'Brien responded to the resolution of the Irish Trades Union Congress's Parliamentary committee, expressing dismay and anger at the attempt to divide Ulster from the rest of Ireland. He called for a great demonstration in Dublin as a national protest against the proposed mutilation of Ireland. This project got as far as John J. Scollan, a Dublin member of the Irish-American AOH (not affiliated with Board of Erin), promising to circularize all the national societies and labor organizations if O'Brien would guarantee his expenses. It was expected that Jim Larkin, James Connolly, Arthur Griffith, Eoin

[48]Bonar Law to Lansdowne, October 8, 1913; Lansdowne to Bonar Law, October 10, 1913; Bonar Law to Long, November 7, 1913, Bonar Law Papers, Beaverbrook Library: 33/5/68, 30/3/16, 33/6/94.

[49]O'Brien to Birrell, November 10, 1913, Davitt Letters, NLI MS. 913.

[50]See Bonar Law to the King, March 8, 1914, Bonar Law Papers, Beaverbrook Library, 33/6/94.

MacNeill, Countess Markievicz, Tom Clarke, and several other extreme Nationalists would attend. Apparently Scollan got as far as securing the support of Sinn Fein and was still awaiting the word of the labor men when O'Brien suddenly called off the meeting on the grounds that there was no symptom whatever of spontaneous public feeling for the project. More than likely his withdrawal was an indication of his reluctance to be seen on the same platform with labor agitators, for whom he had as much distaste as did Dillon and Redmond. No doubt the distaste would have been mutual.[51]

His pathetic appeals for an Imperial convention ignored, O'Brien adopted the only constitutional course open to him in the final, irrevocable division on May 25. He, along with Healy and his little band of followers, abstained from voting on a bill which, as long as it was clogged by an amending bill, was "a Bill for the murder of Home Rule." His reward for this adherence to principle was misrepresentation in Ireland as an opponent of Home Rule and the decimation of his All-for-Ireland forces in the ensuing local government elections. The fate of the amending bill in the Lords confirmed his worst fears when on July 8 an amendment was passed providing for the permanent exclusion of Ulster. One did not need to wonder what would happen in six years if a general election were to return the Tories to power. Dunraven, disillusioned by the futility of the conference idea, sounded the proper note of impending disaster to O'Brien late in May: "It is too late. We are sitting on the very edge of a volcano and unless something occurs pretty soon to avoid an immediate catastrophe I do not see what chance a conference has."[52] The rumbling of the "guns of August" was certainly not what he had in mind.

[51]Scollan to O'Brien, March 25 and 31, 1914; O'Brien to Scollan, April 3, 1914, UCC William O'Brien Papers, Box AS.
[52]Dunraven to O'Brien, May 22, 1914, NLI William O'Brien Papers, NLI MS. 8554/15.

NINE

The Destruction of the
Irish Parliamentary Party

THE DECLARATION of war on August 4, 1914, found O'Brien, Redmond, and their followers rallying to the cause of the Empire. One could not have expected otherwise, considering their repeated expressions of loyalty to the Crown over the years. The whole thrust of O'Brien's conciliation policy was, as he often stated, "to complete the pacification of Ireland and her incorporation . . . in this Empire in spirit as well as in substance." O'Brien's wife was less politic in her interpretation of his action, being convinced that since his mother-in-law resided in Paris, O'Brien would do something "to give her and me pleasure by advising the Irish people to stand firm with the allies."[1] In any event, on the very day war was declared, O'Brien's *Cork Free Press* printed Dunraven's call to the government to draw off its troops stationed in Ireland and trust to Irishmen defending themselves in words almost identical to Redmond's declaration in the House of Commons on the previous day.

In the following weeks O'Brien's readers were told that the war had welded the Irish people together and that to secure Home Rule it was necessary to join with Britain in her hour of need. All this was in preparation for an All-for-Ireland League prowar rally at the Cork City Hall on September 2. The platform was one to excite a journalistic fit from the *Leader*—William O'Brien flanked by Lord Bandon, Lord Barrymore, and the Protestant Bishop of Cork. Barrymore, who had resisted for years O'Brien's conciliatory advances, was more than glad to cooperate on a recruiting platform. Redmond declined the invitation to join the demonstration, as did the Redmondite Lord Mayor of Cork (O'Brien had recently lost his majorities in both the Cork Corporation and the Cork County Council). O'Brien's statement speaks for itself:

[1] See unpublished reminiscences of Sophie O'Brien, NLI MS. 4217 (1914).

Every man worth his salt . . . has got to step into the fighting line as the comrade of two-thirds of the population of Europe in beating back the . . . bar-
barians . . . In fighting England's battle in the particular circumstances of this
war, I am convinced to the heart's core that we are fighting for Ireland's liberty
. . . Whatever armed help Ireland is to offer will have to take its orders and its
discipline from the War Office.[2]

There was no way, of course, in which O'Brien could have remained
silent without disavowing the policy of conciliation for which he had
long endured the whips and scorn of the Nationalists. As the enlistment
notices reminded the public, "to do nothing is to say 'No.'"

When Redmond took it upon himself to pledge the Irish nation to defend his part of the British Empire, he was not being presumptuous. In
the following months thousands of Irishmen flocked to the colors, ignoring the propaganda of Sinn Fein. Even the King's Own Scottish
Borderers, who had shortly before been branded as murderers for the
Bachelor's Walk "massacre," were cheered by the Dublin populace on
their departure for the front, although this also may have indicated rejoicing at their removal (Dublin had a notoriously bad record on
recruiting).

The loyal advice O'Brien gave his fellow countrymen had fatal consequences for his further influence in Irish affairs. In one blow he had
alienated his supporters among the Cork Nationalists. Frank Gallagher,
his editor, had attempted to dissuade him from this decision. Gallagher
was worried about the effects such open siding with Britain would have
on the All-for-Ireland League which he (Gallagher) felt was capable of
becoming an important section of the freedom movement. Almost immediately after the speech, the League began to melt away, and the
Cork Free Press declined catastrophically in circulation, to become moribund in 1915. In his book on those fateful years, Gallagher (under the
pseudonym David Hogan) states that many of the staff and printers of
the *Cork Free Press* were Sinn Feiners. One wonders how really committed they were, however, for immediately the war was declared the
paper devoted much of its space to the glorious exploits of the army
and, as a crowning insult to the traditions of a Nationalist press which
the younger O'Brien had done much to foster, began to print a section
on RIC affairs.[3]

[2]*Cork Free Press*, September 3, 1914.
[3]D. Hogan, *The Four Glorious Years* (Dublin, 1953), 224–225. (Note: Gallagher took up
arms as an IRA fighter in the Black and Tan period). For O'Brien's own admission of the
disappearance of the All-for-Ireland League, see O'Brien to M. Roycroft, no date (1916),
UCC William O'Brien Papers, Box AS.

O'Brien, however, was not to be denied, and while Asquith was shilly-shallying on the question of putting Home Rule on the Statute Book, he circulated a memorandum to all the members of Parliament setting out the terms of a settlement by consent. It called for concessions to the federalists and concessions to the Protestant minority at a time when the majority of the Irish people were crying for concessions to Irish Nationalism: "It is the essential vice of the present Bill that it does not contain a single provision of any substance to meet the deeply marked historical and geographical particularism of this block of one-fourth of the population." Therefore, he proposed that Ulster be given a direct suspensory veto on any bill of the Irish Parliament and, further-more, that the minority be given increased representation, up to at least 60 votes in the 164-member House of Commons.[4] But conferences had proven to be particularly futile in the recent past—the constitutional conference of 1911, the Buckingham Palace conference of 1914—and now the parties involved were too committed to their supporters to allow for free discussion, even if they had wanted a conference. Finally, however, the urging of Redmond and O'Connor moved Asquith to ac-tion, and on September 9 he promised Redmond that the bill would become law immediately, that an amending bill to deal with Ulster would be left over until 1915, and that the operation of the Government of Ireland Act would be suspended for a fixed period which Redmond presumed would be one year.[5] In reality, as one observer noted, Ireland was presented with "an undated check, given with the assurance that when it was presented the nominal amount would not be at the bank."

Recruiting

O'Brien, like the party leaders, accepted the Suspensory Act which ac-companied the royal assent to the Home Rule Bill on September 18. He did so out of loyalty in a time of war, but he could hardly have been pleased to do so. Redmond had what he wanted, the semblance of vic-tory, and Carson could hardly be in any doubt as to the greater victory

---

[4]O'Brien's "Memorandum on the Solution of the Home Rule Crisis," copy in Asquith Papers, Bodleian Library, MS. Asquith 39, folio 253.

[5]Redmond to Devlin, September 9, 1914 (copy), J. F. X. O'Brien Papers, NLI MSS. 13418–477/folder 36. Shortly before the one-year period was to expire, Denis Gwynn (later

he had achieved. The event unleashed the recruiting fervor of the Nationalists, and soon O'Brien, Redmond, Dillon, Devlin, O'Connor and others were seeking to make good Irishmen out of their followers by putting them into British uniforms. Redmond led off with the noted recruiting speech at Woodenbridge on September 20, having promised Field Marshal Roberts earlier in the month that he would deliver his exhortation as soon as Home Rule became law.[6] The *Cork Free Press* on the next day printed O'Brien's warning contained in a letter to an Irish-American journal: "Whether Home Rule is to have a future will depend upon the extent to which Nationalists in combination with Ulster Covenanters, do their part in the firing line on the fields of France." Dillon was no less profligate with Irish blood, condemning at Ballaghaderreen on October 4 the Sinn Fein attacks on Irish soldiers, protesting against the doctrine that a soldier in the British army could not be a good Irishman, and exhorting the Irish people to keep faith with England.[7]

The result of all this goading of Irishmen to join the ranks was a split in the Volunteer movement. Yet this split still showed how vastly outnumbered were the so-called Sinn Fein elements in the organization. Of the 167,000 Volunteers, almost 158,000 went along with Redmond as the newly-styled National Volunteers, in an apparent endorsement of the recruiting policy. This loyalty to the Empire, however, did not result in any accession of strength to the party apparatus. This could usually be measured by the condition of the party organization in America, and by the end of 1914 the situation there was extremely desperate. M. J. Ryan, the national president of the UIL of America, had gone over to its opponents. Bourke Cockran, who at one time or another had been wooed for funds by Redmondite and O'Brienite alike, felt the turning point had been reached with the acceptance of exclusion and must have shocked Moreton Frewen with the observation that "if a revolt were started in Ireland I think the Irish in America would support it to a

---

Redmond's biographer) published an article in *New Ireland* demanding Home Rule by September 1915. Redmond wrote him a stern letter on this proposal which Redmond said was "quite untenable in argument, and extremely mischievous" and a cause of embarrassment and trouble to the Party (Redmond to Gwynn, July 13, 1915, Redmond Papers, NLI MS. 15192/8).

[6] Lord Roberts to Bonar Law, September 11, 1914, Bonar Law Papers, Beaverbrook Library, 34/6/35.

[7] *The Times,* London, October 5, 1914.

man." The *Irish World,* so loyal in 1912, was attacking the party once more. And, most serious of all, contributions from American supporters were nonexistent.[8]

Neither did the success of Redmond in capturing the Volunteer movement result in increased enlistments. The stupidity and arrogance of the War Office in refusing to cater to Irish sentiment and allow the organization of specific "Irish" regiments did much to dampen the initial enthusiasm for the war effort. Figures prepared for the Cabinet early in 1917 show how ineffective were the appeals of all the "recruiting sergeants" of both sections of the Irish Parliamentary party:

	Total Enlistments Aug. 4, 1914–Dec. 2, 1916	Percentage of Male Population Represented by Enlistments[9]
England	2,911,474	17.24
Wales	183,500	17.32
Scotland	410,350	17.45
Ireland	108,388	4.96

Throughout 1915 increased Sinn Fein activity and the proliferation of antienlistment and anticonscription propaganda rendered the political climate highly volatile. O'Brien was alarmed by the increasing unrest, perhaps not realizing that to a large extent he himself had been responsible for the progressive alienation of youthful Irishmen from the constitutional movement. For five years he had carried on an unrelenting campaign of hate against the Irish party, constantly resurrecting dead

[8]Cockran to Frewen, March 25, 1914 (copy), Cockran Papers, NYPL Box 17. T. B. Fitzpatrick (treasurer, UIL of America) to Redmond, December 15, 1914, and March 5, 1915; P. Egan (vice-president, UIL of America) to Redmond, June 18, 1915, Redmond Papers, NLI MS. 15236/7.

[9]Extract from Appendix (Table 1) in PRO, CAB/23/1, War Cabinet no. 41, January 23, 1917. The figures for Ireland do not include enlistments from the Dublin Metropolitan Police area (Dublin city and parts of counties Dublin and Wicklow). These are estimated at 21,412 for approximately the same period, thus increasing the percentage figure in column 3 above to about 6 percent. However, these figures do not tell the full story of the involvement of Irish manpower in the war. For instance, they do not include Irishmen recruited in Great Britain. Also, at the outbreak of war, some 60,000 Irishmen were either serving in the army and navy or had rejoined as reservists. In addition, many thousands worked in British munition plants and other war-related industries. But even though another 25,000 or so were recruited during the remaining two years of the war, the enlistments in Ireland fell far short of requirements: as late as October 1916, an estimated 161,000 Irishmen were considered "available for military service." The failure of Lord French's recruiting drive in 1918, coupled with the resistance to conscription, demonstrate how little available Irishmen really were. [For various official reports on recruiting, see House of Commons: cd. 8168 (1914–16), 39; cd. 8390 (1916), 17. also, *Parliamentary Debates,* 105 (15 April 1918), 42].

issues in the interest of his own personal bitterness. Now his following had deserted him and had gone over to the revolutionary party. The County Inspector (RIC) reported to headquarters in 1915 that the Irish Volunteers (the IRB faction) in West Cork were composed of men who had formerly given their allegiance to O'Brien's All-for-Ireland League:

They are active propagandists, bitterly disloyal, and if only for their negative effect on recruiting, are potential dangers. They are almost entirely composed of farmers' sons, of military age, who before the war were followers of Mr. O'Brien, M.P., but who are now in opposition to his war policy. Their organisers are known suspects, and their cry against conscription and war taxes appeals to the O'Brienite farming classes.[10]

Deprived of any public support whatsoever, O'Brien took up the federal scheme he had all along thought too advanced for the Protestant Unionists who, he had convinced himself, were only awaiting the magical moment to show themselves. The time had come, he thought, for yet another association, but, as he explained to the disillusioned Frewen, the initiative would have to come from others. This time the talisman was to be a Federal Conciliation Association to be modestly started by influential Irish Unionists. "Neither Redmond nor Carson, nor, of course, myself, need be in the first instance brought in," he wrote rather presumptuously. Two months later, in May 1915, he suggested that as a Unionist savior to rouse the Irish gentry there could be none better than Walter Long—better still, if he were appointed Lord Lieutenant with a cabinet seal.[11] It should be remembered that Walter Long was one of the most active propagandists against Home Rule, federalism, or anything at all purporting to weaken the Union in the slightest way. O'Brien, however, had not taken leave of his senses, as one might be forgiven for thinking. He had a genuine fear of partition, and no one realized better than he that the "settlement" already approved by the party could only result in the permanent exclusion of Ulster. This eventuality hardly seems to have troubled the Nationalist leaders at this stage. Though Frewen did eventually get to see Carson, the scheme, of course, came to nothing. Nevertheless, O'Brien persisted in his utopian projects, even to the extent of canvassing quite politically insignificant individuals to take a lead.

As the year 1915 drew to a close, the issues that concerned Irish

[10]B. MacGiolla Choille, *Intelligence Notes, 1913–18* (Toronto, 1970), 147–148.
[11]O'Brien to Frewen, March 10, 1915 (copy), NLI William O'Brien Papers, NLI MS. 8557/5; O'Brien to Frewen, May 21, 1915 (copy), Macdonagh Papers, NLI MS. 11440/3.

politicians were not Home Rule and conciliation but conscription and recruiting. The reorganization of the Cabinet during the summer sent a shiver through the Nationalist ranks. The fear that conscription might be part of a new government policy was hardly allayed by the fact that Carson was now a member of the Cabinet and that none of the chief officials in the Irish Administration—the Lord Lieutenant, the Chief Secretary, the Undersecretary—was an Irishman. Redmond had been offered a Cabinet post but, naturally, could not have added this supreme capitulation to his list of surrenders. The Nationalists lost no time in warning the government that vigorous resistance would be offered to any conscription policy. In this they represented the feelings of all Irish Nationalists, including the O'Brienites. Though it is highly probable that Redmond personally would not have objected to conscription's being applied equally in Ireland and England, he was in no position in 1915 to flout Irish opinion on this subject as he had done on recruiting at the outbreak of the war. During the autumn conscription became virtually the sole topic of conversation in rural districts. In order to minimize the danger, the party began to take a renewed interest in recruiting: if enlistments could be increased, conscription would not be necessary.

Redmond's recruiting fervor had reached such a pitch that opponents began to taunt him as the "recruiting sergeant" for the British army. In December 1915 he wrote to his Cork supporter J. J. Horgan of his desire to attend the Lord Lieutenant's proposed recruiting conference in that city: "Of course O'Brien will be present but that would not deter me unless it would offend our people . . . When I am ready to meet Carson etc. etc. it seems to me absurd to refuse to stand on the same platform as O'Brien."[12] The plan never materialized, not because of the dislike of the Cork Redmondites for sharing anything with O'Brien but because of the effect such a meeting would have on the dwindling body of Nationalist supporters, large numbers of whom had defected to Sinn Fein. This did not deter Redmond from doing the War Office's work elsewhere. On February 2, 1916, in the first of many such meetings, he shared a recruiting platform at Galway with the Lord Lieutenant, Birrell, the Marquis of Sligo (one of the largest landowners in Ireland), and several M.P.'s. It was a particularly slavish performance—praise for the RIC; chastisement for the war-shy farmers; pleas to maintain the army; joy at the numbers of men with the colors;

[12]Redmond to Horgan, December 4, 1915, Horgan Papers, NLI microfilm p. 4645.

contempt for antiwar propagandists; a call for an Irish Press Agency for recruiting; and a warning that to break faith with England would be "to prove ourselves a nation of reckless, irresponsible, unthinking men, utterly unworthy of self-government."[13] These gatherings were marked by a noticeable absence of clergy.

O'Brien did his share of recruiting also. On February 19, the *Cork Free Press*, allegedly manned by Sinn Fein members, printed Dunraven's arrogant letter condemning the Irish "loafers" for not doing their bit. But others also wanted recruits. Patrick Pearse, the spirit of the "Irish" Ireland which had passed O'Brien by, sent out his own call in May 1915:

We want recruits because we believe that events are about to place the destinies of Ireland definitely in our hands, and because we want as much help as possible to enable us to bear the burden. The political leadership of Ireland is passing to us—not, perhaps, to us as individuals, for none of us is ambitious for leadership and few of us fit for leadership; but to our party, to men of our way of thinking; that is, to the party and to the men that stand *by Ireland only* . . . [14]

This ringing cry epitomizes the revulsion that disillusioned Nationalists had come to feel for the cringing constitutionalism that had blighted the hopes of the younger generation. Not long after that call and with fewer recruits than expected, Pearse and his separatist republicans entered the General Post Office in Dublin and sounded the death knell of the Irish party.

The Easter Rising

O'Brien received the news of the Easter Rising of April 1916 with predictable horror. Gallagher relates that O'Brien, who was isolated in London at the time, wired an editorial deploring the revolt as "heartbreaking folly," believing it to be Socialist in origin and led by sansculottes and the down-and-outs. Apparently the reaction led to a stormy scene between O'Brien and his editor, who went over to London to remonstrate. Only the threat of resignation by the entire staff, according to Gallagher, induced O'Brien to moderate his views and agree not to adopt an anti-Sinn Fein policy. Nevertheless, the editorial when it appeared was most severe:

[13]*Freeman's Journal*, February 3, 1916. Redmond achieved his apotheosis on St. Patrick's Day, when he reviewed a battalion of the Irish Guards in the company of the King and Queen and Kitchener. Redmond was pinned with shamrock by the Queen herself (*ibid.*, March 18, 1916).

[14]P. H. Pearse, *Political Writings and Speeches* (Dublin, 1952), 121.

All Irishmen who have any sense of proportion will regret more deeply than it is possible to describe that such events have happened. The object which lay behind the inauguration of the Irish Volunteer movement was from the very first a misguided one. It was idealistic and—impossible. In war time above all others it was sheer lunacy ever to hope that it could succeed . . . For the leaders of this expedition [the abortive landing of German firearms on the coast of Kerry] and for those who actively cooperate with them here at home there must be nothing but immediate condemnation. They were men of no mental balance.[15]

The Easter Rising had taken everybody by surprise, the constabulary most of all. Only a week before it occurred the Inspector General had reported to Sir Matthew Nathan, the Undersecretary, that "apart from the disloyal and mischievous activity of the Sinn Fein faction, the state of Ireland was on the whole fairly satisfactory."[16] Actually, the authorities were justified in their complacency. The number of separatists was small, and before the event it was quite common for groups of them to be abused by the wives and relatives of soldiers at the front. Nor did this change during the immediate aftermath. Robert Brennan, a leader of the Wexford Republicans, related how he and his comrades were received after their arrest: "The crowd left no doubt in our minds as to what they wanted done to us . . . I was surprised to see a number of Redmondite Volunteers in green uniforms mingling with the British soldiers. They joined the British in jeering at us."[17] Numerous rural and urban councils and boards of guardians, all controlled by Home Rulers, passed resolutions condemning the insurrection. Only Laurence Ginnell, the Independent Nationalist member of Parliament, immediately protested the executions. Dillon, hitherto noted for his attacks on Sinn Feiners, made a spirited defence of the bravery of the insurrectionists, but only on May 11 when the executions were nearly over. Irish Nationalists, Redmondite and O'Brienite alike, were incapable of understanding that Irish nationality in Pearse's concept was a spiritual thing, not the negotiable merchandise of the Parliamentarian. Had they realized so, they would not have "opened for business" again as rapidly as they did. When General Sir Nevil Macready on May 1 invited Redmond to a recruiting conference with Carson, the Irish leader indicated his willingness but not "for a few

[15]Hogan, *The Four*, 226; *Cork Free Press*, April 29, 1916.
[16]SPO, CBS–IG Reports 1908–1920, carton no. 15 (Report for March 1916).
[17]R. Brennan, *Allegiance* (Dublin, 1950), 73.

days," when it would be more propitious. This reply came after the executions of Pearse, Thomas Clarke, and Thomas MacDonagh.[18]

Though the party was eager to stop further executions, the motive appeared to be related to the concern for its own survival. When Redmond proposed to Dillon that he (Redmond) raise a question in the Commons on the effect of the executions, Dillon was careful to point out the complexities involved: "I very much dislike the form of your proposed question. It would *not* be true to say in a general way that 'the executions which have taken place have produced profound popular resentment in Ireland,' and such a statement would be contentious." On the next day, the May 9 meeting of the party in London condemned the rising as mad, futile, and "a dangerous blow at the heart and hopes of the party."[19]

Dillon, of course, had grossly understated the situation. Within a few days of the execution of fifteen leaders the inevitable reaction set in, and overnight "assassins" became "martyrs." O'Brien on reflection conceded privately that the rebellion was "the inevitable revolt of the unselfish young men of Ireland against the shameful collapse of Parliamentarianism."[20] Dillon said as much to C. P. Scott, in terms that scarcely concealed his true feelings:

The executions had converted the Sinn Fein leaders from fools and mischief-makers, almost universally condemned, into martyrs for Ireland. Redmond . . . had largely lost his influence in Ireland . . . [with the danger that] Nationalist Ireland would be divided between the Sinn Feiners and the O'Brienites who were now striking an attitude of ultrapatriotism.[21]

O'Brien's *Cork Free Press* soon began to present an altogether favorable attitude toward Sinn Fein, presumably because of the influence of its editor. Though the paper continued to point the lesson that physical force had been proved useless and that what was needed was a united constitutionalism, the editorials took on a distinctly heroic

[18]Macready to Redmond, May 1, 1916, Redmond Papers, NLI MS. 15262/5. Dillon and Redmond were prepared to accept the executions of the leaders, especially of Connolly and Kent. Their major concern, apart from the rescue of the constitutional movement, was for the rank and file, especially for any wrongly-arrested AOH men (see Dillon to Redmond, April 30 and May 2, 1916; Redmond to Dillon, May 1, 1916, Redmond Papers, NLI MS. 15182/22). Dillon had the highest praise for the Undersecretary: "but for him the Castle would have been taken" (Dillon to Redmond, May 2, 1916, *ibid.*).

[19]Dillon to Redmond, May 8, *ibid.*, MS. 15182/22. For the minutes of the Irish party meeting, see NLI MS. 12082.

[20]O'Brien to Father Madden, May 20, 1916, UCC William O'Brien Papers, Box AS.

[21]C. P. Scott, *Political Diaries of C. P. Scott*, edited by T. Wilson (London, 1970), 206.

view of the rebels and damned Redmond and the Irish M.P.'s for their anti-Sinn Fein utterances. Possibly O'Brien himself was gratified at Birrell's evidence to the Hardinge Commission on the causes of the Easter Rebellion that "the sneers of the O'Brienites and the daily 'naggings' of the *Irish Independent* contributed to the political eclipse of Home Rule."[22] Home Rule was identified with the party, and O'Brien hated the party with an abiding fury. The public's reaction against the party, however, did not serve to restore O'Brien's political fortunes. No one heeded his call to supersede the Hardinge Commission by a tribunal composed of the prime ministers of Canada, Australia, South Africa, and others to investigate a settlement of the Irish question by consent. In June he called a meeting in Cork to protest partition as a warning to Lloyd George, who had just been commissioned by Asquith to take up the Irish problem. The meeting was a disaster and marked the finish of O'Brien's career as a popular politician. The gathering was broken up by Cork Republicans, who drowned out O'Brien's every word with shouts and songs.

O'Brien kept his paper going for another few months, though the financial burden was almost intolerable. At the very beginning, in 1910, the amount of capital subscribed to the paper had not been enough to keep it going for more than a few months. Only Dunraven's help and O'Brien's own enormous advances kept it alive over the years. Now with the war depleting his wife's investments and the remainder soon to be lost by the confiscations of the Bolsheviks in Russia, it was becoming impossible to maintain the paper.[23] The militant tone of the *Cork Free Press* in its final months was in marked contrast to the tone of the party press and, according to Healy, was a matter of some concern to H. E. Duke, Birrell's replacement as Chief Secretary. One reader expressed his thanks to O'Brien, who cannot have been overjoyed at the nature of the audience to which his paper was appealing: "The *Cork Free Press* is doing good work which is much appreciated by those of Republican sympathies. Since Easter it is being sought for in many districts in which it was previously not circulated."[24] The editorial in the issue of

[22]*Cork Free Press*, May 27, 1916.

[23]For details of the financing of the *Cork Free Press*, see copies of O'Brien's letters to various correspondents dated for February and March 1916 in UCC William O'Brien Papers, Box AS. Information on Mrs. O'Brien's war losses are in Lord Eversley to O'Brien, February 5, 1923, *ibid.*, Box AT. [Note: It was Eversley (Shaw-Lefevre) who introduced O'Brien to his future mother-in-law].

[24]T. M. Healy, *Letters and Leaders of My Day* 2:576; Hogan, *The Four*, 228; J. M. Kennedy (Thurles) to O'Brien, October 1, 1916, UCC William O'Brien Papers, Box AS.

September 30, however, betrayed all the hesitance about embracing Sinn Fein that had distinguished O'Brien's attitude over the years. "It is to the Sinn Fein party that Ireland must now look to mould the future of her people," the editorial began and then went on to dismiss the idea of a republic or of armed revolt. Sinn Fein could not desert the constitutional path that had won great legislative victories in the past. Rather, the physical force leaders should throw in their lot with those Nationalists who were contesting the next election. These statements also reflect the general confusion among the Parliamentarians as to the nature and purpose of Sinn Fein. The real exponents of physical force had been those IRB and Citizen Army elements which had carried out the Easter rebellion. They were Sinn Feiners only in the sense that any nationalist who was not a follower of Redmond or O'Brien was so. But the leaders had all been executed and the rank and file were in jail, without leadership and organization. Those who found inspiration in the political component of Griffith's doctrine may have been republicans or separatists, but they were not necessarily physical force men. As originally conceived by Griffith, Sinn Fein offered the solution employed by Hungarian separatists against the Habsburgs in 1862 when they refused to attend the Reichsrat, denied there was a link with any other Habsburg dominion other than the personal one of a common monarch, and asserted full freedom to dispose of Hungarian affairs. The Habsburg dissolution of the Hungarian Diet was answered by a campaign of passive resistance which won the famous 'compromise of 1867'—the establishment of the dual monarchy. Adapted to Irish circumstances, this tactic would require the withdrawal of Irish MPs from the Imperial Parliament, their joining with locally elected officials in a newly constituted National Council, and a willingness to passively resist any British retaliation. In the aftermath of the Rising, it seemed a solution practical enough to attract the majority of those disillusioned with traditional parliamentary tactics. Ulster Unionists on the other hand might have drawn the conclusion that their place in a dual-monarchy Ireland would parallel that of the repressed minorities in post-1867 Hungary.

All O'Brien's previous attempts to use Sinn Fein for his own purposes foundered on the question of the withdrawal from Parliament. It was his inability to desert Westminster even in the face of disappointment and betrayal that had prevented O'Brien's association with the youthful elements of the *new* Ireland over the past ten years. Even as late as October 1916, Herbert Pim, a well-known Irish Volunteer organizer and member of Sinn Fein, invited O'Brien to withdraw his followers from Westminster and work with Sinn Fein in Dublin. O'Brien refused and instead had one of his supporters contest the seat made vacant in West Cork by the death of Gilhooly. His candidate lost to the Redmondite. In Cork City, his fortunes were no better. Since the hostile reception given his prowar rally in that city in September 1914, he could have been under few illusions regarding the Republican nature of Cork Sinn Fein. Now, in 1916, he was unable to make even a public appearance to air his views—his antipartition rally of June, as we have seen, was broken up by Republicans. Finally, in December 1916, O'Brien lost the last effective link with his constituents when he stopped publishing the *Cork Free Press*. To keep the paper alive since 1910 had cost him £30,000 of his wife's savings.[25]

The Home Rule Crisis

William O'Brien was among those canvassed by Lloyd George for suggestions on a settlement of the Irish question. On May 31, 1916, he sent a memorandum to George on the now-familiar strain of a settlement by conciliatory conference.[26] Couched in the vaguest terms, it called for some future, undefined federal arrangement as the most practical choice, for no solution could contemplate the partition of Ireland. But, he felt, the setting up of any provisional government in Ireland "while the present high fever lasts" was out of the question. Actually, his real preference, he added, was for "slower and better matured action" but this (presumably some tame devolutionary measure) was also left unexplained. For the moment it would suffice to obtain a parliamentary resolution, "passed with anything approaching to unanimity," for a settlement by consent. This, he expected, would appeal to young Irishmen in Ireland and America and win over Carson, Bonar Law, and Long. In addition, enough harmony would ensue so that both groups of Volunteers, North and South, could be formed into a National Guard, which would be fertile ground for recruits for the British army.

We do not know what Lloyd George thought of O'Brien's

[25] Pim to O'Brien, October 25, 1916; W. O'Brien to M. O'Brien, June 15, 1916, UCC William O'Brien Papers, Box AS.

[26] O'Brien to George, May 31, 1916, Lloyd George Papers, Beaverbrook Library, D/14/1/44.

suggestions, but it is tempting to assume that he wished his real Irish antagonist were the airy O'Brien rather than the hard-faced Dillon. Quite obviously, O'Brien had missed completely the lessons of the Easter Rising, which, indeed, had changed everything. His concept of Irish nationality was not quite as indestructible as he used to profess, and his concern continued to be mainly to lull the apprehensions of Unionists. The minimal nature of his demand for the satisfaction of Irish hopes is evident from a letter he wrote to Frewen two weeks before he outlined his suggestions to George. In stressing the high-level conference idea, he explained to Frewen that any settlement could only take effect when the war was over and should be "on the lines of making the Irish Unionists an invulnerable power and even (if they have the sense) the possible ruling power in an Irish Parliament."[27] The solution he envisaged, still essentially devolutionary, could never have satisfied the aspirations of an immeasurably strengthened Sinn Fein movement.

Among his observations was one of the few percipient recommendations on the problems of the Irish working class to emanate from Irish Nationalist politicians—the elimination of the Dublin slums. "The horrors of the Dublin slums," he wrote "contributed materials to the recent Rebellion greater than all other causes put together." No one at the time could have been unaware of the horrible living conditions of the working classes in Dublin where over 20,000 families lived in one-room tenements. O'Brien's solution to this problem, however, set one social reform measure against another, for the money to finance urban housing was to come from the saving of the government's contribution under the National Insurance Act of 1911 if that measure were repealed insofar as it applied to Ireland. Since the repeal of that legislation would abolish the vested interest of Devlin's Board of Erin, a registered friendly society under the act, one hopes that O'Brien's new-found concern for the urban poor was not motivated by his desire to inconvenience his enemies.

Meanwhile, those Southern Unionists so much coddled by O'Brien were using all their efforts to press the government into repression in Ireland. As they had formerly flooded England with propaganda against Home Rule, they now attempted to stir British resentment with the details of Irish "disloyalty." Lloyd George told Dillon that he had to use his influence to prevent some of the more gruesome letters from

[27]O'Brien to Frewen, May 17, 1916, NLI William O'Brien Papers, NLI MS. 8557/5.

reaching some newspapers.[28] Walter Long, who O'Brien thought would rush to a conference if invited, was the most vigorous opponent of any settlement and an important force within the Cabinet for preventing capitulation by the government on Ulster or for bringing the Home Rule Act into force before the end of the war. Lord Midleton, acknowledged leader of the Southern Unionists, was more concerned about keeping the five hundred or more Sinn Fein prisoners in the Frongoch internment camp than solving the Irish question. On May 25 a great meeting of Midleton's groups was held in Dublin to impress on the government their opposition "to instituting a new system of Government in Ireland which shall be binding after the war."[29] This group included names often mentioned by O'Brien as essential for inclusion in his conciliation gambits—Lords Barrymore, Kenmare, Bessborough, Beresford, and Desart. That other great Unionist association the Irish Unionist Alliance was also actively spreading propaganda against concessions.

As for Dillon and Redmond, they were equally blind in expecting the government to cede to Nationalists in a time of war the control of even three provinces, when the overriding concern of the Irish Administration was the prevalence of civil disorder. In Ireland it was becoming increasingly evident that those same Nationalists were fast losing the trust of the people. No one was more aware of this than Dillon—a startling change from his unaccustomed optimism of a few weeks before. His gloomy letters to O'Connor were driving that bland character to despair. The major concern of the Nationalist leaders was whether the June convention of the Ulster Nationalists would endorse the agreement they had just come to with Lloyd George—the *temporary* exclusion of Ulster and immediate Home Rule. The chances of this were not good, as O'Connor related to George:

Up to the present the signs are all bad outside Belfast where Joe [Devlin] and good sense are strong . . . Redmond will probably play his trump card in announcing his resignation if they [Cardinal Logue and the bishops] vote the Settlement down; and this will leave these gentlemen face to face with the Red Spectre, which is now the certain and only alternative of the Settlement. Dublin (and other parts of the country) are much worse than I thought. Sinn Feinism has become an infection and almost universal mania—not only among the masses but also among some of the middle classes.[30]

[28]George to Dillon, June 10, 1916, Lloyd George Papers, Beaverbrook Library, D/14/2/24.
[29]See Midleton to Asquith, May 26, 1916 (copy), *ibid.*, D/14/1/26.
[30]O'Connor to George, no date (assigned to June 11, 1916), Lloyd George Papers, Beaver-

The Nationalists, with the help of Devlin's skill at convention-packing and the threat of Redmond's and Dillon's resignations, duly got the approval of temporary exclusion from the Ulster wing of their movement.[31] However, the Irish party was merely a pawn in the weighted game of chess being played behind the scenes. The alternating threats and pleading of the Irish party leaders were as nothing compared to the unbending resolve of Unionists Carson, Lansdowne, Selborne, and Long, along with their less resolute allies Chamberlain, Bonar Law, and Curzon. Asquith and Lloyd George, even had they desired (which is not at all certain), could not have moved such a mountain of resistance. On July 22 the government confirmed to a shattered Redmond what O'Brien had been maintaining for three years: that the temporary exclusion of Ulster was an impossibility. Even Lloyd George's devoted secretary felt he had behaved badly and had not played the game with his Irish supporters.[32]

O'Brien received the news with great bitterness and gave a stinging rebuke and prophetic warning to the government two days later in a speech in the House:

If once Ireland were, by the votes of its own representatives to accept dismemberment, that act could never be undone except by a bloody revolution . . . The work, I am afraid, will have to be left to other men and other times. The real cause of the recent rebellion in Ireland was not pro-Germanism or German gold. The real cause was that you have driven all that is best and most unselfish among the young men of Ireland to despair of the constitutional movement by all your own bungling, your ignorance, your double-dealing in reference to Home Rule in this House, but, above all by the methods by which you have

---

brook Library, D/14/2/27. O'Connor was the "softest" of all the leaders on the integrity of the Irish demand. In March he had indicated to Scott his desire that George's offer to join the coalition should be accepted by the party (Scott, *Political Diaries*, 188). In June, he condemned the way in which "all kinds of empty-headed rural Councils" were passing resolutions against exclusion (O'Connor to George, June 16, 1916, Lloyd George Papers, D/14/3/5).

[31]The meeting was held in Belfast on June 23, and the voting indicates the patent injustice of the simple majority-vote rule. The figures for Antrim and Down testify more to Devlin's power than to the self-denial of the voters.

	For	Against		For	Against
Armagh	62	32	Down	117	13
Antrim	129	7	Fermanagh	36	58
Derry	67	60	Tyrone	64	85
			Totals	475	255

(NLI MS. 708, Report of July 3, 1916, meeting of National Directory.)

[32]F. Stevenson, *Lloyd George, A Diary* (London, 1971), 109.

governed Ireland during the last six months. You have thereby filled the hearts of multitudes of the best men of our race with loathing of Parliamentaryism, British or Irish, and by an inevitable reaction you have raised up another more formidable secret society whose ideals are, at all events, pure, and who have proved their courage to fight and die like men for these ideals.[33]

Though O'Brien was ever fearful of agreement on the exclusion of Ulster, nevertheless he greeted the breakdown of the recent negotiations with unconcealed delight. For the moment, the national and geographical integrity of Ireland were out of danger. In an article in *Nineteenth Century* in September he dismissed as future solutions both partition and any settlement negotiated by the professional politicians, especially the Redmondites who by their agreement on Ulster had forfeited the right to dictate any further action to the Irish people. The thing to do was to appeal for a settlement by conference over the heads of the politicians and party wire-pullers, just as in 1902 the Land Conference Committee had appealed over the heads of the Landowners' Convention. Ever generous to the "historic necessities" of the Unionists, he proposed as a basis for agreement: (1) a disproportionately increased number of Ulster M.P.'s in the Irish Parliament, and (2) right of appeal against Irish legislation to the Imperial Parliament. It took one of his beloved Southern Unionists to inform him (O'Brien could hardly be convinced) that the Protestant opponents of partition were so not because of a love for Home Rule but because of a desire to maintain intact the Union. The parallel of the Land Conference was rightly dismissed—that meeting did not have an iota to do with Home Rule. Besides, any solution which was designed to give a larger representation to any faction than was justified by numbers was of course entirely impractical.[34]

Unlikely as O'Brien's solution was, his basic idea of a conference had some relevance to the impasse that had been created on Home Rule. Shortly after the appearance of his article in *Nineteenth Century*, Lord Wimborne, the Lord Lieutenant, sent his own suggestions to Lloyd George for a "conference of representative Irishmen of all parties" to be assembled in Ireland under the chairmanship of an Imperial referee, possibly Louis Botha, Prime Minister of the Union of South Africa.[35]

[33] *Parliamentary Debates* 84 (24 July 1916): 1455–56.

[34] W. O'Brien, "Is There a Way Out of the Chaos in Ireland?," *Nineteenth Century*, 80 (September 1916), 489–506; H. W. Blake, "Reflections of a Southern Unionist," *Nineteenth Century*, 80 (October, 1916), 734–739.

[35] Wimborne to George, November 6, 1916, Lloyd George Papers, Beaverbrook Library, E/3/9/2.

But there were other pressures that also tended to divert government minds from the preoccupations of war—the growth of Sinn Fein, now the general appellation for all the extraconstitutionalist forces in Ireland. General Sir John Maxwell, "executioner" of the 1916 leaders, was recalled under pressure in November 1916 and replaced by General Sir Bryan Mahon, an Irishman. Immediately Sinn Fein propaganda took on new life, and several new Nationalist and Republican journals appeared. The continued internment of many of the Nationalist rank and file excited popular sympathy for the movement, while in America there was a complete swing in favor of Sinn Fein.[36] The Chief Secretary used this shift in popular opinion as one of the excuses for releasing the internees. Late in December the Cabinet met to discuss the question. It was clear that Imperial and American pressures were the paramount considerations:

From the Imperial point of view, the War Cabinet were more especially influenced by the fact that, according to reliable information, failure to release the prisoners earlier contributed largely to the defeat of the proposals for Compulsory Service in Australia . . . (also) they considered it would be desirable to take any action which might tend to foster the impression in the U.S., as well as at home, that the new Government was approaching the Irish question in a generous but not timorous spirit.[37]

Hoping that official mercy might facilitate the application of conscription to Ireland, Lloyd George, Prime Minister since the recent fall of Asquith, accordingly released the Irish prisoners. The reception accorded them on their arrival in Dublin left no doubt as to the general sympathy for Sinn Fein. In marked contrast to the scorn which the rebels received the previous April, wild cheering was the order of the day. It also afforded an opportunity for many public bodies to rescind the resolutions they had earlier passed condemning the Rising. Next, on February 5, 1917, Sinn Fein won a sweeping victory at a by-election in North Roscommon, the successful candidate refusing, as was the policy, to take his seat at Westminster. This was as much a concern to the government as to the despairing Irish party.

The mounting unrest in Ireland, the defection of the younger priesthood to Sinn Fein, and, in April 1917, America's entry into the war, were potent reasons for making another attempt at negotiation.

---

[36]For a despairing assessment of the affects on the party of the growth of Sinn Fein sentiment in America, see O'Connor to Devlin, August 1, 1917, J. F. X. O'Brien Papers, NLI MSS. 13418–477, folder 36.

[37]PRO, Cabinet Minutes, CAB/23/1, War Cabinet no. 14, December 21, 1916.

Lloyd George began to regret he had not "played the game" the previous summer and informed Carson of his difficulties, citing the pressure of representations from the American and Australian governments, countries with sizeable Irish populations. It seemed that another conference was in the offing.

Early in March, W. S. Adams, the Prime Minister's secretary in the War Cabinet, reviewed the critical situation in Ireland. It would have brought supreme gratification to O'Brien had he known that Adams cited Dunraven's Land Conference as evidence of good to be obtained from a meeting of interested Irish parties. Adams's report, prepared for the War Cabinet, contained the first reference to what was soon to emanate from Lloyd George as a possible solution—an Irish Convention. In order to counter the political influence of Sinn Fein, which, as Adams noted, had revolutionary, Republican, anticapitalist, Socialist, and nonrevolutionary elements, the government should take the initiative by expressing the wish "that Irishmen, representative of different parties, should meet together to consider the position of Ireland, and to see if they can reach any arrangement for the peace and well-being of their common country . . . This purely Irish Convention or Conference should sit in Ireland."[38]

Despite the fact that none of O'Brien's conference suggestions had so far been taken up, he was not one to be discouraged. While the Prime Minister was laying the ground for the ill-fated Irish Convention, O'Brien had sent a lengthy memorandum to Bonar Law reflecting the spirit of Lord Wimborne's call for a conference of representative Irishmen of all parties. This proposal envisaged an Advisory Committee composed of the Lord Mayor of Dublin; the Lord Chief Justice; the Protestant and Catholic Archbishops of Dublin; two peers of the realm; the chairman of the general council of County Councils; W. Redmond; W. M. Murphy (owner of the *Independent* and bane of the Dublin working class); Colonel James Craig (the Ulster diehard); Lord Northcliffe (proprietor of *The Times*); and General Gough (the hero of the Curragh mutiny)—but not one Sinn Feiner. A greater insult to Irish Nationalists of the new school, let alone the timid Nationalists of the Irish party, would be difficult to conjure up.[39] The actual proposal showed that O'Brien had not advanced one whit from the Empire-conscious posi-

---

[38]Adams to Lloyd George, March 1, 1917, Lloyd George Papers, Beaverbrook Library, F/63/1/1.

[39]Holograph copy of O'Brien's memorandum attached to letter of Craig to Bonar Law, March 28, 1917, in Bonar Law Papers, Beaverbrook Library, 81/4/33.

tion of his All-for-Ireland days. The Imperial Parliament was to be supreme in other than domestic affairs. The Irish Senate and House of Commons were to be given extraordinarily facile means of appeal against any legislation of the Irish Parliament. And there was to be double representation for most Ulster constituencies.

Egregious as O'Brien's solution was, it was certain, however, that the Irish problem could only be solved among Irishmen themselves. No action, however, had been taken on Adams's suggestion, so the latter repeated his call for an immediate initiative by the government.[40] On May 16, 1917, Lloyd George at last took the bit between his teeth and wrote to the Irish leaders, O'Brien included, suggesting two solutions for the Irish question. One was impossible to accept, for it contemplated exclusion of Ulster. The other was for "a convention of Irishmen of all parties for the purpose of producing a scheme of Irish self-government."[41] O'Brien's agreement to the holding of a convention was considerably dampened on the following Monday (May 21), when it became clear during the debate in the Commons that the convention would consist of a large number of individuals from the ranks of the Nationalist organization, or, as O'Brien branded them, "a mob of Hibernian partisans." What he meant by a convention, of course, was a small group of a dozen or so notables similar to the Advisory Committee he had outlined in his suggestions to Bonar Law two months earlier, though now it suited his purpose to claim a place for Sinn Fein in the persons of either Arthur Griffith or Professor Eoin MacNeill.[42] In addition, any agreement come to by such an august body should, he felt, be submitted to the Irish people by referendum. He did not explain, however, how the Northern Protestants could accommodate that suggestion to their covenant against Home Rule in any form. Therefore, believing that the inclusion of a large bloc of either Ulster Unionist or Nationalist opinion could only result in deadlock or a partition compromise, he repudiated the basis on which the convention was to be set up. Sinn Fein, via Eamon de Valera (its new leader and a surviving hero

[40]Adams to George, April 16, 1917, Lloyd George Papers, Beaverbrook Library, F/63/1/4.

[41]For details of Lloyd George's proposal and the setting-up of the convention, see R. B. McDowell, *The Irish Convention 1917–18* (Toronto, 1970), chapter 2. O'Brien's initial acceptance of the convention idea is in O'Brien to George, May 17, 1918, Lloyd George Papers, Beaverbrook Library, F/41/9/2.

[42]See O'Brien to W. M. Murphy, May 31, 1917, NLI William O'Brien Papers, NLI MS. 8557/9. O'Brien was supported in this stand by W. M. Murphy, proprietor of the antiparty *Irish Independent*.

of the Easter Rising), also refused to join, recognizing, as O'Brien did, the impossibility of conciliation between diametrically opposed groups. Apparently Griffith, who had incurred some disfavor from Republicans of de Valera's stamp because of his insistence on the old Sinn Fein program of the restoration of the Constitution of 1782, leaned toward O'Brien's small convention plus referendum, but now, as in 1910, Griffith was powerless to chart a moderate course. All attempts, official and otherwise, to get O'Brien to change his mind failed, as he adhered to the opinion conveyed to the Chief Secretary in his initial refusal to attend the Convention:

From all I hear, it is useless to hope to dissuade your colleagues from the so-called "Irish Convention" they have resolved upon . . . I am afraid the great body of Irish nationalists will be left no escape from the conclusion that the proposed Convention will be held for Anglo-American war purposes and upon lines which are bound to aggravate instead of composing the present troubles.[43]

The boring details of the Irish Convention, generally regarded as one of the great nonevents of Irish history, do not concern us here. O'Brien maintained his silence as the proceedings ground to a halt, a silence shared by Healy and which the latter whimsically remarked might be mistaken by the public for statesmanship. At one point, O'Brien weakened in his resolve to the extent that he promised his wife he would join the gathering "if the Bishops delegate Four Stalwarts to fight partition tooth and nail." Then again he trusted the people to prevent any capitulation. "I am now perfectly confident," he wrote to Dunraven, "the people will smash the [partition] plot and will not even allow the Convention to assemble in Dublin without a bloody riot." On another occasion he felt constrained to agree with Healy that the country should give Sinn Fein its chance, since it could at least do no worse than "the stinking crew" it would replace.[44] In the event, the convention died of inanition and failed to solve anything. It would only have been poetic justice had it been held at the Royal College of Surgeons building, as planned, instead of at Trinity College; fortunately, Dillon, it seems, saved the affair from the ridicule that would have depicted the convention as the corpse of Ireland on the dissecting table!

Of more immediate concern in the spring of 1918 was the possibility

---

[43]O'Brien to Duke, May 24, 1917, *ibid.*, MS. 8506/12.

[44]O'Brien to Healy, August 18, 1917, *ibid.*, MS. 8556/14; O'Brien to Dunraven, June 21, 1917, *ibid.*, MS. 8554/16; O'Brien to Sophie O'Brien, June 13, 1917, Sophie O'Brien Papers, NLI MS. 4217. There were, in fact, many instances both in Cork and in Dublin where Redmond and Devlin had to flee threats of physical violence from Republicans.

of conscription in Ireland. Ever since the war began, Irish politicians, O'Brien included, had strenuously supported the recruiting effort in Ireland. Even the Irish hierarchy, with the exception of Dr. O'Dwyer, Bishop of Limerick, exhorted Irishmen in their 1916 Lenten pastorals to "do their duty." It is equally clear, however, that there would be no such support for the application of compulsory military service to Ireland. Both Redmond and Dillon had let it be known in the Commons in late 1915 and early 1916 that the conscription of Ireland would never be tolerated as long as Ireland was denied Home Rule. These warnings were repeated from time to time in the following two years. Thus, when rumors of Lloyd George's intentions began to circulate in Ireland in March 1918, a united opposition began to develop. The expected blow struck on April 9 when the Prime Minister, smarting over the failure of the Irish Convention and faced with the German spring offensive on the Western front, introduced in the Commons a Military Service Bill which, among other provisions, extended the military service acts to Ireland. Immediately, at the instigation of the Dublin Corporation, Lord Mayor Laurence O'Neill issued a call for a conference of representative Irishmen to arrange an all-Ireland opposition to conscription. O'Brien's last speech in the House of Commons on April 16 was a bitter denunciation of the government and of conscription.

The conference was duly held in the Mansion House on April 18 and 19. Nowhere was the character of united opposition to George's bill more evident than in the improbable gathering in that famous edifice: O'Brien and Healy, representing the defunct All-for-Ireland League, flanked by Dillon and Devlin (Redmond had died in the previous month), along with de Valera and Griffith representing Sinn Fein and three representatives from Labour. When invited by O'Neill, apparently on the insistence of de Valera, O'Brien's first reaction was to question why antiwar Unionists had not been invited. O'Neill's crushing reply was that he could not find any. At the conference itself O'Brien could not resist the temptation to introduce a wider platform for discussion even though the Lord Mayor, who presided, had clearly indicated in his invitation that only the question of conscription would be considered. As if in final acknowledgment of the futility of conciliation, O'Brien pressed for a combined Parliamentary-party–Sinn-Fein call for Dominion Home Rule, but this was rejected by the Sinn Fein representatives. Next he baited the Parliamentary representatives with the proposal that Griffith be allowed to run without opposition for the va-

cant East Cavan constituency, at which Dillon quite naturally threatened to withdraw from the conference.[45]

In the event, a united declaration did issue from the conference,
denying the right of the British government to impose compulsory
military service in Ireland and warning that the passage of the Conscription Bill (it became law on April 18) would be a declaration of war
on the Irish people. Concurrent with a similar statement by the Irish
bishops, Irishmen were called on to resist "by the most effective means
at their disposal," and pledges against the "blood tax" were administered at Sunday masses throughout the country on April 21.
Much more effective was the national strike of organized labor (the first
general strike in Ireland) in all areas outside northeast Ulster on the
following Tuesday—no trams, trains, van deliveries, newspapers,
restaurants, theaters, drink, tobacco. Conscription was shelved, and
some months later when the need for recruits became urgent, Lloyd
George could no longer get a timorous Cabinet to agree to issue the
Order in Council which was needed to introduce conscription. By then,
however, the war was virtually at an end, and no Irishman had to pay
the blood tax by compulsion, though many had paid it voluntarily in
the previous four years. O'Brien's own post mortem on the confrontation did not conceal his pleasure at the predicament of the Irish party.
Claiming that it was Sinn Fein alone who saved the country from conscription, he exulted that their reward would be total victory in the imminent general election.[46]

In those last months of O'Brien's political career, the disappointments mounted. Already his friend Hutcheson-Poë had endorsed
the exclusion of Ulster in a letter to *The* (London) *Times* on April 13,
1917. All the disappointments of the past years seemed to culminate in
his parting with his closest collaborator on conciliation, Dunraven, in
January 1918. A few days before, the latter had made an about-turn
and endorsed Midleton's proposal at the Irish convention excluding the
customs from the purview of any All-Ireland Parliament. Toward the
end, O'Brien alienated Frewen because of his (O'Brien's) rejection of
federalism by adopting Dominion status as the only possible solution of

[45]Earl of Longford, and T. P. O'Neill, *Eamon De Valera* (New York, 1971), 72. L. O'Neill to
O'Brien, April 10 and 13, 1918, NLI William O'Brien Papers, NLI MS. 7998; O'Brien to
Darrell Figgis, May 1, 1918, *ibid.*, MS. 11440/4; O'Brien to L. O'Neill, June 22, 1918, *ibid.*,
MS. 8506/3. See also O'Brien's unpublished manuscript on the Irish Free State, *ibid.*, MS.
4210.

[46]O'Brien to Dean O'Connor, July 28, 1918, NLI William O'Brien Papers, NLI MS.
8506/3.

the Irish problem. He also alienated his other federalist friends by his opposition to conscription. Despite the breakdown of the Parliamentarianism he had so long forecast, O'Brien refused to the end to discard his own constitutionalist principles and so held back from endorsing the Sinn Fein policy of abstention. Nevertheless, as the most important general election in Irish history was about to take place, he refused, like Healy, to fight Sinn Fein, convinced that the only dignified course was to stand aside and let Sinn Fein exert its pressure on England to come to terms. Thus, at the end, he was spared the humiliation which was administered, much to his delight, to the discredited members of the Nationalist party he had helped to build. It only remained to write an epitaph. No one could find fault with the obituary notice Healy obligingly provided:

We have got our *congé* and I move that a warm vote of thanks be inscribed on our tombstones![47]

[47]Healy to O'Brien, October 12, 1918, NLI William O'Brien Papers, NLI MS. 8556/21.

TEN

The Torch Is Passed

THE SWEEPING victory of Sinn Fein in the general election of December 1918 did not come as any surprise to O'Brien. He had concluded that the Irish party had already lost its mandate to rule by the acceptance of partition—even allegedly temporary partition—in June 1916. Thus, when Sinn Fein issued a call shortly before the election requesting all the Irish representatives to resign in a body before the dissolution, O'Brien acceded in the grand manner. His letter published in the *Irish Independent* on October 14 explained that his refusal to stand was because neither he nor any one else had authority to speak for Ireland in the existing circumstances. An unrepresented Ireland would teach other nations the disgust and contempt felt by Irishmen for the "dual hypocrisy of conscription by coercion and Home Rule by coercion." Sean T. O'Kelly, later President of the Irish Free State, congratulated him on the "splendid tone" of the letter and also requested his aid in ensuring that the representatives of labor in Cork would leave the field free to a decision between Sinn Fein and the Irish party at the forthcoming elections. O'Brien's polemical ability was again put to good use by Sinn Fein through the circulation of his pamphlet *The Downfall of Parliamentarianism,* just published in time for the election. It was a screed against the Parliamentarianism that "eats the bread of English party managers." In a complete contradiction of his own moderate approach to Home Rule over the past decade, O'Brien based his new hopes on the Wilsonian formula of the right of self-determination by small nations and now openly commended Sinn Fein to the electorate.[1]

The response of the official Irish party was the opposite of O'Brien's.

[1]Sinn Fein acknowledgments of O'Brien's aid are in O'Kelly to O'Brien, October 14 and 19, 1918, Macdonagh Papers, NLI MS. 11439/6; P. O'Siothchain (secretary of Sinn Fein) to O'Brien, November 27, 1918, UCC William O'Brien Papers, Box AS.

Dillon (leader of the party since Redmond's death the previous March) rallied his followers against a force he believed had been demoralized by the apparent collapse of Germany. H. A. L. Fisher, who spent a month in Ireland as Lloyd George's investigator in September 1918, reported an interview he had had with Dillon, describing him as a "despondent, bitter politician . . . as fully convinced of the necessity of keeping order and of controlling the dangerous forces at present at work in Ireland as the most stringent Unionist." Fisher also perceived the basic weakness of the party, citing the general complaint of the total absence of popular young men of ability and the fact that the party was quite unrepresentative of Irish culture.[2]

Before the election the combined Parliamentary forces of Redmondites, O'Brienites, and one or two Independents held seventy-eight Nationalist seats, the remaining twenty-five Irish seats being filled by Ulster Unionists (eighteen) and Sinn Fein (seven). After the election, which was not contested by O'Brien's All-for-Ireland group, Sinn Fein was successful in seventy-three constituencies, while the remnants of the once-proud Nationalist party could boast a mere six Irish seats, only one of which was outside of Ulster. Indeed, this number would have been less had not four seats, uncontested by Sinn Fein, been "awarded" by Cardinal Logue to the Irish party, to prevent Unionist victories in triangular contests. This electoral reverse also included the defeat of Dillon by de Valera, the symbolic victory of the new over the old. As for O'Brien, he could feel gratified that he had done his part to drive a nail in the coffin of the Parliamentarianism he hated by cooperating with Sinn Fein in those hectic final months of 1918.

With the Sinn Fein victory in the elections, O'Brien, for all intents and purposes, went into retirement to his Mallow home. Though differing from his enemies in the defunct Parliamentary party on many fundamental issues, he was at one with them in regarding the British connection in some form or other as inevitable. If he preached a withdrawal from Parliament, it was only as a temporary expedient to pressure the government. If he endorsed Sinn Fein, it was only to give his youthful successors the chance to complete what their fathers had set out to do—to confer upon the Irish people full legislative and executive control of all purely Irish affairs. But now, not step-by-step Home Rule or the

[2]F. S. L. Lyons, *John Dillon* (London, 1968), 446; Fisher to George, October 11, 1918, Lloyd George Papers, Beaverbrook Library, F/16/7/29. For further evidence of Dillon's loathing of Sinn Fein (which he never concealed), see Duke of Atholl to J. T. Davies, April 29, 1918, Lloyd George Papers, Beaverbrook Library, F/94/3/45.

Dominion status lately taken up by O'Brien, but rather an Irish Republic was the solution demanded by the new representatives. Griffith's original policy of self-determination under the Crown—his "Hungarian" policy—had fallen victim to the "irrational" program of de Valera and his Republican zealots. Accordingly, instead of attending Westminster, Sinn Fein sent invitations to all the successful candidates in the recent election to gather in Ireland's own self-erected Parliament Dail Eireann on January 21, 1919, in the historic Mansion House in Dublin. By including the Unionist representatives in this invitation, the Republicans at least showed they possessed a sense of humor. Naturally, only those Sinn Feiners who were not in prison under the renewed coercion of Lord French showed up at the gathering. The declaration issued by the thirty-man assembly ratified the establishment of the Irish Republic and pledged themselves and the Irish people to make that declaration effective "by every means."

O'Brien had little realization that the gun would be the medium of producing an Irish settlement. Rather, he calculated that the "Lloyd George gang and his Government" would be replaced so that a New Zealand or Newfoundland settlement (O'Brien's new *idée fixe*) could be effected.[3] Therefore, on July 5, 1919, he took it upon himself to convey to the Prime Minister the certainty that Sinn Fein would not block the way of any offer by the government of Dominion status. The basis of this hopeful missive was a letter from an unnamed associate who "had an opportunity of seeing ——— who is really a fast friend of ours and is the right-hand man of de Valera." No clue is given as to the identity of O'Brien's informant, but, considering O'Brien's veracity, there is no reason to doubt that some erring soul in Sinn Fein circles misled himself and O'Brien as to the integrity of the Republican demand. The "right-hand man" may have been Professor Eoin MacNeill, for in an earlier letter to Healy, O'Brien states: "I had a long and interesting chat with [W. M.] Murphy who heartily approved the suggestion made in my letter. So does [Eoin] MacNeill whom I also saw. He [MacNeill] is quite sure Dominion Home Rule would settle the question and is only restrained from saying so publicly for a reason you will understand. He

---

[3]O'Brien to Dunraven, January 7, 1920, UCC William O'Brien Papers, Box AT. O'Brien had a poor opinion of Lloyd George, and when the latter replaced Asquith in 1916, O'Brien made the hopelessly wrong judgment that George would be no improvement "either for war or peace purposes" (O'Brien to Frewen, December 7, 1916, MacDonagh Papers, NLI MS. 11440/4). In the same letter to Frewen he stated: "I have never doubted that he [George] is an imposter—and as weak as water." In the latter judgment he was, perhaps, only half-wrong!

assures me de Valera is of the same opinion."[4] But until the strange and
tragic circumstances of the treaty negotiations December 21, there was
never any whittling-down of the demand for a thirty-two-county Irish
Republic. In fact, Sean T. O'Kelly had specifically rejected the
possibility of Sinn Fein's adoption of Dominion status when he wrote to
O'Brien in September 1918, "It may be that some day the 'half-loaf'
policy might again be adopted by the majority of nationalists but just
now there seems no likelihood of such measures being listened to."[5]

Over two years of guerrilla warfare were to pass before the policy of
the "half-loaf" was to reappear with such tragic consequences.
Meanwhile, the Republicans set up their own civil administration, including Land Courts, Land Banks, and arbitration machinery for industrial disputes. Even the aging Dunraven could not but admire the
"polite, considerate and gentlemanly" raiders for arms who contrasted
very favorably with the "outrageous 'black and tan' police."[6] O'Brien
retained enough of his native rebelliousness to admire the fight the
"boys" were waging against the Black and Tans, as did Healy who by
his legal defence of prisoners became a trusted friend of the "Sinns."
Actually, the introduction of the odious auxiliary police was necessi-
tated by the collapse of that old bastion of British power, the Royal
Irish Constabulary. The state of that body had been bad since 1913,
when Birrell reported to Asquith that there were practically no recruits
and that resignations were pouring in. By 1920 the RIC had apparently
become half informers to Sinn Fein and, according to Fisher's reliable
information, was "on the verge of a breakup at all events in the South."[7]

The one thing the British government was resolved not to do was to
make concessions to the demand for an Irish Republic. This latter
dream receded immediately the Government of Ireland Act established
a separate Ulster Parliament in December 1920. For O'Brien, this was
the disastrous culmination of the concessions to Ulster yielded by Redmond and his associates early in 1914. Partition had at last become a

---

[4]A copy of O'Brien's letter to Lloyd George, including an extract from the mysterious
letter, is in the Macdonagh Papers, MS. 11440/1. See also O'Brien to Healy, June 9, 1918,
NLI William O'Brien Papers, NLI MS. 8556/20.

[5]O'Kelly to O'Brien, September 19, 1918, MacDonagh Papers, NLI MS. 11439/6.

[6]Dunraven to Frewen, September 10, 1920, Frewen Papers, LC Box 53. Though Dunraven
lamented his inability to shoot a pheasant or two for dinner (all his guns had been taken),
that catastrophe was more than balanced by the excellent order which he claimed Sinn Fein
administered at race meetings, and the like.

[7]Birrell to Asquith, October 28, 1913, Asquith Papers, Bodleian Library, MS. Asquith 38,
folio 243; Fisher to George, July 21, 1920, Lloyd George Papers, Beaverbrook Library,
F/17/1/6.

political fact. From that point on the pressure mounted for an equal settlement for the South. Lloyd George himself announced in the Commons in March and April 1921 that negotiations could begin as soon as the Republicans were prepared for an agreed settlement. In May, Horace Plunkett's Irish Dominion League sent a memorandum to Lloyd George signed by a galaxy of notables requesting, among other alternatives, full Dominion status for a united Ireland.[8] Though rejected by both sides, this effort at least demonstrated how far along the road to Home Rule such Unionists and timid devolutionists as Plunkett, Lord Monteagle, and Nugent Everard had traveled. Had they adopted this position a decade earlier when O'Brien was pleading for their assistance in ensuring their own survival, it is probable that the Ulster Unionists could never have become the sole deciding voice on the question of Irish Home Rule.

Meanwhile, the Republicans utilized the electoral machinery of the Government of Ireland Act (ignored in the South) to return unopposed Republican candidates in every county and borough of the twenty-six counties as a demonstration of national unity against the partition of Ireland. Something of a crossroads had now been reached: on the one hand, Ulster had been formally excised from eventual control by an Irish Parliament; on the other, the Irish people in the twenty-six counties had given an overwhelming endorsement to the Republican position. When the King opened the first session of the Ulster parliament on June 22, the decision had already been reached to treat with the rebels.[9] Within six months an Irish "settlement" (the Anglo-Irish "treaty" of 1921) had been reached which endorsed partition, accepted Dominion status, and split the Republican movement from top to bottom. The settlement also arranged for a Commission to adjust the boundary between the two new states in Ireland, which the Irish negotiators expected would report in the South's favor. These hopes were not to be realized.

During the ensuing civil war, O'Brien's sympathies were with de Valera's group, though he did not believe in using force to secure the abrogation of the treaty. In this, of course, he was only being consistent,

[8]Plunkett to Lloyd George, May 9, 1921, Lloyd George Papers, Beaverbrook Library, F/42/10/6.

[9]Healy, Governor General of the Irish Free State from December 1922, wrote to O'Brien in 1926 of a discussion he had had with the King on the events of 1921: "The King told me he would not have gone to Belfast unless he received a promise that negotiations with 'the South' would be opened afterwards" (Healy to O'Brien, March 2, 1926, NLI William O'Brien Papers, NLI MS. 8556/31).

for the Republican position, like O'Brien's, was opposed to partition in any form. O'Brien maintained to the end that the Treaty would have to be replaced by a more lasting settlement encompassing the whole of Ireland in some common bond of friendship with the British Empire. For him the English government, not the Irish nation, had won the victory, as is clear from his letter to his old friend and supporter, Father Clancy:

The Republican youngsters are irrational—even idiotic—in their way of protesting against "the treaty" but their instincts are those of sound Irish nationalists of the old school, and too many of their opponents are camouflaged Mollies of the worst place-hunting brand—The bosh about a "free Ireland a Nation" and an evacuation by the English will not impose upon any thinking Irishman . . . England retains a larger "English Pale" than ever before she was able to keep since the Norman Invasion.[10]

Significantly, O'Brien was not nominated for the Irish Senate by William Cosgrave, president of the Dail since the deaths of Griffith and Michael Collins in August 1922. When J. J. Walsh, the Postmaster General, requested his permission to propose his name for the Senate seat, O'Brien publicly declined the offer: "It would be a reversal of the work of my whole life to do anything that could be interpreted as a recognition of the partition of our nation. The partition crime . . . must be undone at any hazard."[11] The same sentiment prevented his congratulating his friend Healy on the latter's appointment as Governor General of a truncated Ireland. Eventually, he came to regard the Cosgrave government with something of the loathing he had formerly reserved for the Irish party. For him, the deaths of Collins and Griffith marked the change from "a Free State Government compulsorily obedient to England but still preponderantly Nationalist, to a Free State Government more and more frankly British and Imperialist."[12]

While the pro-treaty government of President Cosgrave was consolidating its rule, O'Brien continued to support the Republicans, who had abandoned their civil war in May 1923 because of the superior force and the resolve of the established government. Late in 1925, when the Republicans were campaigning against the "sellout" to Britain consequent upon the breakup of the Boundary Commission, O'Brien was

[10]O'Brien to Father Clancy, December 23, 1922, *ibid.*, MS. 8506/6. The Pale, of course, was Ulster, where a British army could always be kept poised for action.

[11]*The Times*, London, November 14, 1922.

[12]See chapter 9 of O'Brien's unpublished manuscript on the foundation of the Irish Free State, NLI MS. 4210. A legible copy of this work in Sophie's handwriting is in NLI MS. 8559.

requested by de Valera to speak at a demonstration in Dublin.[13] With the same prescience with which he had earlier condemned temporary exclusion as a farce, O'Brien repudiated the much-touted Boundary Commission as "a false and fraudulent pretence."

His support of the Republican position did not go unrecognized, and during 1926 he was requested by Republican election agents to speak or write on behalf of candidates at by-elections. It was even rumored early in February 1927 that he would contest Cork City in the forthcoming Dail elections in de Valera's interest. Actually, O'Brien was invited by a branch of Fianna Fail (de Valera's new Constitutional Republican party) to let his name go forward for adoption as a candidate.[14] However, O'Brien's platform days were over, for he was almost seventy-five and in his last year of life, having been in Ireland's battle for almost half a century. Like Davitt before him, O'Brien ended his days in fierce hatred of an England that denied full nationality to his countrymen. It was bitter irony, indeed, that one who had striven so long and at such personal cost in pursuit of an Irish settlement under the Crown should finally exalt the ideals of Republicans and revolutionaries and share with them a loathing of the Imperial connection. Among his last political acts was his public endorsement of Fianna Fail in a letter which that party publicized as an electioneering pamphlet. It shows clearly how far he had advanced from his former Parliamentarian commitment to the old Home Rule bogey:

The approaching general election is to be above all else a life or death struggle between the nationality of Ireland and her perversion to the ideals of British Imperialism . . . To our last breath our choice must be with an Independent Ireland, sovereignly free from shore to shore, as against a Britonized Ireland split into two insignificant provinces of an alien British Empire.[15]

William O'Brien died while on a visit to London on February 25, 1928. His sudden and peaceful death made one opponent reflect how remarkable it was that one who had led so tempestuous a life should have so peaceful an end. Of his colleagues of earlier days, only Healy and T. P. O'Connor were left—Dillon, Redmond, and Davitt having already passed away. The funeral was held in his native Mallow and

[13]De Valera to O'Brien, December 2, 1925, NLI William O'Brien Papers, NLI MS. 7998. A telegram from O'Brien was read at the demonstration.

[14]D. Lehane to O'Brien, May 12, 1927, UCC William O'Brien Papers, Box AU. The Cork Constituency Executive of Fianna Fail had earlier passed a resolution expressing a desire for O'Brien's return to Irish public life.

[15]See election handbill in NLI William O'Brien Papers, NLI MS. 7998 (June 1927).

was private, in accordance with O'Brien's request. However, this did not prevent the attendance of a small group of mourners from the former Buckley estate on the Galtee mountains. It was a fitting mark of respect from the inhabitants of what fifty years before had marked the scene of O'Brien's first crusade in the fight to make Ireland what it had lately become—a land of occupying owners.

Epilogue

"O'Brien would thrust his hand into a furnace if it would serve Ireland." So wrote T. M. Healy, and it is a just comment on O'Brien's life's work. Few Irish politicians of his era risked more than he did for the tenants of rural Ireland. Even his bitterest enemies would have found it difficult to withhold admiration for the unflinching courage with which the frail, sickly agitator of the 1880s braved numerous prosecutions and several imprisonments in the stormy battles of the land war. Throughout that decade the name of William O'Brien served as a constant reminder to the people of Ireland that British policies in their land were being tested according to the standards and re-quirements of Irish Nationalism. Indeed, had it not been for O'Brien's fanaticism, self-sacrifice, and journalistic flair, the Irish party in those years would have had little to show for its long confrontation with coercion-minded governments. Thus, O'Brien's value to the national cause in this early period cannot be underestimated. He conducted his land agitation with a singleness of purpose and a disregard of personal comfort that were matched only by one other, his friend John Dillon. In an era when the tradition of the monster meeting still dominated politics, his demagoguery and fiery Nationalist rhetoric played on the feelings of Irish audiences in a manner reminiscent of Daniel O'Connell himself. If he used violent methods, it was, as he explained, only to secure a hearing for moderation.

The greater part of his life was one of steady achievement in Irish politics—the long-sustained invective of *United Ireland;* the organization of the National League; the defence of the tenants; the creation of the United Irish League; the reunion of the Nationalist party. By far his greatest success was, of course, the part he played in the events leading to the Land Act of 1903, which transferred almost one-third of the soil of Ireland to its rightful owners. It was not the great conciliatory instru-ment he had hoped for because by 1914 almost 40 percent of the more than half a million holdings in Ireland were still not owner-occupied.

Yet, his instincts in supporting this great social legislation were surer than those of his enemies in the party, for the Act started a process of land transfer which not even the hesitancies of the Republican "government" of 1919–1921 could arrest.[16] O'Brien lived to see the "Hogan" Act of 1923, which made compulsory the sale and purchase of all the land not yet dealt with and reduced to fourteen years purchase the high purchase terms he had championed, to his cost, twenty years earlier. He was fortunate not to have lived to see the repudiation of the land-purchase annuities by the Fianna Fail government in 1932: his last public letter was against schemes to stop payment of land annuities.

The 1903 Act was a landmark in O'Brien's career, for it set him on the trail which was to make him a pariah in Irish Nationalist politics. At that point he discarded his "violent" stance and broke with his party to take up what was even in his own time recognized to be a chimera—the inducement of a Home Rule consciousness in Irish Unionists. From that point onward we also begin to detect certain defects of character which had been hidden during those years when intense activity, wide respect, and a place in the councils of the party provided outlets for his highly imaginative, romantic nature. When his colleagues refused to share his belief that by some strange mutation a Land Conference of Protestant Unionist landlords and Catholic tenant representatives had somehow become a platform for Home Rule, he threw caution to the winds and began to heap on them the abuse he had earlier reserved for coercionists and land-grabbers. The manner in which he converted honest differences of opinion into a personal vendetta not only diminished his own political stature, but by recalling the evils of the earlier party split, it did much to discredit the constitutional movement in the eyes of a younger and more impatient generation of Irish Nationalists. The depth of his hatred of the party is nowhere better revealed than in the wholly unjustified explanation he gave for the failure of conciliation in 1903: "a wholly vicious incapacity [of the party] to collaborate with English Toryism in doing the work of Ireland."[17] Yet it had been that same Toryism, allied to Ulster Unionism, which fought tooth and nail against Home Rule in 1886 and 1893, discovered treachery in the paltry devolution scheme of 1904, and threatened red war against any attempt to impose Irish self-government after 1912.

[16]For an account of how the "city-minded" Republican government sent special commissioners to troubled areas to patrol estate walls, to enforce decrees for rent, and to arrest or order out of the country leaders of local land agitation (something not even Balfour at his worst dared to do), see P. O'Donnell, *There Will Be Another Day* (Dublin, 1963), 12.

[17]W. O'Brien, *The Parnell of Real Life* (London, 1926), 93.

O'Brien's financial independence really turned out to be quite a dis-advantage, for without it he could not have sustained his long, bitter squabble with his former colleagues or created a political organization to chase the rainbow of conciliation. Not that the conciliation policy was wrong in itself. To give O'Brien his due, he saw more clearly than others, or at least recognized the fact that there were but three main ways to solve the Irish question—exterminate the Unionist one-fourth of the population, exterminate the Nationalist three-fourths, or create conditions under which both sections could advance together in a shared independence. O'Brien, unfortunately, had undermined his capacity to champion the conciliation policy. Ulster Unionists could hardly be blamed for remembering him as the hate-monger of *United Ireland* or the warhorse of the Plan of Campaign. Nor could they forget how he guided the electoral machinery of the United Irish League to shut out Unionists, wherever possible, from representation in local government in the elections which followed the Local Government Act of 1898. Worse still, he defeated his purposes by the implacable fury with which he assailed his unconvinced opponents among the Nationalists, a one-sided condemnation which refused to see in the Unionist minority—even in the 280,000 Southern Unionists—an ap-parently ineradicable disregard for the patriotic feelings which motivated their Catholic fellow countrymen. His voice was an unavail-ing one in a political atmosphere which, since 1898, tended to shut out non-Nationalists from all positions of control in boroughs and councils outside of the few Ulster Protestant counties. Only the electoral machinery of the Parliamentary party could arrest this divisive develop-ment, and Dillon's ascendancy in party management would ensure that that effort would never be made. It is difficult, however, to fault Dillon for his realistic appraisal of factors in the ascendancy mentality which O'Brien dismissed from consideration.

Lack of political judgment, therefore, was another of O'Brien's failings, and what contributed to this more than anything else was the lack of any well-developed idea of what Home Rule really meant. The party, no less than O'Brien, had always been content to follow the lead of English politicians on that score. Furthermore, Irish politicians had never really reckoned with the problem of Ulster in its relation to a Home Rule Parliament. But, as the representatives of the majority, why should they have concerned themselves with any considerations that would make a mockery of Home Rule? After all, whatever guarantees and safeguards might be proper for the minority were surely upheld in

successive Home Rule bills by the legislative veto of the Lord Lieutenant, by clauses protecting religion and education, and by the ultimate
sanction of the Imperial Parliament. The nineteenth-century Home
Rule debates clearly reveal the confusion about what constituted a
"final settlement" of this question. In general, Irish party members
were prepared to accept the step-by-step approach, at which the most
notable attempt was the abortive Irish Council Bill in 1907. O'Brien, on
the other hand, went further than most in whittling down the minimal
demand—whatever that might mean. Even as late as May 1916 we find
him calling for "slower and better matured action" than that evidenced
by the "suspended" legislation of 1914, action which he claimed would
provide the national harmony essential to the recruiting drive! Thus,
his commitment to the goal of Irish independence had become secondary to his desire to conciliate the Protestant minority. Before 1916, the
Irish party did not face Ulster's fears because to do so was to negate
Home Rule. O'Brien met them after 1903 because he chose to
downgrade Home Rule. But, unlike his colleagues, he refused, or was
too blind, to see that Home Rule in any shape or form was anathema to
Ulster. With a fanaticism reminiscent of his younger days, he continued
to wage his hopeless campaign virtually alone except for the help of a
tiny handful of devolutionary-minded Southern Unionists, a class instinctively distrusted by the people at large and shunned by the party
machine. The party, on the other hand, while accepting interim gains,
jealously eyed the more alluring goal of a final settlement, and in this, of
course, it was supported by the masses and outdistanced by the nascent
Irish movements epitomized by Sinn Fein. O'Brien's error was not
alone that he underestimated the political obstacles, but that he also ignored the harsh realities of Ireland's struggle for self-respect. He might
well consider Home Rule a sentiment as long as social wrongs were rife,
but by doing so he concealed the fact that the concept of nationality had
acquired a life of its own through the aura of spiritual necessity im-
parted to it by Thomas Davis and John Mitchel and nourished by
Patrick Pearse. Home Rule, or independence, could no longer be put
off—least of all by the rather promiscuous use of conferences between
Unionists and Nationalists. In such negotiations, Nationalists would inevitably meet the representatives of the ascendancy with cap in hand
amid a chorus of Orange denunciation in the wings.

Neither O'Brien nor his colleagues in the Irish Parliamentary party
envisioned the use of physical force to attain national ends. They did
their political best to exorcise the revolutionary spirit that stalked the

"Irish" Ireland of the late 1890s and after. O'Brien must bear his share of the responsibility for persisting in Parliamentary methods when duplicity and betrayal were the end result, though in this he was less culpable than Redmond and some others whose actions went far to vitiate the credibility of the constitutional approach. When appeals to the British conscience failed and appeals to an international conscience were not possible, Parliamentarians like O'Brien might have recognized that constitutionalism had been strained to its limits with the failure of 1914. The conclusion seems inescapable that, given the revitalized Nationalism of "Irish" Ireland in the early twentieth century, only violent methods could advance the Irish cause beyond the paltry concessions contemplated at Westminster.

The Home Rulers may well be entitled to the encomium of Arthur Griffith that "the task of William O'Brien's generation was well and bravely done. Had it not been so the work men are carrying out in this generation would have been impossible." Yet, their partisan bitterness, self-serving politics, and constricted concept of Irish nationality have relegated them to the outer darkness of a historical limbo which renders their names and deeds forgotten and ignored by the present generation of Irishmen. O'Brien himself scarcely comprehended the many-sided cultural movement that emerged at the turn of the century, and his memoirs give no indication of the seething Republican and revolutionary forces coming to the surface in the second decade of the present century.[18] Not the Home Rulers but the men of 1916, 1867, and 1848 are now revered in the litany of Irish Nationalism. The failure of O'Brien's generation, responsibility for which must be charged alike to Nationalist, Ulster Unionist, and British Imperialist, unleashed destructive forces which blighted the lives of the rising politicians of the younger generation and froze the Irish question into a mold that even fifty more years and the "lessons of history" have not thawed. As we view the latest "battlefield" in Irish history, that in Northern Ireland, we can discern the same hopes and fears which spurred on an earlier generation of Irishmen and we can equally recognize, lurking in the background, the nemesis of politicians who cannot lead, leaders who cannot produce victories, and victories which cannot achieve peace.

[18]O'Brien saw O'Casey's *Juno and the Paycock* for the first time in 1926 and, with the occluded vision of his contemporaries, considered it "one of the most disgusting experiences I ever had in my life . . . There was not absolutely a single tolerable sentence . . . drunkenness, indecency, blasphemy, cowardice—it is to me amazing how any Irish audience could have stood it" (W. O'Brien to Sophie O'Brien, April 14, 1926, UCC William O'Brien Papers, Box BI).

Appendix A

AGRARIAN OUTRAGES IN IRELAND, 1850–1913

Year	Total Agrarian Outrages	Percentage of all Crimes (Agrarian and Other)	Incidence of Major Outrages				
			Threatening Letters and Notices	Homicides	Arson and Cattle Abuse	Firing at a Person	Assaults on Bailiffs and Process-servers
1850	1,362	13	517	18	380	18	3
1851	1,013	11	395	12	241	13	3
1852	907	11	364	6	272	15	1
1853	469	9	170	1	131	9	—
1854	334	7	114	5	110	4	—
1855	255	6	66	6	84	5	—
1856	287	7	99	6	83	6	—
1857	194	5	78	4	45	5	—
1858	235	7	98	6	59	1	—
1859	221	6	91	5	58	1	—
1860	232	7	87	4	34	6	—
1861	229	6	105	4	42	4	—
1862	363	8	211	8	63	3	—
1863	349	9	166	2	80	6	—
1864	304	10	145	2	76	3	—
1865	178	7	73	4	59	2	—
1866	87	4	32	—	35	3	—

Appendix A (continued)

Year	Total Agrarian Outrages	Percentage of all Crimes (Agrarian and Other)	Threatening Letters and Notices	Incidence of Major Outrages			
				Homicides	Arson and Cattle Abuse	Firing at a Person	Assaults on Bailiffs and Process Servers
1867	123	6	53	2	43	3	—
1868	160	6	72	4	39	1	—
1869	767	25	480	10	29	16	—
1870	1,329	30	624	7	53	11	—
1871	373	13	195	6	30	6	—
1872	256	8	144	5	43	6	—
1873	254	11	137	5	40	4	—
1874	213	10	94	5	48	4	—
1875	136	7	67	11	13	2	1
1876	212	10	97	5	47	7	2
1877	236	10	99	5	30	4	1
1878	301	12	128	8	62	3	1
1879	863	25	553	10	85	8	13
1880	2,585	46	1,576	8	311	24	37
1881	4,439	57	2,606	22	511	66	45
1882	3,433	55	2,300	27	425	58	9
1883	870	35	479	2	184	9	—

Appendix A (continued)

Year	Total Agrarian Outrages	Percentage of all Crimes (Agrarian and Other)	Incidence of Major Outrages				
			Threatening Letters and Notices	Homicides	Arson and Cattle Abuse	Firing at a Person	Assaults on Bailiffs and Process Servers
1884	762	31	423	—	167	7	1
1885	944	35	512	7	153	12	7
1886	1,056	32	516	10	176	16	11
1887	883	33	385	8	179	19	11
1888	660	30	316	7	128	14	2
1889	534	28	232	1	124	11	1
1890	519	27	241	6	108	15	—
1891	472	25	245	2	132	8	1
1892	405	22	219	4	107	7	—
1893	380	19	195	—	97	7	1
1894	276	15	152	2	67	3	—
1895	261	16	133	2	65	4	2
1896	251	15	125	2	82	6	—
1897	247	15	119	2	74	3	—
1898	243	13	112	1	79	3	—
1899	246	13	121	3	72	3	1
1900	280	16	151	2	70	3	—
1901	246	14	127	1	79	1	—

Appendix A (continued)

Year	Total Agrarian Outrages	Percentage of all Crimes (Agrarian and Other)	Incidence of Major Outrages				
			Threatening Letters and Notices	Homicides	Arson and Cattle Abuse	Firing at a Person	Assaults on Bailiffs and Process Servers
1902	253	15	143	2	63	2	—
1903	195	12	97	1	51	1	—
1904	206	13	124	—	39	1	—
1905	279	15	155	2	56	2	4
1906	234	13	120	—	58	3	1
1907	372	18	199	—	54	9	—
1908	576	25	290	1	76	15	—
1909	397	18	210	1	63	15	—
1910	420	18	211	—	82	13	—
1911	324	15	149	2	59	12	—
1912	307	14	149	—	58	5	—
1913	192	9	93	1	36	7	—

NOTES: Agrarian outrages were classified into three main categories: offences against the person (homicides, shooting, assault); offences against property (robbery, arson, cattle abuse); offences against the public peace (intimidation, oath-taking, resisting the law). The third category invariably comprised the largest number of offences, with "threatening letters" representing the bulk of them. For example, from 1879 to 1890 over 55 percent of all agrarian crime represented such intimidatory notices.

SOURCES: Data compiled from the following sources in SPO (Dublin):

1850–82: Irish Crimes Records, 1877–1882, Return of Outrages, Vol. 8. B.W.P.2/4
1883–1913: Police and Crime Records, 1848–1920, Carton no. 4 (Police Reports 1886–1915)

Appendix B:

NUMBER OF FAMILIES EVICTED IN IRELAND, 1849–1911

Year	Evictions	Year	Evictions	Year	Evictions	Year	Evictions
1849	16,686	1865	924	1880	2,110	1896	695
1850	19,949	1866	795	1881	3,415	1897	624
1851	13,197	1867	549	1882	5,201	1898	561
1852	8,591	1868	637	1883	3,643	1899	454
1853	4,833	1869	374	1884	4,188		
1854	2,156			1885	3,127	1900	443
1855	1,849	1870	548	1886	3,781	1901	314
1856	1,108	1871	482	1887	3,869	1902	288
1857	1,161	1872	326	1888	1,609	1903	311
1858	957	1873	671	1889	1,805	1904	226
1859	837	1874	726			1905	197
		1875	667	1890	1,842	1906	242
1860	636	1876	553	1891	1,098	1907	165
1861	1,092	1877	463	1892	907	1908	229
1862	1,136	1878	980	1893	1,018	1909	168
1863	1,734	1879	1,238	1894	75		
1864	1,924			1895	671	1910	147
						1911	97

NOTES: The rate of evictions should be kept in perspective. For instance, some 90,000 families were evicted between 1849 and 1880, and of these over 21,000 were readmitted to their holdings. However, in the 1870s the actual number of evictions and clearings effected, after allowing for tenant and caretaker readmissions, amounted to only 3,400 (i.e., 0.57 percent of an estimated 600,000 holdings). (See B. L. Solow, *The Land Question and the Irish Economy, 1870–1903* (Cambridge, Mass. 1971). 55–57.)

SOURCES: SPOT, CBS: Intelligence Notes 1906–1914 (Carton No. 2 Summary Report for 1910/11).

Appendix C:
A COMPARISON OF IRISH HOME RULE BILLS

Principal Provisions	Bill of 1886	Bill of 1893	Bill of 1912
1. Legislative			
a. Legislative body under the Crown:	Two Orders: First Order, 103 members (75 elective and 28 peerage, the former elected for ten-year term by electors of high property qualification) Second Order, 204 members (elected for five-year term under existing franchise)	Two Houses: Council, 48 members (elected for eight-year term by electors of high property qualification) Assembly, 103 members (elected for five-year term under existing franchise)	Two Houses: Senate, 40 members (nominated initially by Lord Lieutenant, then elected for five-year term under existing franchise) Commons, 164 members (elected for five-year term under existing franchise)
b. Settling of disagreement:	by joint majority vote if bill reintroduced after dissolution or lapse of three years whichever is longest	by joint majority vote if bill reintroduced after dissolution or lapse of two years	by joint majority vote if bill reintroduced in next session
c. Restrictions on Legislature	no power to make laws regarding: the Crown peace or war defence	no power to make laws regarding: as in 1886 " "	no power to make laws regarding: as in 1886 " "

Appendix C (continued)

Principal Provisions	Bill of 1886	Bill of 1893	Bill of 1912
c. Restrictions on Legislature: (continued):	treaties	"	"
	titles of honor	"	"
	treason, alienage or naturalization	"	"
	trade, navigation, quarantine beacons, lighthouses, etc.	as in 1886 (see *d*)	as in 1886 (see *d*)
	coinage, weights, etc.	as in 1886	as in 1886
	copyrights, etc.	"	"
	establishment or endowment of religion	as in 1886	"
	undenominational constitution of national schools	"	"
d. Exceptions to Restrictions on Legislature	—	inland trade and navigation	religious belief or ceremony as a condition of marriage; as in 1893
e. Representation in Imperial Parliament:	none	80	42

Appendix C (continued)

Principal Provisions	Bill of 1886	Bill of 1893	Bill of 1912
f. Powers reserved to Imperial Parliament:	erection of forts and dockyards	for three years: Relations of landlord/tenant and purchase/letting of land	until Resolution for Transfer passed by Irish Parliament: Old-Age Pension Acts 1908/11, National Insurance Act 1911, Labor Exchange Act 1909, Post Office, Savings Banks, and Friendly Societies (minimum ten years) in perpetuity: collection of taxes, land purchase
2. Executive			
a. The Crown (i.e. Imperial Parliament) as represented by:	Lord Lieutenant (having veto power and aid and advice of Executive Committee of Irish Privy Council)	as in 1886	as in 1886
b. Term of office of Lord Lieutenant:	indefinite	six years	six years

Appendix C (continued)

Principal Provisions	Bill of 1886	Bill of 1893	Bill of 1912
3. Finance			
a. Taxation:	under Irish control (except customs and excise)	as in 1886 (after six years)	power to vary Imperial taxes and impose new taxes,[1] power to impose custom duties on articles subject to Imperial Customs Duty[2]
b. Revenue:	gross revenue collected in Ireland from Irish and Imperial taxes and Crown Lands (cost of collection to be borne by Irish Parliament)[3]	true Irish revenue derived from Imperial taxes, revenue from Irish taxes and Crown Lands, and Imperial grant of one-third annual cost of Irish police	Sum transferred from Imperial Treasury consisting of: revenue derived from Irish taxes plus fixed annual grant from Imperial Parliament[4] (cost of Reserved Services to be borne by Imperial Parliament)
c. Ireland's contribution to Imperial Exchequer:	a fixed annual maximum, which might be diminished, but which could not be exceeded, revisable in thirty years. (1886=£3,242,000)	for six years: Ireland to pay one-third of *true* revenue raised in Ireland (1893=approx. 1/27 of total Imperial expenditure)	when total revenue equals total charges for three consecutive years, Joint Exchequer Board to fix equitable contribution by Ireland to

Appendix C (continued)

Principal Provisions	Bill of 1886	Bill of 1893	Bill of 1912
3. *Finance* (continued)		after six years: entire scheme to be revised	common expenses of United Kingdom
4. *Judges:*	appointed by Irish government	as in 1886[5]	as in 1886
5. *Police:*	Dublin Metropolitan Police (DMP) under Imperial control for two years; Royal Irish Constabulary (RIC) under Imperial control while it exists; Ireland to have power ultimately to create new force under control of local authorities	DMP/RIC under Imperial control as long as they exist; locally controlled police to be gradually established by Irish government to replace old forces	police under control of Irish government[6]

1. Irish Parliament not allowed to vary rate of income tax except on incomes above £5,000 per annum.
2. I.e., alcohol, tea, coffee, sugar, tobacco, cocoa.
3. Total cost, 1886=£1,500,000. Imperial Treasury was to pay any surplus over £1,000,000 until the cost was reduced to that point.
4. £500,000 per annum for three years, thereafter diminishing by £50,000 per annum until reduced to £200,000.
5. For six years, Irish Supreme Court judges to be appointed by Imperial Parliament.
6. RIC under Imperial control for six years.

Bibliography

The materials mentioned here are organized in the two major categories of "Primary Sources" and "Secondary Sources." Under those two headings, they are grouped as follows:

PRIMARY SOURCES—The William O'Brien Papers; Other Collections of Private Papers; State Papers; Pamphlets; Newspapers and Periodicals; Contemporary Memoirs, Diaries, and Other Contemporary Narratives; and Parliamentary Records.

SECONDARY SOURCES—General; Biography; and Special Subjects.

Primary Sources

The William O'Brien Papers

There are two repositories for the William O'Brien Papers. The larger collection is deposited in the Library of University College, Cork. It consists of about forty cardboard boxes totaling several thousand letters arranged in chronological order and covering O'Brien's entire political career. This collection is not of a value consonant with its size, much of the correspondence being of minor local significance and containing very little of interest from O'Brien's many political associates. Of greatest interest were the boxes containing the correspondence and records of the early years of the United Irish League, the more important of these being Boxes AIA, AIB, AJA, AJB, AJC, AKA, AKB, AKC, and AM.

Much more rewarding is the smaller collection at the National Library of Ireland, in Dublin, particularly MS. 8554 (Dunraven letters 1902–1926), MS. 8555 (Dillon letters 1890–1902), MS. 8556 (Healy letters 1910–1927), and MS. 10496 (Redmond letters). Other interesting items of miscellaneous correspondence are in MSS. 7998, 8506, and 8557. A further boon of this collection is the fact that it contains a considerable number of O'Brien's letters copied in Sophie's legible hand. The value of this becomes evident when one deals with O'Brien's almost incomprehensible scrivenry in other private collections.

I have designated references as "UCC William O'Brien Papers" and "NLI William O'Brien Papers," to indicate their sources as University College, Cork, and the National Library of Ireland, respectively. Since each NLI manuscript generally contains a number of folders for each separate group of letters, the folder number has been included when referenced. For example, MS. 8555/12 indicates MS. 8555, folder 12.

Other Collections of Private Papers

The Davitt Papers and the Dillon Papers are in private custody in Dublin, the former in the hands of Professor T. W. Moody of Trinity College and the latter in the possession of the Dillon family. These have not generally been available to scholars for some time, and I was refused permission to peruse them for this work. However, the Dillon Papers have been the basis of a recent biography by Professor F. S. L. Lyons, and his work, *John Dillon*, has been used in this research.

In Ireland

1. In the National Library of Ireland, Dublin:

Blake Papers. Microfilm copies of originals in the Canadian National Archives, Ottawa. These copies are in eight reels, letters from William O'Brien being in microfilm p. 4683.

F. S. Bourke Collection. MSS. 10702 and 10731.

Bryce Papers. Letters, mainly covering his tenure as Chief Secretary—chiefly MSS. 11012, 11014, 11015, 11016.

Croke Papers. Microfilm copies of originals in Cashel Diocesan Archives.

Davitt Letters. An odd collection consisting of MSS. 913, 914, and 2159. The first two are bound volumes, and, while consisting mainly of letters of Davitt to O'Brien, they include a number of letters from other individuals.

Gill Papers. A very large, uncatalogued collection of over twenty metal boxes from the years 1871 to 1923. The most important for this study deal with the Plan of Campaign and the Parnell Crisis. Most of the correspondence is extensively damaged by fire.

A. S. Green Papers. MS. 15089 proved useful for letters of Antony MacDonnell to Mrs. Green during the years 1902–1916.

Harrington Papers. Contains many items of interest for the history of the Irish National League. Manuscripts of particular use for this research were MSS. 8576–8578.

Horgan Papers. Microfilm reel of letters to Redmond's political associate in Cork.

Macdonagh Papers. Letters to O'Brien from various correspondents with many copies of O'Brien's letters (MSS. 11439, 11440, 11442).

J. F. X. O'Brien Papers. The general correspondence is in MSS. 13418–477 consisting of five unmarked metal boxes containing many items relative to the financial history of the Irish National Federation and the United Irish League.

Sophie O'Brien Papers. A small and not important collection. MS. 4210 is a draft of O'Brien's unpublished work on the Irish Free State.

Redmond Papers. A huge, catalogued collection, indispensable for the later history of the Irish Parliamentary party. The manuscripts used are too numerous to list here. The letters from William O'Brien are in MS. 15212.

Miscellaneous manuscripts. MS. 708 (minute book of the National Directory of the United Irish League) and MS. 10907 (documents relating to
the Land Conference).
2. In the Royal Irish Academy: MS. 24/D/37 (documents relating to New
Tipperary).

In Britain

Asquith Papers, Bodleian Library, Oxford.
Balfour Papers, British Museum. An important collection for the "official"
view of the Plan of Campaign. The relevant Add. MSS. are mainly
49826–30 (Irish Office Letter Books); 49808–12 (Ridgeway Letters);
49807 (Buller Letters); 49803–04 (Wyndham Letters).
Bonar Law Papers, Beaverbrook Library, London.
Buller Papers, Public Record Office, London. Relating to Buller's tenure as
Special Commissioner and Undersecretary in Ireland.
Campbell-Bannerman Papers, British Museum.
Carnarvon Papers, Public Record Office, London.
Lloyd George Papers, Beaverbrook Library, London.
Herbert (Viscount) Gladstone Papers, British Museum.
MacDonnell Papers, Bodleian Library, Oxford.
Murray of Elibank Papers, National Library of Scotland, Edinburgh.
Plunkett Papers, Plunkett Institute, Oxford.
St. Loe Strachey Papers, Beaverbrook Library, London.

In the United States

Bourke Cockran Papers, New York Public Library.
Moreton Frewen Papers, Library of Congress.
Henley Papers, Pierpont Morgan Library, New York. Contains a small
number of interesting letters from George Wyndham on his sojourn as
Chief Secretary (MS. MA 1617:R–V).

State Papers

State Paper Office, Dublin

The vast collection of official papers is the main source for the records of
agrarian agitation and political unrest in Ireland. The papers used for this
research record the years 1885–1916 in the following main classifications:
Chief Secretary's Office, Registered Papers.
Crimes Branch Special Files, 1890–1920. Correspondence among the upper
echelons of the RIC relating to secret societies and the constitutional
movement.
Inspector General's Reports, 1898–1920. Summary reports on political un-
rest by the Inspector General, RIC.
Intelligence Notes, 1895–1914. Miscellaneous reports and statistics on the
Nationalist movement.
Irish Crimes Records (Return of Outrages).
Police and Crime Records, Crimes Branch Special, 1887–1917. Reports of
divisional commissioners and district inspectors.

Police and Crime Records, 1848–1920. Police reports on Irish National League.

Public Record Office, London

1. The Colonial Office records in many cases supplement the information available in the records of the State Paper Office, Dublin. The records found useful for this study include:
   C. O. 903/1. Intelligence notes relating to Plan of Campaign estates.
   C. O. 903/2 Intelligence notes relating to Nationalist movement and operation of the Crimes Act.
2. Cabinet Papers, 1886–1889. War Cabinet, 1916–1917.

Pamphlets

Lehane, Con. *Ireland's Burden Under British Boards*. Dublin, 1905.
Lynch, S. J. *Some Observations on Congestion in Ireland*. Dublin,1908.
National Library of Ireland Pamphlet Collection IR 3330941/i8. *Landowners' Convention Reports*. Dublin, 1888–1919.
———IR 3330941/p7. *Property Defence Association Reports*. Dublin, 1881–1887.
Norman, H. *Bodyke*. London, 1887.
Redmond, John. *The Chicago Convention*. London, 1886.

Newspapers and Periodicals

Belfast Newsletter
Connaught Telegraph (Castlebar)
*Cork Accent
Cork Constitution
Cork Examiner
*Cork Free Press
Freeman's Journal (Dublin)
Irish Daily Independent (Dublin)
*Irish People (Dublin)

Irish Times (Dublin)
Leader (Dublin)
Nation (Dublin
Northern Whig (Belfast)
Sinn Fein (Dublin)
The Times (London)
**United Ireland (Dublin)
United Irishman (Dublin)

*Published by William O'Brien.
**Edited by William O'Brien 1881–1886.

Contemporary works of reference

Annual Register, 1880–1918. London.
    Dod's Parliamentary Companion, 1883–1918. London.
Hart's Army List, 1887–1890. London.
Irish Year Book, 1922. Dublin.
May's British and Irish Press Guide, 1883. London.
Thom's Directory, 1880–1918. Dublin.
Thom's Irish Who's Who. Dublin, 1923.

Published Works of William O'Brien

Autobiography

Recollections. New York, 1905.
An Olive Branch in Ireland. London, 1910.
Evening Memories. Dublin, 1920.

The Irish Revolution. London, 1923.

Biography, Essays, and Fiction
When We Were Boys. London, 1890.
Irish Ideas. London, 1893.
A Queen of Men. London, 1898.
Edmund Burke as an Irishman. Dublin, 1924.
The Parnell of Real Life. London, 1926.

Pamphlets and Articles in Periodicals
"Are the Irish Evicted Tenants Knaves?" *New Review* 7 (October 1892):385–396.
"Mr. Morley's Task in Ireland." *Fortnightly Review* 52(November 1892): 585–594.
"Was Mr. Parnell Badly Treated?" *Contemporary Review* 70(1896): 678–694.
"Was Fenianism Ever Formidable?" *Contemporary Review*, 71 (1897): 680–693.
"Ireland and the Transvaal." *Contemporary Review* 92 (1907): 536–547.
"The Breakdown in Ireland." *Nineteenth Century* 62(July/August 1907):16–39, 323–344.
"The New Power in Ireland." *Nineteenth Century* 67 (March 1910):424–444.
"Is There a Way out of the Chaos in Ireland?" *Nineteenth Century* 80(September 1916): 489–506.
"The Irish Sybil's Books." *Nineteenth Century* 81 (April 1917): 945–960.
"Parnell and His Liberal Allies." *Nineteenth Century* 83(January 1918):170–183.
The Downfall of Parliamentarianism. Dublin, 1918.
The Responsibility for Partition. Dublin, 1921.

Memoirs, Diaries, and Other Contemporary Narratives
Becker, Bernard H. *Disturbed Ireland*. London, 1881.
Birrell, Augustine. *Things Past Redress*. London, 1937.
Blunt, Wilfrid Scawen. *The Land War in Ireland*. London, 1912.
———.*My Diaries*. London, 1932.
Bodkin, M. McDonnell. *Recollections of an Irish Judge*. London, 1914.
Brennan, Robert. *Allegiance*. Dublin, 1950.
Chamberlain, Austen. *Politics from Inside, 1906–1914*. New Haven, Conn., 1937.
Chamberlain, Joseph. *A Political Memoir, 1880–1892*. Edited by C. H. D. Howard. London, 1953.
Colles, Ramsay. *In Castle and Court House*. London, 1911.
Davis, Thomas. *Essays and Poems: With a Centenary Memoir, 1845–1945*. Dublin, 1945.
Davitt, Michael. *The Fall of Feudalism in Ireland*. New York, 1904.
Devoy, John. *Devoy's Post Bag, 1871–1928*. Edited by W. O'Brien and D. Ryan. 2 vols. Dublin, 1948 and 1953.
Dunlop, Andrew. *Fifty Years of Irish Journalism*. Dublin, 1911.
Dunraven, Earl of (Windham T. W. Quin). *The Legacy of Past Years*. London, 1911.

————. *Past Times and Pastimes*. 2 vols. London, 1922.

Ginnell, Laurence. *Land and Liberty*. Dublin, 1908.

Harrington, Timothy. *A Diary of Coercion*. Dublin, 1888.

Healy, T. M. *Letters and Leaders of My Day*. 2 vols. New York, 1929.

Hogan, David. *The Four Glorious Years*. Dublin, 1953.

Horgan, J. J. *Parnell to Pearse*. Dublin, 1948.

Hussey, S. M. *Reminiscences of an Irish Land Agent*. London, 1904.

Jeans, William. *Parliamentary Reminiscences*. London, 1912.

Kettle, Andrew J. *The Material for Victory*. Edited by L. J. Kettle. Dublin, 1958.

Lloyd, Clifford. *Ireland Under the Land League*. London, 1892.

Lucy, Sir Henry. *Diary of the Salisbury Parliament, 1886–1892*. London, 1892.

————. *Diary of the Home Rule Parliament, 1892–95*. London, 1896.

————. *The Balfourian Parliament, 1900–05*. London, 1906.

McCarthy, Justin. *Reminiscences*. Vol 2. New York, 1899.

————. *An Irishman's Story*. London, 1904.

Midleton, Earl of (W. St. John Brodrick). *Ireland—Dupe or Heroine*. London, 1932.

————. *Records and Reactions, 1856–1939*. London, 1939.

Morley, John. *Recollections*. 2 vols. London, 1921.

Morris, W. O'Connor. *Memories and Thoughts of a Life*. London, 1895.

O'Brien, Lord Peter. *Reminiscences*. Edited by G. O'Brien. London, 1916.

O'Brien, Sophie. *Golden Memories*. 2 vols. Dublin, 1929.

O'Connell, Daniel. *Selected Speeches of Daniel O'Connell*. Edited by John O'Connell. 2 vols. Dublin, 1854.

O'Connor, T. P. *Memoirs of an Old Parliamentarian*. 2 vols. London, 1929.

O'Donnell, F. Hugh. *A History of the Irish Parliamentary Party*. 2 vols. London, 1910.

Pearse, Padraic H. *Political Writings and Speeches*. Dublin, 1952.

Plunkett, Sir Horace. *Ireland in the New Century*. London, 1904.

Scott, C. P. *Political Diaries of C. P. Scott*. Edited by T. Wilson. London, 1970.

Shaw-Lefevre, G. *Incidents of Coercion*. London, 1889.

————. *Gladstone and Ireland*. London, 1912.

Sheehan, D. D. *Ireland Since Parnell*. London, 1921.

Stevenson, F. *Lloyd George, A Diary*. Edited by A. J. P. Taylor. London, 1971.

Sullivan, A. M. *Old Ireland*. New York, 1928.

Sullivan, T. D. *Recollections of Troubled Times in Irish Politics*. Dublin, 1905.

Temple, Sir Richard. *Letters and Character Sketches from the House of Commons*. London, 1912.

Parliamentary Records

Evicted Tenants Commission: Report and Minutes of Evidence. House of Commons (1893–94), 31.

Hansard, *Parliamentary Debates*. Third, Fourth, and Fifth series.

Men of Military Age in Ireland. House of Commons: cd. 8390 (1916), 17.

Prison Treatment of William O'Brien, MP. House of Commons: c. 5698 (1889), 61.

Report on Recruiting in Ireland. House of Commons: cd. 8168 (1914–16), 39.

Secondary Sources
General

Beckett, J. C. *The Making of Modern Ireland, 1603–1921.* London, 1966.
Ensor, R. C. K. *England, 1870–1914.* London, 1936.
Halevy, E. *A History of the English People in the Nineteenth Century.* Vol. 6: *The Rule of Democracy, 1905–14.* 2d ed., rev. London, 1952.
Lampson, G. Locker. *A Consideration of the State of Ireland in the Nineteenth Century.* London, 1907.
Lyons, F. S. L. *Ireland Since the Famine.* London, 1971.
Mansergh, N. *The Irish Question, 1840–1921.* Rev. ed. London, 1965.
Moody, T. W., and Martin, F. X. (eds.) *The Course of Irish History.* New York, 1967.
Paul, Herbert. *Modern England.* Vols. 4 and 5. London, 1905, 1906.

Biography

Banks, Margaret A. *Edward Blake, Irish Nationalist, 1892–1907.* Toronto, 1957.
Bourke, Marcus. *John O'Leary.* Tralee, 1967.
Delany, V. T. H. *Christopher Palles, His Life and Times.* Dublin, 1960
Digby, Margaret. *Horace Plunkett.* Oxford, 1949.
Greaves, C. Desmond. *The Life and Times of James Connolly.* London, 1961.
Gwynn, Denis. *The Life of John Redmond.* London, 1932.
Longford, Earl of (Frank Pakenham) and O'Neill, Thomas P. *Eamon De Valera.* New York, 1971.
Lyons, F. S. L. *John Dillon.* London, 1968.
Macdonagh, Michael. *The Life of William O'Brien.* London, 1928.
Mackail, J. W., and Wyndham, G. *Life and Letters of George Wyndham.* 2 vols. London, 1925.
Magnus, P. *Gladstone.* London, 1954.
Melville, C. H. *Life of General Sir Redvers Buller.* Vol. 1. London, 1923.
Murray, Arthur C. *Master and Brother.* London, 1945.
O'Brien, R. Barry. *The Life of Charles Stewart Parnell.* 2 vols. London, 1898.
O'Luing, Sean. *Art O'Griofa.* Dublin, 1953.
Petrie, Sir Charles. *Walter Long and His Times.* London, 1936.
Ryan, Desmond. *The Man Called Pearse.* Dublin, 1919.
Sheehy-Skeffington, F. *Michael Davitt.* London, 1967.
Sullivan, Maev. *No Man's Man.* Dublin, 1943.
Thorold, A. L. *The Life of Henry Labouchere.* London, 1913.
Walsh, Patrick J. *William J. Walsh, Archbishop of Dublin.* Dublin, 1928.

Special Subjects

Ausubel, Herman. *In Hard Times.* New York, 1960.
Black, R. D. Collison. *Economic Thought and the Irish Question, 1817–80.* Cambridge, 1960.
Bonn, Moritz J. *Modern Ireland and Her Agrarian Problem.* London, 1906.

Brown, Thomas N. *Irish-American Nationalism*. New York, 1966.

Buckland, P. J. "The Southern Irish Unionists, the Irish Question, and British Politics, 1906–14." *Irish Historical Studies* 15(March 1967): 228–255.

Burn, W. L. "Free Trade in Land: An Aspect of the Irish Question." *Transactions of the Royal Historical Society*, 4th series, 31(1948): 61–74.

Cambray, Philip G. *Irish Affairs and the Home Rule Question*. London, 1911.

Clarkson, J. Dunsmore. *Labour and Nationalism in Ireland*. New York, 1925.

Connolly, James. *Labour in Irish History* (paperback). Dublin, 1967.

Cullen, L. M. "Problems in the Interpretation and Revision of Eighteenth-Century Irish Economic History." *Transactions of the Royal Historical Society* 17(January 1967):1–22.

Curtis, L. P., Jr. *Coercion and Conciliation in Ireland, 1880–92*. Princeton, 1963.

D'Alton, Ian. "Southern Irish Unionism: A Study of Cork Unionists, 1884–1914." *Transactions of the Royal Historical Society* 23(January 1973): 71–88.

Dunraven, Earl of (Windham T. W. Quin). *The Outlook in Ireland*. London, 1911.

Fanning, J. R. "The Unionist Party and Ireland, 1906–10." *Irish Historical Studies* 15(September 1966):147–171.

Glaser, J. F. "Parnell's Fall and the Nonconformist Conscience." *Irish Historical Studies* 12(September 1960): 119–138.

Henry, R. M. *The Evolution of Sinn Fein*. Dublin, 1920.

Howard, C. H. D. "Joseph Chamberlain, Parnell and the Irish 'Central Board' Scheme, 1884–5." *Irish Historical Studies* 7(September 1953): 324–361.

Hurst, Michael. *Parnell and Irish Nationalism*. London, 1968.

Larkin, Emmet. "The Roman Catholic Hierarchy and the Fall of Parnell." *Victorian Studies* 4(June 1961): 315–336.

————. "Mounting the Counter-Attack: The Roman Catholic Hierarchy and the Destruction of Parnellism." *Review of Politics* 25(April 1963): 157–183.

————. "Launching the Counterattack" (Part 2 of "The Roman Catholic Hierarchy and the Destruction of Parnellism"). *Review of Politics* 28(July 1966): 359–383.

Lyons, F. S. L. *The Irish Parliamentary Party, 1890–1910*. London, 1951.

————. *The Fall of Parnell, 1890–91*. Toronto, 1962.

————. "The Irish Unionist Party and the Devolution Crisis of 1904–5." *Irish Historical Studies* 6(March 1948): 1–22.

————. "John Dillon and the Plan of Campaign, 1886–90." *Irish Historical Studies* 14(September 1965):313–347.

————. "The Machinery of the Irish Party in the General Election of 1895." *Irish Historical Studies* 8(September 1952): 115–138.

McCaffrey, L. J. "Isaac Butt and the Home Rule Movement: A Study in Conservative Nationalism." *Review of Politics* 22(January 1960): 72–95.

Macardle, Dorothy. *The Irish Republic*. New York, 1965.

McCready, H. W. "Home Rule and the Liberal Party, 1899–1906." *Irish Historical Studies* 13(September 1963): 316–348.

Macdonagh, Michael. *The Home Rule Movement*. Dublin, 1920.

McDowell, R. B. *The Irish Convention, 1917–18*. Toronto, 1970.

MacGiolla Choille, B. *Intelligence Notes, 1913–16*. Dublin, 1966.

Martin, F. X. (ed.). *Leaders and Men of the Easter Rising: Dublin 1916*. Ithaca, N.Y., 1967.

Maxwell, T. Henry. *The Irish Land Acts, 1903–09*. Dublin, 1910.

Micks, W. L. *History of the Congested Districts Board*. Dublin, 1925.

Montgomery, W. E. *History of Land Tenure in Ireland*. Cambridge, 1889.

Moody, T. W. "The New Departure in Irish Politics, 1878–79." In Essays in British and Irish History in Honour of James Eadie Todd, edited by H. A. Cronne, T. W. Moody, and D. B. Quinn. London, 1949.

Norman, E. R. *The Catholic Church and Ireland in the Age of Rebellion, 1859–73*. London, 1965.

O'Brien, Conor Cruise. *Parnell and His Party, 1880–90*. Oxford, 1957, corrected impression 1964.

———— (ed.). *The Shaping of Modern Ireland*. Toronto, 1960.

O'Broin, Leon. *The Chief Secretary*. Hamden, Conn., 1969.

O'Donnell, Peadar. *There Will Be Another Day*. Dublin, 1963.

Palmer, Norman Dunbar. *The Irish Land League Crisis*. New Haven, 1940.

Phillips, W. Alison. *The Revolution in Ireland, 1906–23*. London, 1923.

Pomfret, John E. *The Struggle for Land in Ireland, 1800–1923*. Princeton, 1930.

Rowland, Peter. *The Last Liberal Governments: 1905–10*. London, 1968.

Solow, Barbara Lewis. *The Land Question and the Irish Economy, 1870–1903*. Cambridge, Mass., 1971.

Strauss, Eric. *Irish Nationalism and British Democracy*. New York, 1951.

Tansill, Charles C. *America and the Fight for Irish Freedom, 1866–1922*. New York, 1957.

Ward, Alan J. *Ireland and Anglo-American Relations, 1899–1921*. London, 1969.

————. "Frewen's Anglo-American Campaign for Federalism, 1910–1921." *Irish Historical Studies* 15(March 1967): 256–275.

Whyte, J. H. "Landlord Influence at Elections in Ireland, 1760–1885." *English Historical Review* 80(October 1965): 740–760.

————. "The Influence of the Catholic Clergy on Elections in Nineteenth-Century Ireland." *English Historical Review* 75(April 1960): 239–259.

Index

269